D0835432

# Chronicle
## of the year
# 1989

# Chronicle of the year 1989

has been conceived and co-ordinated by Jacques Legrand

### Editor: Henrietta Heald

**Picture Editor:** Ruth Darby

**Writers:** Hazel Bedford, Peter Bently, Jerome Burne, Robert Carvel, Jonathon Green, Godfrey Hodgson, Robert Jones, Peter Lewis, John Miller, Louis Nevin, Denis Pitts, Warren Pitts, Paul Wilkinson

**Editorial Production:** Bronwen Lewis, Joan Thomas, Chris Allman, Laura Hicks, John McCormack

**Production co-ordination:** Henry Marganne *(Manager)*
Martine Colliot, Alan Turpin

**Computer Systems:** Catherine Balouet

**Artwork:** Bull Publishing Associates Ltd.

**Administration:** Barbara Levinson

### Editor-in-Chief: Derrik Mercer

---

# How to use this book

This book follows the formula of what is in many ways its parent volume – *Chronicle of the 20th Century*. It reports the events of the year as though they had just happened, thereby enabling people to keep up-to-date with our fast-moving times. To help readers follow developments, which can rarely have been more dramatic than in 1989, there is not only an index but also a system of cross-references which link news reports and events in the weekly summaries. These cross-references appear as arrows pointing to the next entry in a specific chain of events. The arrows point only forwards in time and work like this.

If a cross-referenced event occurs in the same month, only the day of that month will appear after the arrow (→ 15, for instance). If the next linked event occurs in another month, then the month will also appear (→ 15/9,

for instance). The arrow can lead to either an entry in the weekly summaries of events or one of the fuller reports. Sometimes an arrow will appear by itself after an entry in the weekly summaries or chronologies of events; this means that the event is covered in one of the reports which appear in the pages adjoining the summary.

The reports of the year's news, recalled here as it happened, are supplemented by summaries of the events in each nation of the world. These summaries also include data about each country such as its size, population, currency and religion. The book ends with an index and a list of agencies which supplied photographs and to whom we extend our thanks for their help in ensuring that this book could be published so speedily.

---

© 1989 Jacques Legrand S.A. International Publishing, Paris, for World English rights.

© Chronicle of the Year 1989, Chronicle Communications Ltd., London.

© Chronicle System. 1986, Harenberg Kommunikation, Dortmund.

First published in 1990 jointly by the Longman Group UK Ltd and Chronicle Communications Ltd.

ISBN: 0-582-05625-X
Typesetting: Berger-Levrault, Nancy, France
Colour processing: Christian Bocquez
Printing and Binding: Brepols, Turnhout, Belgium

Chronicle Communications Ltd.,
154 Clerkenwell Road,
London EC1R 5AD.

Longman Group UK Ltd.,
Longman House,
Burnt Mill,
Harlow,
Essex CM20 2JE.

# Chronicle
## of the year
# 1989

Longman
Chronicle

| Su | Mo | Tu | We | Th | Fr | Sa |
|----|----|----|----|----|----|----|
| 1  | 2  | 3  | 4  | 5  | 6  | 7  |
| 8  | 9  | 10 | 11 | 12 | 13 | 14 |
| 15 | 16 | 17 | 18 | 19 | 20 | 21 |
| 22 | 23 | 24 | 25 | 26 | 27 | 28 |
| 29 | 30 | 31 |    |    |    |    |

**1. UK:** An opinion poll gives Neil Kinnock the worst personal rating since he became Labour leader (→2/2).

**1. US:** Intelligence officials accuse two West German firms of helping Libya build a chemical weapons plant.→

**1. US:** European Community trade sanctions are imposed in response to a ban on imports of hormone-treated US meat.

**2. Sri Lanka:** Ranasinghe Premadasa is sworn in as president (→11).

**2. Brazil:** It is reported that an area of rain forest the size of Belgium was burnt by cattle-ranchers in 1988.

**3. UK:** In a £2.4 billion deal, BP buys back more than half of Kuwait's 21.6 per cent BP shareholding.

**3. UK:** Albert Roux, chef of La Gavroche restaurant, appears in court for breach of food hygiene rules (→23/3).

**4. UK:** NHS review leaks suggest that hospitals will be urged to opt out of health authority control (→27).

**4. S Africa:** Eugene Terre-blanche's right-wing Afrikaner Resistance Movement heads for a split over his links with a blonde journalist (→16).

**5. Zaire:** Former Ugandan leader Idi Amin is detained in Kinshasa after arriving on a false passport (→12).

**5. UK:** Manufacturers Proctor and Gamble and Peaudouce announce plans to produce "green" disposable nappies.

**6. India:** Two Sikhs are hanged for the murder of Indira Gandhi.

**6. US:** Photographic evidence is produced that the US jets acted defensively in shooting down the Libyan MiGs (→18).

**6. UK:** In a wave of City redundancies, Chase Manhattan bank sacks 135 staff.

**7. Paris:** A 14-nation conference on chemical weapons opens (→8).

**DEATH**

**7.** Michinomiya Hirohito, emperor of Japan (*29/4/01).→

# America shoots down Libyan jets

**Jan 5.** US Navy jets shot down two Libyan MiG-23 fighters yesterday about 70 miles (112 kilometres) off the Libyan coast. The Pentagon said they fired in self-defence, but the Libyan president, Muammar Gadaffi, called it "premeditated aggression". He threatened revenge for what he called "US terrorism", and demanded an emergency meeting of the UN Security Council.

Yasser Arafat, the leader of the Palestine Liberation Organization, said the incident would "reflect negatively" on the prospects for peace in the Middle East.

Frank Carlucci, the US defence secretary, explained that two F-14 Tomcats were providing combat air patrol for the aircraft carrier USS *John F Kennedy* 127 miles north of the Libyan coat and close to the south-west corner of Crete.

The two Libyan MiGs approached in a hostile manner, and when they were 14 miles away the US section leader gave the order to shoot them down with air-to-air missiles. The Libyan pilots parachuted into the sea.

In a recent TV interview, President Reagan refused to rule out a US attack on a suspected Libyan chemical weapons plant, which Gadaffi says is for manufacturing pharmaceuticals. Yesterday, Mr Carlucci denied any connection between the plant and the shooting down of the MiGs (→6).

*An American F-14 Tomcat jet of the type used in the Libyan shoot-down.*

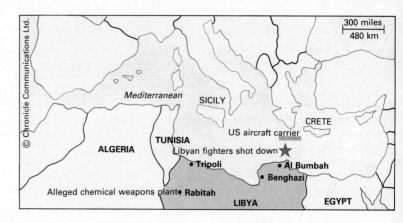

© Chronicle Communications Ltd.

300 miles / 480 km

Mediterranean · SICILY · CRETE · US aircraft carrier · ALGERIA · TUNISIA · Libyan fighters shot down · Tripoli · Al Bumbah · Benghazi · Alleged chemical weapons plant Rabitah · LIBYA · EGYPT

## Row continues over junior doctors' hours

**Jan 5.** Britain's junior doctors – many of whom have to work 80-hour shifts – last night received the support of senior colleagues for a campaign to cut their working week by an average of 14 hours.

The British Medical Association (BMA) Council, which represents consultants and GPs as well as junior medics, unanimously backed a resolution put by Dr Graeme McDonald, chairman of the BMA juniors, that "an average of 72 hours per week should be the maximum necessary for postgraduate training".

This move will be welcomed by the Medical Practitioners' Union, which is campaigning to have junior doctors' weeks eventually cut to 60 hours. Junior doctors claim they work on average about 86 hours a week, about double most people's working week. Rotas mean some doctors can work almost solidly for over three days, and they can be on call for 104 hours at a time.

The BMA Council resolution requires Dr John Marks, BMA Council chairman, to seek an urgent meeting with the health secretary, Kenneth Clarke, on the matter.

David Mellor, the health minister, angered doctors three days ago when he blamed "quite unacceptable" rotas of 90 to 100 hours a week on inconsiderate consultants. He had earlier accused junior doctors of telling "fishermen's tales" about long hours.

## Chinese police beat African students

**Jan 5.** After a week of racial tension in Beijing – in which police used electric pig probes and batons to break up demonstrations – 500 African students in Chinese universities are staging a boycott of their classes. More of the 1,500 black students may join the strike today.

Trouble flared at a Christmas Eve dance in Nanjing when police questioned Chinese girls partnering Africans. Black students barricaded themselves in their hostel in protest and were stormed by police. Chinese students in Beijing are demanding punishment for Africans whom they accuse of "harassing" Chinese women.

# Royals stay away from Lockerbie service

**Jan 4.** Today the grief-stricken people of Lockerbie – the small Scottish town shattered 14 days ago when a Pan Am jumbo jet smashed on to its quiet streets – listened in silence to a memorial address given by Professor James Whyte, Moderator of the Church of Scotland.

They were joined by 200 relatives of the dead passengers, and by Pan Am staff who had flown in from all over the world. Margaret Thatcher and other political leaders attended the service, but the royal family was not present.

The moderator said the "carnage of the young and innocent" should be repaid by justice, not retaliation. Those who could not get into Old Dryfesdale church stood outside in the freezing Scottish rain and heard his words by loudspeaker (→5).

*Mourners unite in grief for the 270 who died in the Pan Am crash.*

# Airport security stepped up after disaster

**Jan 5.** Security procedures at all British airports are to be radically revised, Paul Channon, the secretary of state for transport, said today. This is a direct consequence of the Lockerbie tragedy last December, in which 270 people lost their lives. The disaster is believed to have been caused by a bomb planted in the baggage compartment of the aircraft.

The overhaul was announced after a meeting between the transport secretary, the National Aviation Security Committee and American aviation experts. Mr Channon said: "I have decided immediately to take further steps to increase the security of cargo, also mislaid luggage, and to take further steps to tighten up the regulations for cabin baggage."

The measures will concentrate on luggage bound for the seven major US airlines which operate through Britain. They may include high technology sniffing and X-ray machines (→10).

**Jan 2. Fidel Castro, the 69-year-old Cuban dictator, gives an impassioned speech to mark the 30th anniversary of the overthrow of the American-backed Batista regime. Strongly opposed to Soviet-style reform, Castro labels glasnost and perestroika "capitalist" and "counter-revolutionary".**

# Emperor Hirohito dies

*Emperor Hirohito: his death brings to an end the "era of bright peace".*

**Jan 7.** The Imperial Son of Heaven, Michinomiya Hirohito, emperor of Japan for 62 turbulent years, died early today at the age of 82. His death, from cancer of the duodenum, was announced in the archaic language of the Japanese court from the steps of the royal palace. Hirohito's son, Crown Prince Akihito, automatically accedes to the chrysanthemum throne although his coronation will not take place for at least two years.

During his reign – designated "the era of bright peace" – Hirohito saw his country evolve from a fiercely militaristic state, defeated after a ruthlessly fought war in which it sought to dominate the Pacific, into one of the world's most powerful economies.

It was not until Japan surrendered in 1945 that Hirohito admitted to his shattered people that he was not a god incarnate. Until then it was considered glorious for his soldiers to give up their lives for him. For the rest of his life, he was portrayed as a simple marine biologist and rarely left the palace.

Some countries – Australia in particular – wanted him tried as a war criminal. However, General Douglas MacArthur, the American supreme commander, chose to rule Japan through its emperor (→29).

# Some charges axed against Ollie North

**Jan 5.** The independent prosecutor in the Iran-Contra case today dropped the serious conspiracy charges against Oliver North, the former White House aide.

The charges – that North was involved in a criminal conspiracy to divert money from secret US arms sales to Iran to the "Contra" rebels in Nicaragua – have been blocked by a White House refusal to release certain classified documents. North still faces lesser charges, among them that he lied to Congress.

Subpoenas were served last week on President Reagan and President-elect Bush ordering them to testify in the case (→31).

# Political bias row over new IBA head

**Jan 6.** The appointment of Lord Chalfont, the 69-year-old right-wing peer, as deputy head of the Independent Broadcasting Authority has provoked an outcry from opposition politicians. Labour's broadcasting spokesman, Robin Corbett, said: "He has been put in there to do the prime minister's business. The government has done a great disservice to broadcasting."

Lord Chalfont, who served as a Labour disarmament minister in the 1960s, now regularly attacks left-wing bias on television; he believes television is an entertainment medium and not good at giving information (→6/9).

# January
## 1989

| Su | Mo | Tu | We | Th | Fr | Sa |
|----|----|----|----|----|----|----|
| 1 | 2 | 3 | 4 | 5 | 6 | 7 |
| 8 | 9 | 10 | 11 | 12 | 13 | 14 |
| 15 | 16 | 17 | 18 | 19 | 20 | 21 |
| 22 | 23 | 24 | 25 | 26 | 27 | 28 |
| 29 | 30 | 31 | | | | |

**8.** Paris: The USSR announces a decision to destroy its chemical weapons (→18).

**9.** Singapore: Lee Kuan Yew is sworn in as prime minister for the eighth time.

**9.** UK: University lecturers start an exam boycott as part of a pay dispute (→17/5).

**9.** UK: BR introduces huge long-distance fare increases.

**10.** Angola: In accordance with an agreement reached last year, the first Cuban troops leave.

**10.** Czechoslovakia: Export of Semtex explosive, believed to have been used in the Lockerbie bomb, is halted (→13).

**10.** UK: Friends of the British hostage John McCarthy mark 1,000 days of his captivity in Beirut.

**11.** Hungary: A law is enacted allowing the formation of political parties (→11/2).

**11.** USSR: 10,000 people rally in Vilnius, the capital of Lithuania, in support of Lithuanian independence.

**11.** Sri Lanka: A state of emergency imposed five and a half years ago is lifted (→12/2).

**12.** Yugoslavia: The republic of Slovenia forms the Democratic Alliance, in opposition to the Communist Party (→28/2).

**12.** Zaire: Idi Amin is deported to Senegal.

**12.** UK: BR announces that London's second Channel Tunnel rail link will be at King's Cross (→26/2).

**13.** Paris: Daniel Barenboim is sacked as artistic director of the new Opera de la Bastille.

**13.** UK: Two journalists posing as cleaners admit gaining unsupervised access to aircraft at Heathrow (→16/2).

**14.** UK: Doctors and scientists call for a ban on some popular brands of baby milk which could cause brain damage.

**DEATH**

**11.** Ray Moore, British disc jockey and radio announcer (*2/1/42).

---

# Bradford Moslems burn "Satanic Verses"

*Salman Rushdie's "blasphemous" book is set ablaze outside the City Hall.*

**Jan 14.** *The Satanic Verses*, a novel by Salman Rushdie, was publicly burnt at a demonstration by more than 1,000 Moslems in Bradford city centre today. There is growing unrest among Moslems in the city, who plan a march on W H Smith's bookshop. Smith's have now withdrawn the book from display, although they say that they will still take orders for it.

The novel came out last year and has been on the bestseller list for three months, with hardback sales nearing 40,000. In 1981 Rushdie, born in India, won the Booker Prize, for which this book was also entered. Its title refers to verses cut from the Koran by the Prophet Mohammed because he believed they were inspired by Satan. It has been banned as blasphemous in India, Pakistan and Saudi Arabia.

Rushdie, who was brought up as a Moslem, says *The Satanic Verses* concerns the struggle between the secular and the religious view of life. Of W H Smith's actions, he said: "This is a very sad day, not only for me but for English literature. If pressure groups can decide that my books should be banned, then it will not be long before different groups decide other authors should not be published." He claims he is being victimized by a so-called Society for the Promotion of Religious Tolerance (→29).

# British minister holds talks with Arafat

*William Waldegrave is welcomed to talks in Tunis by the PLO leader.*

**Jan 14.** An historic meeting in Tunis between Yasser Arafat and William Waldegrave, a British Foreign Office minister, was today denounced by Israel. A spokesman said that Britain's "pro-PLO attitude" prevented it from performing a meaningful role in the resolution of the Middle East conflict. Yesterday was the first time that a British minister had met the leader of the Palestine Liberation Organization.

During a break in talks, Waldegrave said that Israel would be "left behind" if it failed to use this chance to join discussions about the future of the Palestinians. He continued: "This year is crucial; there is a window of opportunity; if we waste it, it may not recur" (→23/3).

---

# Reagan makes his farewell to America

**Jan 11.** "We've done our part" in an "American miracle" of economic recovery and progress towards world peace. That was the keynote of President Reagan's farewell speech to the US people tonight. "I won the nickname the Great Communicator," Mr Reagan said. "I wasn't a great communicator, but I communicated great things."

He made no mention of the less than great things about his eight-year administration. He said nothing, for example, about his early warnings of what turned out to be an imaginary "window of vulnerability" to Soviet missiles or about the Iran-Contra scandal (→20).

# Former Belgian premier disappears

**Jan 14.** Fears are mounting that Paul Vanden Boeynants, a former Social Christian prime minister of Belgium who has mysteriously disappeared from his home, may be the victim of a terrorist kidnapping. In calls to Belgian television and radio stations, two previously unknown radical groups have claimed responsibility. Vanden Boeynants, who is aged 69 and suffers from a heart condition, is reported to need constant medication when under stress (→17).

**The Lord Mayor of London cuts a one-ton cake to celebrate the 800th birthday of his office.**

# Carnage as Boeing jet crashes on to motorway

*Rescue teams battled through the night to rescue survivors trapped in the wreckage of the devastated airliner.*

## Pilot shut down "wrong engine"

**Jan 11.** Preliminary evidence from the inquiry into the British Midland 737 crash last Sunday suggests that the starboard engine, which was shut down during flight, was in fact in good working order.

In a speech to the House of Commons yesterday, the transport secretary, Paul Channon, said: "About 15 minutes into the flight, the pilot reported a fire in the starboard engine. The fire was apparently successfully dealt with and the captain asked for permission to divert to East Midlands airport for an emergency landing."

However, while the inquiry team has identified "evidence of a fire in the left engine", Mr Channon went on, they found no sign of fire or mechanical problems in the starboard engine.

Some survivors of the disaster, in which 44 people died, reported that the pilot said he was going to close down the starboard engine minutes before the crash.

While Boeing and the engine manufacturers have made it clear that shutting down an engine is "pilot-initiated action", Boeing captains have said that it would be almost impossible for a pilot to shut down the wrong engine. Investigators have interviewed Captain Kevin Hunt in his bed in Leicester Royal Infirmary, where he is being treated for a broken back.

Residents in the area of the disaster have been asked to look out for aircraft debris which may aid the inquiry (→15).

## More than 40 people killed just half a mile from runway

**Jan 9.** In Britain's second major air disaster in under a month, a British Midland Boeing 737 airliner crashed into a grass embankment next to the M1 motorway between Nottingham and Leicester last night. Of the 117 passengers and eight crew on board, at least 40 are known to have died, but 70 have been rescued.

The pilot of the 737, on a flight from Heathrow to Belfast, had reported engine difficulties and was lining up for an emergency landing at East Midlands airport. But the plane – delivered to British Midland just 12 weeks ago – came down in flames one mile south of junction 24 of the motorway and less than half a mile away from the village of Kegworth.

Peter Wragg, who lives near the site of the accident, saw the plane descend: "Flames came out of the port engine, it was very much nose up and wing down as it struggled for height on the final approach; there was a lot of noise as if it was a backfire."

Terrified motorists watched from cars as debris was strewn across three lanes of motorway. Nearly 100 firemen and 30 ambulance crews rushed to the scene, but two hours later people were still trapped in the wreckage. Air accident investigators, already busy with the bombing of Pan Am flight 103, which crashed on to Lockerbie 18 days ago, arrive today (→11).

## Gorbachev challenges Communist Party

**Jan 10.** Mikhail Gorbachev, the Soviet leader, set the scene for this spring's unprecedented elections by warning his Communist Party that it had no God-given right to rule. Gorbachev told the central committee that the party had to earn its position as the political vanguard of Soviet society.

The meeting adopted a list of candidates from whom l00 leading party officials will represent the party in the new Congress of People's Deputies. Gorbachev said the party's election manifesto would be based on the policy of *perestroika*, or reconstruction.

He reassured party conservatives alarmed by the pace and direction of some of his reforms that the election – which, for the first time, will offer a choice of candidates – was not a "chaotic process but a most important mass campaign" (→18).

## Free shares for Abbey National members

**Jan 11.** Some five and a half million savers and borrowers with the Abbey National Building Society are being wooed in a bid to give the biggest ever boost to wider share ownership in Britain. They are each to get free shares thought to be worth about £280, as long as they give a big enough majority for Abbey's conversion to a company.

Abbey will have more shareholders than any company if the conversion goes through. Moreover, other building societies may follow suit. Sir Campbell Adamson, the chairman of Abbey, said: "The day of the mutual society has passed." Some Abbey members, however, are determined to maintain the mutual tradition. Alec Leaver, the chairman of their pressure group, Abbey Members Against Flotation, attacked today's move as a bribe to win votes (→11/4).

# January

## 1989

**15.** Bangladesh: A train crash kills 120 and injures over 1,000.

**15.** UK: A fault is found in the fire-warning equipment of a Boeing 757 (→20).

**15.** USSR: Moscow imposes direct rule on Nagorny Karabakh, the Armenian enclave in Azerbaijan.

**16.** Prague: Police attack demonstrators for the second day running.→

**16.** UK: The appeal court is ordered to review the convictions of the four jailed for the 1974 Guildford pub bombings (→17/10).

**17.** UK: The football world unites to oppose plans in the Football Spectators Bill for compulsory ID cards (→22/4).

**17.** Brussels: The Socialist Revolutionary Brigade seeks a ransom for the former premier, Vanden Boeynants (→14/2).

**17.** Miami: Martin Luther King day is marked by riots in a black area as visitors arrive for the Superbowl.

**18.** W Germany: The government says that West German firms helped to build a Libyan chemicals plant.

**18.** UK: A 60-year-old Nottingham man is jailed for sexual offences against eight of his grandchildren.

**19.** UK: Viraj Mendis fails in his final appeal to avoid deportation to Sri Lanka.→

**20.** US: An engine falls off a Boeing 737 as it takes off from O'Hare airport, Chicago (→22).

**20.** UK: The Al Fayeds' takeover of Harrods store avoids referral to the Monopolies Commission (→31/3).

**21.** S Africa: The Afrikaner Resistance Movement gives a vote of confidence to Eugene Terreblanche.

### DEATHS

**15.** Wilf Slack, West Indian-born England cricketer (*12/12/54).

**18.** Bruce Chatwin, British writer (*13/5/40).→

**21.** Leslie Halliwell, British film encyclopaedist (*23/2/29).

---

# Bush is sworn in as 41st US president

*The new president shares a joke with his former boss at the inauguration.*

**Jan 20.** With his hand on the same bible as that used for George Washington's swearing-in 200 years ago, George Herbert Prescott Bush was today sworn in as the 41st president of the United States.

The oath was administered in the time-honoured ceremony on the steps of the Capitol by the chief justice, William Rehnquist, and in front of the new first lady, Barbara Bush, and the outgoing president and Mrs Reagan.

President Bush thanked his predecessor for "the wonderful things you have done for America". The old master of the one-liner said simply: "Carry on." Like Jimmy Carter in 1977, Mr and Mrs Bush twice got out of their new armour-plated limousine to walk part of the ceremonial route up Pennsylvania Avenue from the White House to the Capitol.

In his speech Mr Bush several times used the phrase "a new breeze is blowing". He pledged by implication that his administration would be more compassionate than the one that preceded it. "My friends," he said, "we are not the sum of our possessions."

Mr Bush hailed the passing of "the totalitarian era". "In man's heart," he said, "the day of the dictator is over" (→26/2).

# Turks sell kidneys to London hospital

**Jan 17.** Istanbul police today arrested a man accused of offering Turkish peasants up to £2,000 to sell one of their kidneys for transplants at a private hospital in London.

Dr Raymond Crockett, who supervised the operations at the Humana Wellington Hospital, said he did not know how donors were found but the operations were legal and without duress. One donor, Ahmet Koc, claimed he was told in Turkey he needed "medical tests" in Istanbul and London to get a job abroad. In London he signed forms he could not read, and it was only after the "test" that he realized he was one kidney short.

# Writer Chatwin dies of tropical disease

**Jan 18.** Bruce Chatwin, the gifted novelist and traveller, died today at the age of 48 from a rare disease of the bone marrow, contracted in China. He left a career at Sotheby's to study nomads and produced his first travel book, *In Patagonia*, which won the Hawthornden prize, in 1977. His first novel, *On the Black Hill*, about the life of Welsh hill farmers, won a Whitbread award. His most popular book was *The Songlines*, about the Australian outback.

# Riot police move into central Prague following demonstrations

**Jan 19.** Czechoslovak riot police occupied the centre of Prague today after using tear gas, water cannon and baton charges to disperse demonstrators chanting the name of Mikhail Gorbachev, the Soviet leader. The police beat and arrested some of the demonstrators, who had taken to the streets to commemorate the death of Jan Palach, the student who set himself alight 20 years ago in protest against the Soviet-led invasion of Czechoslovakia.

A few days ago Czechoslovakia became one of the 35 nations acceding to the Helsinki East-West human rights accord. Some of those arrested belong to the Charter 77 human rights group (→21/2).

*Police form a human cordon across Wenceslas Square after quelling protests.*

# Court uproar after ANC judgements

**Jan 16.** There was uproar in South Africa's supreme court today after three members of the banned African National Congress (ANC) were given stiff jail terms for treason and terrorism.

Judge Hekkie Daniels had just left the courtroom after sentencing Ebrahim Ismail Ebrahim, Mandla Maseko and Simon Dladla to 20, 23 and 12 years respectively, when supporters of the three men began chanting and shouting black nationalist slogans and songs.

Suddenly, in defiance of the ANC sympathizers in the court, Louise van der Walt, one of the prosecution lawyers and often a counsel for the apartheid state against its opponents, shouted: "Long live the AWB!" The AWB, or *Afrikaner Weerstands Beweging* (Afrikaner Resistance Movement), is the neo-Nazi white extremist group led by the controversial Eugene Terreblanche.

As her colleagues tried to calm her down, Mrs van der Walt blurted out, in Afrikaans: "Why do you silence me when others are allowed to sing out?" She was more tight-lipped outside the court, where relatives of the ANC men comforted one another. Ebrahim, aged 51, is the most senior ANC figure jailed since Nelson Mandela and seven other leaders were imprisoned in 1964 (→21).

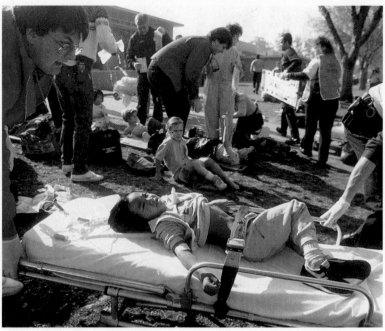
*The young victims of the Californian gunman receive emergency treatment.*

# American schoolchildren gunned down

**Jan 17.** Five children died today and 30 pupils and teachers were wounded when a gunman, dressed in combat fatigues and brandishing an AK-47 assault rifle, launched an unprovoked attack on a crowded school playground in Stockton, California.

The gunman, who was also wearing a flak jacket and carrying two automatic pistols, fired 50 shots into the playground, then shot himself in the head. He died later in police custody. Police, who have not named the killer, have offered no motive for the attack, the third apparently random mass murder in America in recent months. Whether the man's uniform, combined with the fact that 70 per cent of the school pupils were Vietnamese refugees, indicates a connection with the Vietnam war awaits further investigation.

Fifteen of the wounded children and teachers are still on the critical list. Ralph Tribble, Stockton's deputy police chief, said: "We have had a very terrible tragedy in our community."

# Soviet Union plans big defence cuts

**Jan 18.** The Soviet leader, Mikhail Gorbachev, fleshed out his arms cuts proposals and disclosed that he would reduce his military budget by 14 per cent to boost a stagnant civilian economy. At a talk in the Kremlin with several leading Western figures, he specified for the first time how the planned cutback of 500,000 men in the Soviet armed forces would be distributed.

Gorbachev said nearly a quarter of a million men would be pulled back from the European front, as well as 10,000 tanks, of which half would be destroyed. The Warsaw Pact intended to shift its forces facing Nato countries into a purely defensive deployment (→2/2).

# Women paid less, do more housework

**Jan 18.** The average working woman is paid less than a man doing an equivalent job, does the bulk of the housework and, should the strain lead to divorce, is two and a half times less likely to re-marry than her ex-husband. So says the latest edition of *Social Trends*, published today by the Central Statistical Office. It also reveals a hardening of attitudes towards gays, extra-marital sex and contraception for under-16s.

**Brian Clough, the Nottingham Forest manager, is said to have hit at least four fans who invaded the pitch after a cup-tie (→ 9/2).**

# Sri Lankan deported from Britain despite massive protests

**Jan 20.** Viraj Mendis was deported to Sri Lanka today, still protesting his claims to be a legitimate refugee from that country's persecution of its Tamil minority. Mendis, who came to Britain as a student in 1973, was taken by force two days ago from the Manchester church in which he had claimed sanctuary for the past two years.

Despite continuing appeals and wide-ranging support, he failed to convince the authorities that he is a genuine refugee. They claim that his pro-Tamil stance is merely a pose and that he is simply an illegal immigrant.

Sri Lanka rejects Mendis's fears and a spokesman stated that he was "an unknown entity here".

*Sanctuary in a Manchester church: Viraj Mendis before he was deported.*

# January

## 1989

| Su | Mo | Tu | We | Th | Fr | Sa |
|----|----|----|----|----|----|----|
| 1 | 2 | 3 | 4 | 5 | 6 | 7 |
| 8 | 9 | 10 | 11 | 12 | 13 | 14 |
| 15 | 16 | 17 | 18 | 19 | 20 | 21 |
| 22 | 23 | 24 | 25 | 26 | 27 | 28 |
| 29 | 30 | 31 | | | | |

**22.** Poland: Solidarity agrees to government terms to end a legal ban on the union (→6/2).

**22.** US: Boeing halts delivery of a new jumbo, the 747-400 (→1/2).

**23.** UK: The Security Service Bill, which puts MI5 on a statutory footing, is given a third Commons reading.

**24.** US: Theodore Bundy, who confessed to killing at least 22 women, is executed in Florida.

**24.** UK: An inquiry begins into allegations of malpractice by the West Midlands Police serious crimes squad (→15/8).

**25.** UK: A green paper for legal reform is published.→

**26.** UK: The government unveils plans to build two new rail tunnels under London.

**27.** UK: Labour leaks a full-scale draft of the NHS white paper.→

**27.** France: The government is rocked by links with an insider-dealing scandal (→16/2).

**28.** USSR: The Memorial Association, which aims to publicize the truth about Stalin's crimes, is launched.

**29.** Pakistan: Benazir Bhutto's People's Party suffers heavy defeats in Punjab by-elections.

**30.** Lebanon: Amal and Hizbollah, the rival Shia groups, sign a pact ending their year-long feud.

**31.** US: Forty potential jurors in the North trial are excluded for knowing too much (→4/5).

**31.** UK: The BBC is fined £2,600 for last year's Legionnaires' disease outbreak, in which three people died (→7/2).

**DEATHS**

**23.** Salvador Dali, Spanish artist (*11/5/04).→

**25.** Lord (David) Basnett, British trade union leader (*9/2/24).

**27.** Thomas Sopwith, British aviation pioneer (*17/1/1888).

**27.** Arthur Marshall, British journalist and broadcaster (*10/5/10).

**28.** Panchem Lama, Tibetan spiritual leader (*1938).

# More than 1,000 die in Soviet quake

**Jan 23.** The Soviet Union is in the grip of another human tragedy, with more than 1,000 people killed by a powerful dawn earthquake which struck the Central Asian republic of Tajikistan. At least two villages were wiped out after being buried by landslides triggered by the shock. The death toll is expected to go much higher.

The earthquake measured 5.5 on the Richter scale, smaller than the Armenian shock only six weeks ago, which registered 6.9. But at its epicentre were two villages which were engulfed by a wall of sand and clay which swept down from the hillsides. In one of the villages 150 families were killed. Local people used picks and shovels in a frantic search for survivors before bulldozers and cranes reached the area.

Soviet television showed pictures of expanses of fresh earth where the villages had been, and groups of grief-stricken Tajiks, some wearing traditional costumes, carrying bodies covered in embroidered cloths. Vast tracts of valuable agricultural land were covered by the layer of mud and sand. Thousands of cattle

*The search for bodies buried by rubble in the Tajikistan earthquake goes on.*

have perished. Bridges were destroyed and electricity supplies and telephone lines severed.

The half a million inhabitants of Dushanbe, the capital of Tajikistan, were woken in terror by the tremors, but no casualties nor damage in the city have been reported. The republic is one of the poorest in the Soviet Union, with a population of

five million, of whom two-thirds live on the land.

It is in the most earthquake-prone area of the entire country and tremors are frequent. The Kremlin is anxious to avoid repeating the organizational chaos and inefficiency which marked rescue efforts at the time of the Armenian earthquake disaster.

# Rebel troops go for power in Argentina

**Jan 24.** Bristling with weapons, a Coca Cola truck crashed through the gates of an infantry barracks in Buenos Aires two days ago, its occupants spraying the guardroom with machine-gun fire. The barracks were captured quickly, but it was not until leaflets were scattered in nearby streets that it became clear that this was a *left-wing* insurrection. Argentina is used to uprisings by disgruntled army officers – there have been three in the past 20 months – but most people believed that the armed left was defeated and destroyed over ten years ago.

The occupation of the barracks – described as a "suicide mission" – has now ended, after fierce fighting which left more than 30 dead. The political implications remain, however, with President Alfonsin forced to involve his distrusted army in a national security council aimed at meeting the left-wing challenge.

# Thatcher outrages lawyers and doctors

**Jan 31.** Mrs Thatcher has embarked on a daring trial of strength with the two professions with most political clout: lawyers and doctors. She is calling for radical reform of their working arrangements. They are indignantly preparing to resist.

In the name of greater competition and a better deal for customers, the government published proposals for abolition of many of the lawyers' restrictive practices.

Solicitors should be able to do work now reserved for barristers. Banks and building societies should share in conveyancing work. A system should be considered for lawyers to charge normal fees for court work only if they win their cases.

A major shake-up in National Health Service financing is also proposed, in a white paper published today. This is aimed at paying doctors and hospitals according to the amount of work they do. There will be tough cost controls.

Backed by doctors' leaders, one Labour MP said: "This is a new

*Kenneth Clarke: health's new deal.*

deal for accountants, not for patients. The health service is being prepared for privatization." Mrs Thatcher repeated the Tory pledge that the NHS is "safe in our hands" and more will be spent on it (→10/3).

# Violence erupts at anti-Rushdie demo

*Moslem marchers seek legal action.*

**Jan 29.** British Moslem leaders said today that they hope to prove that Salman Rushdie's book *The Satanic Verses* breaches the English law of blasphemy.

The common law of blasphemy covers Christ and Christianity, but as it considers it a crime to insult God it could conceivably be applied to Islam. Ali Mohammed Azhar, a barrister, said Moslem leaders would, if necessary, "go all the way to the European Court".

The move comes hard on the heels of the biggest demonstration so far against the author. There were violent scenes yesterday at the protest in London's Hyde Park, which brought together 8,000 Moslems from all over Britain (→12/2).

# Salvador Dali dies, aged eighty-four

**Jan 23.** Salvador Dali, the artist whose personal life was almost as bizarre as his paintings, died today at Figueras in Spain. He was 84. Dali went to Madrid to study art in 1921 but was expelled in 1926 for irresponsible behaviour. However, he had aroused the attention of the leading surrealists and soon began painting his famous distorted dream-like shapes and landscapes.

Gala, Dali's wife of 50 years, calmed his at times hysterical moods. After her death in 1982 he withdrew even more into himself, and after a fire at his castle he needed constant care. Although criticized for making (and allowing others to make) vast sums from his paintings, Dali will be remembered as the greatest of the surrealists.

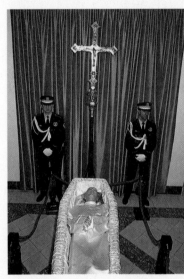

*Salvador Dali: supreme surrealist.*

# Wandsworth jail in the hands of police

*Police and their dogs move into Wandsworth to take control of the prison.*

**Jan 30.** More than 200 police were drafted into Wandsworth prison in south London when warders walked out after refusing to work new shift patterns.

They patrolled the jail under the direction of 36 senior prison staff. There were several disturbances, including two small fires and an assault on an assistant governor.

Members of the Prison Officers' Association in the jail said that the Home Office had imposed new working practices while negotiations with the union were still in progress.

Wandsworth is known for militancy among its warders, who dislike the government's Fresh Start plan to cut overtime (→1/2).

# Cricketing nations agree on South Africa

**Jan 24.** Cricketing nations today reached a compromise over South Africa in an attempt to prevent a split between white and black Test matches. Any player who actively participates in South African cricket after 1 April faces a five-year ban from international competi-tion. In return, nations such as India and the West Indies' states will wipe the slate clean and grant entry permits to players with previous South African links. This winter's England tour of India was called off over the South African issue (→1/8).

# Duke to go to funeral despite opposition

**Jan 29.** Former Japanese PoWs, many of whom worked on the notorious "death railway" in Thailand, are threatening to oust the Duke of Edinburgh as patron of the Burma Star Association if he goes to the funeral of Emperor Hirohito next month.

An official of the association said that he had received hundreds of protest calls from his members. The duke took over when Lord Mountbatten, the former patron, was killed by an IRA bomb. Louis Turner, the 75-year-old secretary of the Aldershot Burma Star branch,

said: "How can someone who is Mountbatten's nephew do this?"

The ex-prisoners' fury has been fuelled by a report in an Australian paper that Japanese soldiers were ordered to supplement their rations by eating the flesh of captured soldiers.

It is on the government's advice that the duke, himself a Far East veteran, is attending the funeral. Although 12,443 British servicemen died in Japanese hands, Britain now has major economic ties with Japan; and Queen and emperor have exchanged visits (→24/2).

# Thatcher rejects Thames TV inquiry

**Jan 26.** Thames TV has been largely vindicated by an independent report published today into its documentary *Death on the Rock*. The programme, an investigation into the shooting of three IRA members in Gibraltar by the SAS last March, was condemned by the government as "trial by television" which contained "damaging inaccuracies". Margaret Thatcher immediately rejected the report and said that the government stood by its original criticisms.

**The ballerina Natalia Makarova sets off on her first visit to the USSR since she defected in 1970.**

# February

## 1989

| Su | Mo | Tu | We | Th | Fr | Sa |
|----|----|----|----|----|----|----|
|    |    |    | 1  | 2  | 3  | 4  |
| 5  | 6  | 7  | 8  | 9  | 10 | 11 |
| 12 | 13 | 14 | 15 | 16 | 17 | 18 |
| 19 | 20 | 21 | 22 | 23 | 24 | 25 |
| 26 | 27 | 28 |    |    |    |    |

**1.** UK: Talks to settle the Wandsworth prison dispute collapse (→6).

**1.** UK: Austin Mitchell is sacked from the Labour front bench over his appointment as an interviewer on Sky TV (→5).

**1.** UK: The Consumers' Association says that tap water in many areas of the UK fails to meet EC standards.

**1.** UK: 1,500 schoolchildren march in London in protest at government plans to introduce student loans.

**2.** US: New allegations about John Tower's private life and business affairs delay a Senate vote on his nomination as defence secretary (→9/3).

**2.** Venezuela: Carlos Perez is inaugurated as president (→28).

**2.** USSR: Pyotr Lushev, Gorbachev's man, replaces Viktor Kulikov as supreme Warsaw Pact commander.

**2.** Greece: A close associate of the prime minister, Andreas Papandreou, is charged in the Bank of Crete scandal (→14/3).

**2.** UK: Edward Heath blames recent leaks of government information on a "corrupt" press office at No. 10.

**3.** China: The government invites Mikhail Gorbachev to visit Beijing (→6/5).

**3.** USSR: Continued high fall-out from Chernobyl prompts the evacuation of 20 more villages in Byelorussia.

**3.** UK: A Right of Reply Bill, allowing people to correct inaccuracies in newspapers, wins a second reading.

**4.** S Africa: The Democratic Party is formed to pursue universal suffrage and attempt to forge links with the ANC (→6/9).

**4.** Lebanon: Israeli troops kill five gunmen in southern Lebanon (→2/3).

### DEATHS

**2.** Sir William Stephenson, British wartime spymaster codenamed "Intrepid" (*11/1/1896).

**3.** John Cassavetes, US film director and actor (*9/12/29).

# Botha resigns as National Party leader

**Feb 3.** P W Botha, who suffered a stroke three weeks ago, stepped down today as leader of the ruling National Party in South Africa, a position he has held for a decade.

Mr Botha, aged 73, will remain as state president, at least until the next whites-only general election, due next March at the latest. His move has surprised the government but there is relief that he has, presumably, averted a future damaging struggle for the presidency.

The National Party's 130 MPs have already chosen a new leader. He is the 52-year-old education minister, Friederik Willem de Klerk, who is considered to be a cautious reformer (→16).

*De Klerk: a new era for Pretoria?*

# Eggs, cheese and chicken pose health risk

**Feb 1.** The Ministry of Agriculture looks set to have egg on its face following reports that it knew of the extent of the salmonella epidemic in raw and partly cooked eggs and poultry a year ago. This was six months before the issue made headlines and ten months before Edwina Currie resigned as health minister after her controversial remark that most egg production was infected with salmonella. The remark outraged farmers and caused egg sales to plummet. Mrs Currie has so far refused to cooperate with a Minis-try of Agriculture probe into the affair. Last week, official – but unpublished – sources confirmed that salmonella had been found in sausages, dog food and even kosher pasta.

There is also growing worry over listeria, another food poisoning bacterium, now a wider danger to health than salmonella, according to the experts. Pregnant women in particular have been advised to avoid soft cheeses, cook-from-frozen chicken meals and prepared supermarket salads (→8).

# Guardian Angels to watch over Londoners

**Feb 1.** Four American vigilantes, who call themselves the Guardian Angels and spend their lives patrolling the high-risk lines of New York's notorious subway system, have arrived to set up a London branch of their organization. The Home Office and London Transport are not keen on the plan, and the Angels spent a day in Special Branch custody before being allowed out of Heathrow airport.

Wearing the distinctive Angel red beret, Curtis Sliwa, the leader of the group, which has won respect from New York commuters, promised full-time patrols on London tubes by the summer. At a crowded meeting in a martial arts club, he promoted well-prepared restraint and told hopeful recruits: "You need to be like Gandhis."

*New York's Guardian Angels go to work on the London underground.*

# Coup brings down Paraguay's dictator

**Feb 3.** Alfredo Stroessner, the brutal dictator of the land-locked republic of Paraguay, is being held in a military barracks tonight after a day of heavy fighting in Asuncion and other Paraguayan towns.

After 34 years of repression, Stroessner faces exile; and tonight his successor, General Andres Rodriguez, leader of the coup, has promised to introduce democracy into the country.

Stroessner, the son of a German immigrant, seized power in an uprising in 1954. His regime has been notorious for its harbouring of Nazi war criminals (→5).

*Andres Rodriguez: the coup leader.*

# Boeing jets to be tested for safety

**Feb 1.** European pressure has prompted an order from the US Federal Aviation Administration that the Boeing company performs safety checks on 1,755 of its jets. All planes delivered since 31 December 1980 are to be checked for faulty wiring and plumbing. The UK Civil Aviation Authority has ordered the checks to be carried out on the 124 Boeing jets run by British airlines.

European concern about Boeing has increased following a suggestion that the air disaster near the M1 motorway in January, in which the pilot shut down his good engine, may have been caused by faulty wiring. No proof of this has yet been found (→8).

# Last Soviet troops leave Afghanistan

**Feb 2.** The nine-year-long Soviet occupation of Afghanistan drew to a close today when the last big Red Army convoy from Kabul set off up the Salang Highway for home. It left to a fanfare of artillery barrage, rockets and machine-gun fire to clear the way of ambushes by the Afghan mujahedin rebels. All 120,000 Soviet military personnel should have left the country within the next ten days.

In Kabul, President Najibullah has called up 30,000 civilians and held a military parade through the city, displaying modern equipment left behind by the departing Soviet military. He told his forces to get ready for a life-or-death struggle against the rebels.

The Russians rolled into Kabul at Christmas 1979, and are leaving behind a nation ravaged by war, disease, hunger and atrocities. More than a million people have died. Six million more, nearly half the pre-war population, have fled their homes to become refugees in Pakistan and Iran. The Soviet dead number nearly 16,000, with some

*Massed Soviet tanks prepare to begin their final withdrawal from Kabul.*

30,000 injured. The Kremlin has never admitted that the war has been a disastrous failure. But it has proved to be expensive, and unpopular at home.

Above all it has had a harmful effect on Moscow's relations with almost every body of international opinion. The Afghan conflict is expected to continue until the rebels are strong enough to bring down the Najibullah regime.

Although his government lacks popular support, the president has the means to hold on for months, possibly years, providing the Kremlin continues to supply him with weapons (→9).

# Hundreds wounded in pre-election violence in Jamaica

**Feb 1.** Streets are blocked by barricades of burning tyres and at least five people are known to have died in election violence here.

Two teenagers, a boy and girl, were killed when police opened fire on members of the Jamaica Labour Party (JLP) in the Fletchers Land district of Kingston. JLP supporters claim that they were fired on without provocation, but the opposition People's National Party is claiming the shots were fired after a mob tried to block a march by one of their candidates.

As police and firemen fight to douse the fires, stones and bottles are flying in Kingston amid fears of the kind of violence that took 700 lives in the 1980 election.

The leadership opponents, Edward Seaga of the JLP and Michael Manley, the former prime minister, signed a peace accord last summer. With Seaga trailing heavily in the polls, it is a fragile peace indeed in Kingston tonight (→10).

# Fraud scandal rocks European Community

**Feb 1.** The European Community is setting up a high-powered anti-fraud squad to try to curb the astronomical losses from swindling. These now amount to £6 billion, according to estimates made during the public hearings into fraud held in Brussels last week by the European parliament. Fraudsters claim export subsidies for goods that never leave port or dishonestly keep import levies. The problem is not so much the small farmer but big organised crime syndicates who are channelling the proceeds into drugs and arms.

# Thousands join pro-Sakharov protest

**Feb 2.** Moscow's elite Academy of Sciences was besieged by 3,000 scientists and research workers today protesting about the way the academy had rigged seats for next month's parliamentary elections in the Soviet Union. The protesters demanded the reversal of a vote which excluded several reformist academicians, among them Dr Andrei Sakharov, from seats in the new Congress of People's Deputies. Dr Sakharov, the father of the Soviet human rights movement, says he supports many of Mikhail Gorbachev's reforms (→22/3).

## Chatlines banned by British Telecom

**Feb 3.** A 12-year-old girl who tried to kill herself after running up a £2,400 phone bill and an 18-year-old who landed his family with a £6,000 bill were among the cases cited by British Telecom today supporting their decision to close down private "chatlines" – a service which allows callers to ring a number and chat to whomever else is on the line. The five main operators of a business estimated to be worth £750,000 a week are believed to be planning to challenge the decision in the courts (→6).

**Marlon Starling (US) beats Lloyd Honeyghan of Britain to take the world welterweight title.**

*Crowds gather outside the Academy of Sciences in support of the reformers.*

13

# February

1989

| Su | Mo | Tu | We | Th | Fr | Sa |
|----|----|----|----|----|----|----|
|    |    |    | 1  | 2  | 3  | 4  |
| 5  | 6  | 7  | 8  | 9  | 10 | 11 |
| 12 | 13 | 14 | 15 | 16 | 17 | 18 |
| 19 | 20 | 21 | 22 | 23 | 24 | 25 |
| 26 | 27 | 28 |    |    |    |    |

**5.** Paraguay: The new leader, Andres Rodriguez, promises elections within three months.

**5.** Pakistan: The country's first successful test of a surface-to-surface long-range missile is announced.

**5.** UK: It is reported that people with negative tests for Aids are being denied life assurance.→

**6.** UK: The Wandsworth prison officers' dispute is settled.

**6.** UK: BT closes chatlines despite legal moves by the lines' operators.

**6.** UK: A construction worker on the Channel Tunnel dies in the second such fatal accident in two weeks.

**7.** Milan: Former tennis star Bjorn Borg survives a drugs overdose.

**7.** UK: Jack Ashley, the MP for Stoke-on-Trent and campaigner for the handicapped, announces his retirement.

**7.** US: The government accuses Israel of a "substantial increase in human rights violations".

**8.** UK: Appearing before the Commons agriculture committee, Edwina Currie refuses to clarify the eggs mystery (→10).

**9.** UK: Brian Clough is found guilty of bringing football into disrepute and fined £5,000.

**9.** UK: Investigators rule out faulty wiring as the cause of the M1 plane crash (→24).

**10.** UK: A government inquiry into all aspects of food poisoning is launched.

**10.** Pakistan: Talks collapse between the Afghan mujahedin about forming an alternative government in Kabul.

**10.** Kabul: The first UN relief supplies are flown in (→15).

**11.** Hungary: The government admits the failure of one-party socialism (→30/5).

**DEATHS**

**5.** Emrys James, British actor (*1/9/30).

**6.** Barbara Tuchman, US historian (*30/1/12).

## Kinnock confirms shift on unilateralism

**Feb 9.** Neil Kinnock tonight confirmed that the new-look Labour Party is moving towards a formal decision to drop unilateral nuclear disarmament from its programme. This will probably be taken at the party's autumn conference. The Labour leader said in a TV interview: "We are the party that has thrown off the past, not in terms of our values and convictions, but in terms of a lot of shibboleths."

Mr Kinnock argued that the unilateralist stance was now outdated because headway had been made with the multilateralist disarmament process. This shift in policy will be passionately resisted by Labour's left-wing and by supporters of the Campaign for Nuclear Disarmament, which Mr Kinnock has proudly backed in the past. The party leadership is determined to dump all policies which lost votes in previous elections and its unilateralist defence one tops the list.

Mr Kinnock explained: "We are doing it from a basis of analysis and

*Neil Kinnock drops a bombshell.*

conscience." He knows that many party members will dub this as a betrayal of socialism, but in Labour's bid to attract middle-ground voters the Red Flag must begin to look pink (→26).

## Afghan guerrillas step up battle for Kabul

**Feb 9.** With the last Soviet troops due to leave Afghanistan within a few days, mujahedin rebels in hills around Kabul have stepped up their rocket attacks on the city's airport.

Seven people were killed yesterday while Soviet transport aircraft flew in food and other supplies for the beleaguered capital. The main airlift home of men and equipment is complete. The Afghan armed forces said they had launched an offensive to clear rebels cutting the vital supply route to the Soviet border. One new weapon being used was a Soviet multiple-rocket launcher with a range of 18 miles.

Meanwhile, mujahedin groups are meeting for the first time, in Pakistan, to try to put together a government that could take over in Kabul if and when the regime of President Najibullah falls (→10).

**Feb 7. A railway viaduct across the River Ness is destroyed as floods caused by torrential rain and exceptional tides wreak havoc in Inverness.**

## First woman bishop consecrated in US

**Feb 11.** The Boston Episcopal church risked schism today by consecrating the first woman bishop in Anglican history. The traditionalists who objected were booed by the 8,000-strong congregation. When asked "Are you persuaded that God has called you to the office of bishop?" the Right Rev Barbara Harris replied with unexpected emphasis: "I *am* so persuaded."

Her blackness was even more important than her sex, according to Rev Paul Washington. In his sermon he said: "The first woman to be consecrated as a bishop? If that's all, you have missed the point. This isn't just a woman, but a woman born of slavery."

*Bishop Harris at a dramatic moment in the history of the Anglican church.*

## New antibody hope for Aids sufferers

**Feb 9.** A new treatment for Aids sufferers, using a man-made antibody, has been developed in San Francisco. The antibody, based on a molecule called CD4, may prove more effective than AZT, the most successful drug so far in fighting the Aids virus, and have less serious side-effects. It could keep the disease at bay for years and markedly lengthen victims' lives, although it will never offer a complete cure. Tests on Aids patients may begin later in the year.

# Boeing jet crashes in the Azores

**Feb 8.** One hundred and forty-four people died today when a Boeing 707 jet crashed into the side of the 2,000-foot-high Pico Alto mountain on the island of Santa Maria in the Azores.

The airliner, owned by the Independent Air Corporation of Smyrna, Tennessee, was en route from Bergamo in northern Italy to the Dominican Republic. It was coming into land at Vila do Porto for refuelling when it crashed. The pilot had apparently decided to use the "visual" approach for landing because the airport has no radar and the alternative landing system would have taken too long in view of the shortage of fuel (→9).

# Solidarity talks with government

**Feb 6.** The jailers sat down with the jailed in Poland today to discuss ways of solving the country's deepening economic, social and political crisis. The round-table talks between the Communist government and the banned trade union Solidarity are expected to last two months. The Solidarity team is led by Lech Walesa, who today shook hands with the man who locked him up in 1981: the interior minister, Czeslaw Kiszczak (→5/4).

# Satellite TV goes on air: but no dishes

*Media magnate Rupert Murdoch shows off a model of his Astra satellite.*

**Feb 5.** The number of TV channels theoretically available to the British public was doubled at a stroke today with the launch of Rupert Murdoch's much touted – by the Murdoch press at least – Sky Television network.

The reality was somewhat less dramatic: because of the near impossibility of obtaining the necessary dish aerial, the number of people actually able to receive Sky Channel, Sky News, Sky Movies and Euro Sport is estimated at around 50,000.

Mr Murdoch, who has already spent £25 million setting up the network, blamed himself for the shortage of aerials and said the opposition to his plans sprung from real British class snobbery. Asked whether more television meant worse, he replied: "In America there are 30 channels, amazing documentaries, excellent serials. When I arrive here all I find late at night is snooker."

Plans were also announced to use one of the 24 radio channels that come with the TV channels to carry the BBC World Service. Meanwhile, Bryan Gould, Labour's trade and industry spokesman, demanded that the Monopolies Commission investigate Mr Murdoch's media empire.

# V&A staff forced to quit in shake-up

**Feb 8.** Staff at the Victoria and Albert Museum are up in arms at a controversial plan to restructure the museum's management.

Last week nine of the museum's senior curators – internationally renowned experts in their fields – were offered redundancy terms by the museum's director, Elizabeth Esteve-Coll, who succeeded Sir Roy Strong on 1 January 1988.

The move comes as part of plans to separate the job of managing the collection from that of research. It follows an official report – rejected by the curators – which claimed that the V&A let objects deteriorate as a backlog of conservation work built up (→17).

*Esteve-Coll: museum's new broom.*

# Landslide victory for Michael Manley in Jamaican election

**Feb 10.** Despite accusations of ballot-rigging and other electoral frauds, Michael Manley, the former prime minister, has won a landslide victory in the Jamaican elections. The colourful and charismatic – and four times married – Manley has won 44 of the 60 electoral seats after a campaign in which ten people were killed and more than 100 injured.

The new prime minister ("my style will be open and consultative") has interests ranging from cricket through classical music to pulp fiction. He told his people tonight that he proposes to establish immediate contacts with President Bush, Mrs Thatcher and the International Monetary Fund.

*The charismatic Michael Manley rejoices in his return to Jamaica's helm.*

# Londoner dies of Legionnaires' bug

**Feb 7.** A man who died on January 25 was killed by Legionnaires' disease, health officials said today. Joseph Sheedy, aged 41, was the first victim of another outbreak in London's West End. Eight other cases have been officially confirmed so far, while 19 more are suspected.

An investigation into the source of the outbreak is centring on 17 air-conditioning cooling towers near Leicester Square, from which environmental health officers think the Legionnaires' bacterium may have been carried in water droplets. Mr Sheedy was a building worker who is thought to have worked on rooftops in the area (→6/3).

| Su | Mo | Tu | We | Th | Fr | Sa |
|----|----|----|----|----|----|----|
|    |    |    | 1  | 2  | 3  | 4  |
| 5  | 6  | 7  | 8  | 9  | 10 | 11 |
| 12 | 13 | 14 | 15 | 16 | 17 | 18 |
| 19 | 20 | 21 | 22 | 23 | 24 | 25 |
| 26 | 27 | 28 |    |    |    |    |

**12.** Islamabad: At least five people are killed and dozens are injured at an anti-Rushdie protest rally. →

**12.** UK: A gang of "steamers" robs 13 passengers on a late-night train from Bedford to King's Cross.

**13.** Japan: Four prominent businessmen are arrested in connection with the Recruit insider-dealing scandal (→25/4).

**14.** El Salvador: Central American leaders agree on a plan to expel the Contras from Honduras (→8/8).

**14.** India: The US company Union Carbide is told to pay £270 million for claims arising from the 1984 Bhopal gas leak.

**14.** Belgium: Paul Vanden Boeynants, the kidnapped former prime minister, is freed after the payment of a £1 million ransom.

**15.** Afghanistan: General Boris Gromov, the commander of the Soviet forces, is the last Soviet soldier to leave.

**16.** France: Roger-Patrice Pelat, a close friend of President Francois Mitterrand, is charged with insider dealing.

**16.** S Africa: Some political prisoners end a hunger strike when the government promises to free 1,000 detainees.

**16.** Sri Lanka: Ranasinghe Premadasa's ruling United National Party wins the general election.

**17.** Iran: President Ali Khamenei tells Rushdie he may be spared if he begs forgiveness (→19).

**17.** Arctic: Scientists say that ozone-depleting chemicals over the North Pole are 50 times greater than expected.

**17.** UK: Eight top scholars accept redundancy terms from the Victoria and Albert museum.

**18.** UK: Eleven paediatricians say that most of the children involved in the Cleveland crisis were sexually abused (→22).

**DEATH**

**17.** Guy Laroche, French couturier (*1921). →

## Evidence mounts against Winnie Mandela

*Winnie Mandela flanked by members of her notorious "football club".*

**Feb 16.** Winnie Mandela, the wife of the jailed African National Congress leader Nelson Mandela, was today publicly denounced by the leaders of South Africa's radical black opposition.

The move, whereby the radical leadership "dissociates itself from Mrs Mandela and her actions", comes after months in which her maverick and arrogant behaviour has proved increasingly embarrassing both to the nationalist cause and to the prestigious name of its jailed leader.

The activities of the so-called "Mandela United Football Club", Mrs Mandela's notorious personal bodyguard, have brought things to a head. The "club" – which never plays football – has been accused of harassing and abusing local people in Soweto, where Mrs Mandela lives, and now it appears to have murder on its hands.

A body found last month with stab marks in its neck has been identified as that of a 14-year-old activist, "Stompie" Moeketsi Seipei, one of four youths kidnapped by the "club" from a Methodist church shelter in December and taken to Mrs Mandela's house.

Accounts of how the boys were beaten – allegedly even by Mrs Mandela herself – have gradually seeped out. The police are investigating (→21).

## Violence mars poll run-up in Sri Lanka

**Feb 12.** At least 45 people died in Sri Lanka at the weekend, in an upsurge of violence during the run-up to parliamentary elections.

The government said that Tamil Tiger separatists killed 37 Sinhalese villagers, including 20 children, in one attack, and Sinhalese militants were blamed for the murder of an opposition candidate in his own home.

The seven-week campaign has so far claimed at least 700 lives. Most of the attacks have been blamed on terrorists from the Sinhalese nationalist group, Janatha Vimukthi Peramuna, which wants an election boycott (→16).

## Political row grows over lawyer's death

**Feb 13.** A major political row is likely to follow the shooting last night of Pat Finucane, a leading Belfast solicitor who specialized in IRA cases. Mr Finucane was killed by gunmen who burst into his north Belfast home. His wife was injured in the attack. The Ulster Defence Association is thought to be responsible. Some Labour MPs fear the shooting may have been triggered by remarks of Douglas Hogg, the Home Officer minister who recently criticized "a number of solicitors in Northern Ireland who are unduly sympathetic to the cause of the IRA". Mr Hogg has condemned the killing.

## Fewer unemployed, but inflation is up

**Feb 17.** Government figures out yesterday show that unemployment has fallen below two million for the first time in eight years. The good news is overshadowed by today's announcement that inflation rose to an annual rate of 7.5 per cent last month. This is the highest rate since August 1982 and is more than double the rate prevailing in the early months of last year. The Treasury said the increase was temporary and due largely to increased mortgage payments.

## Cassette player hid Lockerbie bomb

**Feb 16.** Police confirmed today that the Pan Am jumbo jet which crashed on the village of Lockerbie last December, killing 270 people, was blown up by a bomb hidden in a radio-cassette player.

It is thought probable that the bomb was loaded on to a Boeing 727 at Frankfurt airport and then transferred to the 747 at Heathrow, although it may have been loaded at Heathrow. The aluminium aircraft baggage container which held the bomb has been identified by police, but forensic experts are still trying to establish in which item of baggage the cassette player was concealed (→23).

**Guy Laroche, the French fashion designer who died this week, was a dominant figure in the world of couture for over 30 years.**

# Khomeini orders Moslems to kill British author

*Khomeini: voice of Islamic justice.*

**Feb 14.** In an unprecedented move, Ayatollah Khomeini, the Iranian leader, today ordered the execution of Salman Rushdie, the British author accused of blaspheming Islam. In an edict broadcast on Tehran radio, the ayatollah said: "I inform the proud Moslem people of the world that the author of *The Satanic Verses* book, which is against Islam, the Prophet and the Koran, and all those involved in its publication who were aware of its content, are sentenced to death."

*The Satanic Verses*, which was published in Britain last September, has already been publicly burnt by angry Moslems. At least five people died in Pakistan at the weekend in a protest rally against the book.

Rushdie's novel takes its title from verses which the Prophet Mohammed ordered to be cut from the Koran because they were inspired by the devil. In one passage particularly offensive to Moslems, prostitutes play out a fantasy that they are the Prophet's wives.

Rushdie, who lives in London, said the strong reaction to the book was based on a misunderstanding: "It is not true that this book is a blasphemy against Islam. I doubt very much Khomeini or anyone else in Iran has read it." He said he took the ayatollah's attack seriously, however, and was considering seeking a police guard (→15).

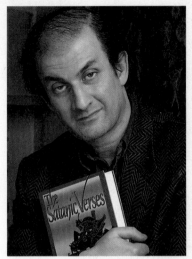

*Rushdie: under sentence of death.*

## Protesters attack UK embassy in Tehran

**Feb 15.** A crowd of demonstrators marched on the British embassy in Tehran today, chanting "Death to England" and "Death to America". Rallying in support of Ayatollah Khomeini's sentence of death on Salman Rushdie, the several thousand protesters broke windows in the embassy, which reopened last November after a year's closure.

The embassy demonstration was part of a day of mourning in Iran to protest against Mr Rushdie's book, *The Satanic Verses*. Senior political figures in the country endorsed Khomeini's call for the author's execution, and the Revolutionary Guard Corps said it was ready to carry out the order. In another de-

velopment, Hassan Sanei, the head of a wealthy Islamic charity organization, offered a $1m reward to any non-Iranian who would "punish this mercenary of colonialism for his shameful act".

There are signs that Khomeini may be using the Rushdie controversy to improve Iran's standing in the Islamic world, following his acceptance of the ceasefire with Iraq in the Gulf war, and to inspire a renewal of revolutionary fervour in the country. Hashemi Rafsanjani, the speaker of the Iranian parliament, said that Khomeini believed that *The Satanic Verses* represented a "well-calculated and extensive plot against Islam" (→16).

## Rushdie in hiding, security stepped up

**Feb 16.** Salman Rushdie has cancelled a three-week tour of the USA to promote *The Satanic Verses* and gone into hiding under police guard. Experts on Islam and terrorism have warned that he may need protection for the rest of his life.

Security has also been stepped up at the London offices of Rushdie's publishers, Viking Penguin, who have issued a statement regretting the distress caused to Moslems by the novel but confirmed that they intend to go ahead with a paperback edition. The hardback edition has already sold 58,000 copies in Britain. A West German firm, however, today joined publishers in France and Italy in abandoning plans to bring out the book.

Police in Britain are intensifying surveillance of known Islamic extremists. They are investigating a remark by Sayed Abdul Quddus, the joint secretary of the Bradford Council of Mosques, that Mr Rushdie "deserves hanging".

A group of prominent writers and journalists, organized by the playwright Harold Pinter, has urged the prime minister to denounce Ayatollah Khomeini's call for Rushdie's death. While condemning the threat as "totally unacceptable", the British government today said it would maintain diplomatic links with Tehran, for the time being at least (→17).

## Briton sentenced for spying in Iran

**Feb 14.** Roger Cooper, the British businessman detained in Tehran for more than three years, has received a heavy sentence for spying, according to Iran's information minister, Mohammed Reyshahri. Although proceedings against Mr Cooper are complete, the minister said, a final judgement would be issued later.

Mr Cooper, who was held in December 1985 while working for a US offshore oil company, has made "confessions" on Iranian TV, but the British government is unaware of specific charges against him. The Foreign Office is seeking to clarify the latest development.

*Roger Cooper – a British spy?*

*Angry Iranians show their determination to win retribution from the West.*

17

| Su | Mo | Tu | We | Th | Fr | Sa |
|----|----|----|----|----|----|----|
|    |    |    | 1  | 2  | 3  | 4  |
| 5  | 6  | 7  | 8  | 9  | 10 | 11 |
| 12 | 13 | 14 | 15 | 16 | 17 | 18 |
| 19 | 20 | 21 | 22 | 23 | 24 | 25 |
| 26 | 27 | 28 |    |    |    |    |

**19.** Iran: Khomeini says Rushdie will not be forgiven even if he repents.→

**20.** UK: The Clapham rail crash inquiry opens.

**21.** Prague: The writer Vaclav Havel is jailed for inciting last month's demonstrations.

**21.** S Africa: Two of Winnie Mandela's former bodyguards are charged with murder.

**22.** UK: The paediatricians who spoke out on the Cleveland crisis admit they made a "mistake".

**23.** Cairo: Eduard Shevardnadze, the Soviet foreign minister, unveils a Middle East peace plan.

**23.** UK: Hugh Annesley is appointed chief constable of the Royal Ulster Constabulary.

**24.** Pacific: A Boeing 747 cargo door blows off at 22,000 feet, sucking 16 to their deaths.

**24.** Japan: World leaders attend the funeral of Hirohito.

**24.** Bombay: An anti-Rushdie protest results in eight deaths and 56 injuries (→26).

**25.** USSR: Thousands march through Tbilisi, the capital of Georgia, calling for independence for Georgia (→10/4).

**26.** N Ireland: Unionists reject an offer of talks with the Irish premier, Charles Haughey.

**26.** Karachi: An explosion linked to the Rushdie affair kills a Pakistani guard at the British Council library.

**27.** UK: David Owen, the SDP leader, rejects calls from the Social and Liberal Democrats for a by-election pact.

**28.** UK: School inspectors warn of a teacher crisis.

**28.** Venezuela: Up to 100 are killed in riots after austerity measures are introduced.

### DEATHS

**22.** Sir Raymond Gower, British Conservative MP (*15/6/16).

**26.** Roy Eldridge, US jazz player (*30/1/11).

**27.** Konrad Lorenz, Austrian polymath (*7/11/03).

## No surprises as Tyson smashes Bruno

*Mike Tyson (r.) has little difficulty in dispatching the great British loser.*

**Feb 25.** Mike Tyson, the champion, predictably defeated Frank Bruno, the British challenger, in their world heavyweight title fight in Las Vegas.

The referee stopped the bout in the fifth round as Tyson battered Bruno with a series of uppercuts to the chin, followed by blows to the body. He stepped in even before Bruno's anxious manager, Terry Lawless, could reach the ring, waving a white towel in surrender.

From the start Bruno never looked likely to trouble the champion, but he showed considerable courage and stamina to stay in the fight after suffering a first-round knockdown.

He lost one point in that round for wrestling the American to the ropes, and was always behind on points. Tyson seemed as if he were taking out all his recent domestic and public problems on the challenger.

The fans gave Bruno an ovation for going so far against so powerful an opponent, and there was immediate talk of a re-match.

But Bruno was initially more concerned about finding his family and going away to recover from the pummelling he had received.

In Leeds a man died after falling through a restaurant window during a row over the result, and in Shrewsbury 12 people were arrested after a hotel brawl when a video link failed.

**Athlete Colin Jackson helps the UK notch up its best-ever medal tally in the European indoor championships, at The Hague.**

## Envoys withdrawn in Rushdie affair

**Feb 22.** Nicholas Browne, Britain's charge d'affaires in Tehran, arrived home today after the British government recalled all its diplomats without officially severing ties. Sir Geoffrey Howe, the foreign secretary, yesterday expelled the Iranian charge d'affaires from London, demanding a full retraction of Khomeini's death threat against Salman Rushdie, the author of *The Satanic Verses*. Iran has ordered its envoys to the EC to return home in response to the decision by EC foreign ministers, supported by President Bush, to withdraw their ambassadors from Iran (→24).

## Poll gives Labour lead over Tories

**Feb 26.** Labour has opened up a one percentage point lead over the Conservatives, according to the latest nationwide opinion poll. This is the first time for more than two years that the government has fallen behind.

Its majority has also been slashed in the true-blue Richmond (North Yorkshire) constituency, where the strongest challenge was from the Social Democratic Party. Midterm blues have now set in for Mrs Thatcher. Voters are telling opinion pollsters and party canvassers that they object more than anything else to proposed National Health Service reforms (→27).

## Tanks in Kosovo as ethnic unrest grows

**Feb 28.** Troops and tanks are moving into the province of Kosovo, Yugoslavia's ethnic hotspot, after a week of strikes by Albanians. Emergency measures were introduced in Kosovo yesterday after the collapse of the local leadership, accused by the Albanians of pursuing pro-Serbian policies. Serbia, the biggest Yugoslav republic, is determined to regain control over the province.

Serbia's campaign is being led by Slobodan Milosevic, an arch nationalist and Serbian Communist Party boss. Hundreds of thousands of Serbs have taken to the streets in Belgrade and elsewhere, alleging that minority Serbs in Kosovo have been suppressed by the ethnic Albanians. An uprising in Kosovo in 1981 led to scores of deaths and martial law (→21/3).

YUGOSLAVIA'S TROUBLED PROVINCES

SLOVENIA — HUNGARY — ROMANIA
Zagreb — VOJVODINA
CROATIA — Belgrade
BOSNIA — SERBIA
Sarajevo
100 miles
160 km
MONTENEGRO — KOSOVO
ITALY — MACEDONIA
ALBANIA — GREECE

© Chronicle Communications Ltd.

# Bush faces row in China

*Deng Xiaoping, the Chinese leader, gets down to talks with President Bush.*

**Feb 26.** President Bush's "happy homecoming" to Beijing has been marred by the Chinese government's refusal to allow a leading dissident to attend a barbecue given by the president and his wife for their Chinese hosts, including the Chinese prime minister, Li Peng.

Astrophysicist Fang Lizhi – a leading advocate of free speech and democratic reform – was stopped by police on his way to the party and told that he and his wife, another prominent dissident, were not on the guest list.

A White House spokesman confirmed that Mr Fang had been invited to the barbecue as an "honoured friend", and Fang told a press conference: "This is a fresh example

that shows the human rights situation in China."

Chinese authorities are clearly furious at what they see as American interference in their affairs. In a strongly worded speech tonight, Zhao Ziyang, the general secretary of the Communist Party, lashed out at dissidents who, he said, advocate "the multi-party politics and parliamentary politics of western countries".

Mr Zhao – regarded by many as a liberal-minded leader – told Mr Bush that men like Fang threatened the Chinese reform programme by playing into the hands of hard-line conservatives. American officials are trying to play down the Fang affair.

**Feb 26. United in opposition to three possible routes being considered by BR, more than 15,000 demonstrators march through London in protest over plans to build a high-speed rail link to the Channel Tunnel.**

# IRA bombs destroy Shropshire barracks

**Feb 20.** Three bombs planted by the IRA devastated an army barracks housing men from the Parachute Regiment.

Only one person was slightly injured in the explosion, after the alarm was raised by sentries who disturbed two men as they planted a fourth device at the Tern Hill barracks near Market Drayton in Shropshire. About 100 pounds of Semtex explosive was used in the attack.

Detectives believe the IRA men are those being sought in connection with the discovery of a bomb factory in Clapham, south London, in December 1988. They may also have been responsible for the bombing of the Inglis barracks in north

London in August the same year. One man died and nine were injured in that incident.

The two Tern Hill sentries challenged the intruders shortly after 3am inside the nine and a half mile perimeter fence.

There was a scuffle before the IRA men fled. One of the soldiers loaded his rifle and fired three shots, but missed.

Soon afterwards a local householder was roused from his bed and his car was stolen at gunpoint. It was later found abandoned ten miles away. The Ministry of Defence rejected suggestions of lax security, claiming that vigilance by their patrol had ensured that no one was killed.

*The dust rises from the Tern Hill barracks, shattered by three bombs.*

# Thatcher and Kohl divided on missiles

**Feb 21.** Mrs Thatcher and Helmut Kohl, the West German chancellor, tonight agreed to differ over modernization of Nato's short-range missiles. The prime minister wants bigger and better ones based on German soil. The chancellor, facing growing domestic pressure to take a softer line with the Soviet Union, prefers to defer a decision. The two leaders issued a statement fudging their discord after two days of talks in Frankfurt. A West German spokesman said: "Neither side wants trouble over this." However, Mrs Thatcher's Iron Lady stance has upset the Germans (→21/4).

# Lockerbie families castigate Channon

**Feb 23.** Relatives of the victims of the Lockerbie air disaster have demanded the resignation of Paul Channon, the transport secretary. This follows a statement by the US Federal Aviation Authority that it issued only 16 warnings about terrorist threats to the Department of Transport last year. Mr Channon had given the impression that the warning received concerning Pan Am flights from Frankfurt was one of so many that it was not considered necessary to alert Heathrow. His comments on the warning's credibility conflict with those from US and West German sources (→21/3).

# March

## 1989

| Su | Mo | Tu | We | Th | Fr | Sa |
|----|----|----|----|----|----|----|
|    |    |    | 1  | 2  | 3  | 4  |
| 5  | 6  | 7  | 8  | 9  | 10 | 11 |
| 12 | 13 | 14 | 15 | 16 | 17 | 18 |
| 19 | 20 | 21 | 22 | 23 | 24 | 25 |
| 26 | 27 | 28 | 29 | 30 | 31 |    |

**1. UK:** It is announced that the trade deficit rose to £1.7 billion in January, the third worst figure on record.

**1. UK:** The Scottish Centre for Economic and Social Research is set up to promote Scottish political ideas.

**1. Yugoslavia:** A curfew is imposed in Kosovo, where protests continue at the alleged intimidation of Serbs (→13).

**1. Israel:** The Likud party wins a sweeping victory in municipal elections.

**2. W Germany:** Police break a ring of hackers alleged to have sold US military computer passwords to the USSR.

**2. UK:** Gareth Morris, the last trade unionist at the Government Communications HQ in Cheltenham, leaves after being sacked.

**2. Venezuela:** Troop reinforcements are flown into Caracas, where at least 200 people have died in riots (→3).

**2. Vietnam:** A group of 75 Vietnamese boat people returns to Vietnam from Hong Kong – the first to do so (→27/6).

**2. UK:** Margaret Thatcher says that the government will ban the use of CFCs in British-made fridges.→

**3. Belfast:** Michael Stone is given a 30-year jail term for last year's killings at an IRA funeral at Milltown cemetery.

**3. UK:** A Czech spy who called himself Erwin van Haarlem and posed as an art dealer is jailed for ten years.

**3. S Africa:** Following prison hunger strikes, 279 political detainees have been freed; about 550 remain in captivity.

**3. Venezuela:** All payments on the country's $32 billion foreign debt are suspended.

**4. Rome:** The Vatican condemns *The Satanic Verses* as blasphemous (→5).

**4. W Germany:** The hitherto fragmented Green Party unites to enter conventional politics.

**4. UK:** At the Tory local government conference, Mrs Thatcher criticizes the handling of the water privatization issue (→18/4).

## Four Palestinians killed in border ambush

*A heavily armed Israeli jeep on border patrol in strife-torn south Lebanon.*

**March 2.** A joint Israeli and Southern Lebanese Army patrol today ambushed and killed four Palestinian guerrillas in Israel's border security zone in south Lebanon. It was the second time in less than two weeks that the Democratic Front for the Liberation of Palestine (DFLP) had attempted operations in the area.

Infiltration by radical Palestinians into the buffer zone could compromise talks between the USA and the PLO – agreed by the Bush administration last December after the PLO leader, Yasser Arafat, publicly renounced terrorism. Diplomatic sources in Washington have said that it will proceed with discussions only if the PLO halts attacks on Israeli targets.

Nayef Hawatmeh, the DFLP leader, said that his group was not accountable for promises made by Arafat. His guerrillas had been planning to attack an Israeli settlement in revenge for the bombing of a DFLP headquarters in which 20 civilians allegedly died.

William Waldegrave, a British foreign minister who was visiting the region, said the issue was not clear-cut. He condemned violence, but made the point that the Israeli troops were on the soil of another country.

## Britain rejects offer of talks with Iran on Rushdie affair

**March 2.** Britain has turned down an Iranian offer of talks on the Salman Rushdie affair, saying there is no point in a meeting until Iran renounces the threat of violence against a British citizen.

In approaches to the Foreign Office, Akunzadeh Basti, the Iranian charge d'affaires in London who arrived back in Tehran yesterday, offered to arrange talks in Geneva – to explain a call by the Iranian parliament for a total break with Britain unless it condemned *The Satanic Verses*.

Britain declined the offer because it appeared to come from only a moderate faction of the Iranian government, while hardliners have shown no sign of conciliation.

Keen to keep open the chance of compromise, Sir Geoffrey Howe, the foreign secretary, speaking in a BBC interview, emphasized that the British government was not upholding freedom of speech because it liked Rushdie's novel: "The book is extremely critical, rude, about us. It compares Britain with Hitler's Germany. We don't like that any more than Moslems like the attacks on their faith."

Another person to receive death threats for allegedly speaking out in defence of Rushdie is Peter Sissons, the Channel 4 newsreader (→4).

## Total defeat for France at English hands at Twickenham

**March 4.** England stormed to their greatest rugby triumph in years today, crushing France by 11 points to nil at Twickenham. Tries by Will Carling and Andy Robinson plus a penalty by Rob Andrew gave England a victory which puts them in sight of the five nations' championship. It was England's first defeat of France for seven years and the first time in 25 years that the French failed to score a single point. Scotland, who beat Ireland 37-21 today, can also win the title, but their final match away to France in two weeks' time seems harder than England's task against a demoralized Wales, still without a single point. However, England have not won in Cardiff for 26 years (→18).

*England muscle in to beat France for the first time in seven years.*

# Europe agrees to ban use of ozone-destroying gases

**March 2.** The 12 member countries of the European Community (EC) have agreed to ban chlorofluorocarbons (CFCs), the industrially produced gases that damage the earth's ozone layer, by the end of the century. At a Brussels meeting they also undertook to reduce CFC production by 85 per cent "as soon as possible". The pact covers the eight CFCs most harmful to ozone.

Britain's representative, Lord Caithness, described the accord as "a quantum leap forward". It goes far beyond the Montreal Protocol of 1987, under which 70 countries agreed to reduce CFC production levels by half by the year 1999.

A protective filter high in the atmosphere, the ozone layer screens out dangerous ultra-violet radiation from the sun. Evidence that CFCs are eating away at it has been growing for several years.

The EC pact comes just days before a London conference on saving the ozone, to be attended by about 100 nations. Some EC members may have wished to pre-empt the London talks, particularly as Britain was initially asking for only an 85 per cent reduction in Brussels. Next week the discussion moves to The Hague, where France, Norway and the Netherlands are hosting a conference (→7).

# Purley crash kills five

*Overturned like a model train: rescue workers with the 12.50 to London.*

**March 4.** Five people died today when one passenger train ploughed into the back of another near Purley in south London. The impact of the crash sent carriages tumbling down the embankment into nearby gardens.

The collision appears to have been triggered by the late departure from Purley of the 12.50am Horsham to Victoria train. Leaving three minutes late, it pulled on to the express line to London when it should have been much further advanced on its journey. The 12.17 Littlehampton to Victoria service smashed into the back of it shortly after it joined the express line. But

the late train should have been safe, provided there were no failures in the signalling system and the driver responded correctly.

A full investigation into the cause of Britain's second major train accident in three months has already begun. David Morgan, the driver of the Littlehampton train, who was taken to hospital with two broken thighs, will be interviewed tomorrow by the BR inquiry team.

The Purley crash, which injured 94 people in addition to the five who lost their lives, has produced disturbing echoes of the Clapham rail disaster last December in which 34 people died (→29).

# Baker to advisers: "I know better"

**March 2.** Kenneth Baker, the education supremo, clashed with his advisers today over his conviction that old-fashioned grammar, long neglected by modern teaching methods, should once more take a central role in English studies.

Compilers of the new national curriculum, which recommends optimum levels of attainment for children as they progress through their education, have placed oral skills above traditional reading and writing attainments.

Mr Baker remains adamant, but he will have a harder time convincing the real experts: Britain's children and their teachers.

# Johnson "started steroids in 1981"

**March 1.** The Canadian athlete Ben Johnson – who lost his 100 metres Olympic gold medal last year for drug-taking – had been using steroids since 1981, his coach, Charlie Francis, told a Canadian royal commission on drugs in sport.

Francis admitted today that he had set up a drugs programme for Johnson and four other athletes at his Toronto club. Supplies were provided by a doctor.

Johnson has always denied the charges against him, but Francis said the athlete knew the steroids he took were performance-enhancing drugs – which had the effect of giving him a metre's advantage over other competitors.

# "We have become a grandmother ..."

*A proud granny faces the cameras.*

**March 3.** Overcome with pride and joy, Margaret Thatcher interrupted her ministerial duties today to tell the world: "We have become a grandmother." In regal style, Mrs Thatcher revealed that her American daughter-in-law, Diane, had given birth to a son: "It is something very deep within you to have a grandson. We are absolutely thrilled." Diane, wife of the premier's son Mark, and baby Michael are doing well after the birth on Tuesday in Dallas, Texas. It was kept a secret until they returned home.

**"Scandal", the film that has revived national fascination in the Profumo affair: Joanne Whalley stars as Christine Keeler, the young temptress whose involvement with both the secretary of state for war, John Profumo, and the Soviet naval attache, Eugene Ivanov, rocked the government in 1963.**

# March

## 1989

| Su | Mo | Tu | We | Th | Fr | Sa |
|----|----|----|----|----|----|----|
|    |    |    | 1  | 2  | 3  | 4  |
| 5  | 6  | 7  | 8  | 9  | 10 | 11 |
| 12 | 13 | 14 | 15 | 16 | 17 | 18 |
| 19 | 20 | 21 | 22 | 23 | 24 | 25 |
| 26 | 27 | 28 | 29 | 30 | 31 |    |

**5.** US: Time Inc and Warner Communications announce plans to merge into the world's largest media empire.

**5.** Syria: Ahmed Jibril, an extremist Palestinian leader, vows to kill Rushdie (→7).

**5.** UK: A new newspaper, *Wales on Sunday*, is launched.

**6.** UK: A fourth man dies in the Legionnaires' disease outbreak in London's West End.

**6.** India: After more than four years in prison without trial, 104 Sikhs are freed.

**7.** Iran: Ties with Britain are unilaterally cut; a diplomatic visit to the jailed businessman Roger Cooper is halted (→8).

**7.** UK: Police find a large quantity of Semtex explosive near Scarborough, where a Tory conference is due to be held.

**7.** UK: Mrs Thatcher closes an international conference on saving the ozone layer, calling for united action.

**7.** UK: Ted Dexter is chosen as chairman of the England cricket selectors (→5/4).

**8.** Afghanistan: Mujahedin guerrilla groups launch their long-awaited assault on the city of Jalalabad.

**8.** Greece: Pressure mounts for the resignation as premier of Andreas Papandreou, linked to the Bank of Crete scandal (→14).

**8.** UK: A number of Iranians are expelled because of the continuing death threat against Rushdie (→16).

**10.** US: Dick Cheney, a Republican congressman from Wyoming, is chosen to replace Tower as defence secretary.

**10.** US: The wife of a US navy captain escapes injury in an apparent revenge bomb attack for last year's shooting-down of an Iranian airliner.

**10.** UK: Comic Relief day sees more than 50,000 charity fund-raising events organized throughout the country.

**11.** UK: Scotland Yard admits finding a list of more than 100 prominent names at an IRA bomb factory in Clapham, south London, last year.

## John Tower grounded by US senate

*Tower as an earthbound Superman.*

**March 9.** The US Senate today dealt a sharp blow to President Bush by voting 53-47 to reject the nomination of Senator John Tower of Texas, the president's choice as defence secretary.

The nomination set off a bitter argument about Tower's fitness for the position, which focused on allegations about his heavy drinking and his behaviour with women. Tower was also alleged to have used contacts made as one of President Reagan's arms control negotiators to bring profitable trade to his consultancy business.

The senator's opponents circulated stories to the media about his getting drunk in Geneva during the arms reduction talks and fondling a secretary at an air force base.

Such charges were robustly dismissed as hypocrisy by the former senator Barry Goldwater. "If they chased every man and woman out of this town who'd shacked up with somebody else or gotten drunk," he said, "there'd be no government."

The Democrats claim that this was no partisan victory. "It wasn't an effort to be harmful to the president," said George Mitchell, the leader of the Democratic majority in the Senate.

The Republicans knew otherwise. "It wasn't a personal loss," said the president's spokesman, Marlin Fitzwater, "it was a partisan loss." (→10).

## New East-West talks begin on arms cuts

**March 6.** East-West negotiations aimed at reducing the military hardware of both sides in Europe opened today in Vienna in a new climate and with a new determination to reach agreement.

Speakers at the Conventional Forces in Europe conference spoke of a growing trust between Nato and the Warsaw Pact largely brought about by new thinking in the Kremlin. The new forum comes after 15 years' fruitless discussion on reducing the two blocs' forces, during which negotiators were unable to agree even on each other's estimates of force strengths.

Both sides are now seeking significant cuts in the number of tanks, guns and armoured vehicles.

**Firemen struggle with the crumpled carriages of two wrecked trains in Glasgow. In Britain's third fatal train crash in three months, two suburban trains crashed head-on, killing two passengers and injuring 51 others.**

## Vatican bank sacks archbishop as head

*Marcinkus at a 1987 Easter service.*

**March 9.** The Vatican has finally agreed to the removal of Archbishop Paul Marcinkus from his headship of the Vatican Bank. The bank lost $66 million in 1988 and is expected to lose even more this year. The losses are the legacy of the bank's involvement with two buccaneering financiers, Michael Sindona and Roberto Calvi.

Chicago-born Marcinkus had a mercurial rise. Unusually for an American, he won the trust of the members of the Vatican's inner circle. So much so that they defended him in the wake of fraud exposes and the scandal following the discovery of Calvi's body hanging from Blackfriars bridge in London. But now big donations are needed to restore finances, and potential US donors insisted on a new bank manager before paying up.

## Home teams take big strides to Rome

**March 8.** England and Scotland today took further steps on the road to Rome and the finals of soccer's World Cup in 1990. England won 2-0 in Albania, while the Scots beat France by a similar score in Glasgow. Both countries now head their qualifying groups.

The Republic of Ireland are still in with a good chance of reaching the finals after a 0-0 draw in Budapest against Hungary. Spain look likely to win Ireland's group, but two nations qualify (→26/4).

# GPs step up protest against NHS reform

**March 10.** Representatives of hundreds of doctors have threatened a wave of mass resignations in protest at the government's proposed new contracts for GPs.

The threats are the latest in a protest movement among Britain's doctors against the government's health service reforms. In one move, 60 local medical committee doctors in Kent, representing nearly 800 GPs in the county, voted for resignation letters to be collected if the government presses ahead with its planned new contract for GPs.

One part of the new contract about which doctors are unhappy is a proposal to pay doctors bonuses for immunizing 90 per cent of children on their lists and for carrying out cervical smear tests on 80 per cent of their women patients. Doctors say this is unfair to GPs who achieve 89 or 79 per cent.

Kenneth Clarke, the health secretary, does not take the resignation threats seriously. "I have heard this ploy before," he said (→ 12).

# Bloody riots mark Tibet anniversary

**March 10.** Despite the enforced "evacuation" of all tourists from Tibet and a news blackout by the Chinese authorities, reports reaching the West speak of at least 16 dead, together with hundreds injured and thousands arrested, as Tibetans marked the 30th anniversary of the first rebellion against Chinese rule.

The last tourists to leave the capital, Lhasa, by air spoke of people being "dragged from their homes in the middle of the night" in their hundreds, even thousands. An Australian traveller talked of hundreds of police and soldiers banging on doors after dark, and a Tibetan woman confirmed briefly by telephone that there had been many arrests.

The protest began several days ago when a group of 13 saffron-robed Buddhist monks unfurled banners outside the Jokhang temple – the holiest Buddhist shrine in Lhasa – and began to shout pro-independence slogans. Within three hours, more than 600 other Tibet-

*A last view of Lhasa taken by a tourist from the Hotel Lhasa on Wednesday.*

ans were involved in a full-scale riot. Shops and offices – including the local Communist Party headquarters – were ransacked and looted. As Tibetan fury grew and the anniversary approached, tourists were asked, politely at first, to leave. Others were ordered out. Since Chinese troops first occupied

Tibet in 1950, Tibetans have suffered economic and religious devastation, particularly under the Cultural Revolution, when the Chinese sought to destroy every vestige of religion in the country. From exile in India, Tibet's religious leader, the Dalai Lama, has appealed to China to negotiate.

# Palestinian uprising claims more victims

*Children walk round the burning blockades in the war-torn streets of Gaza.*

**March 7.** The Palestinian *intifada*, or uprising, against Israeli occupation brought violent scenes to fervently nationalist areas on the West Bank and in Gaza today.

In the village of Nablus on the West Bank an 18-year-old Arab was shot dead, allegedly for failing to stop for an Israeli patrol. The army also blew up the homes of two

men who were suspected of involvement in the killing of an Israeli sergeant.

In Gaza there were violent confrontations over the death of an Arab during interrogation. Roads were blocked with burning tyres and troops stoned. Hospital staff said 36 people needed treatment for gunshot wounds (→13/4).

# BR reveals Channel tunnel link route

**March 8.** The rail link from the Channel tunnel will run through Peckham in south London on its way to terminals at Waterloo and King's Cross, British Rail announced today. The journey from the coast will take less than 40 minutes in trains travelling at 140mph.

Although about 65 per cent of the route will pass through tunnels, it is still expected that the plan will arouse widespread hostility; BR has offered to buy up 900 homes in the 240-metre corridor which will be blighted by the new route.

But angry residents are only one of BR's problems. It is still not clear how the necessary £1.7 billion pounds – £500 million more than

originally estimated, when no digging has even begun – will be raised. BR are inviting private sector consortiums to "tender for construction and possible ownership".

BR board member John Welsby said that passengers would be expected to bear the brunt of the costs but went on to say: "We have not sought or been offered funding from public sources. If there was a shortfall then we we'd talk to the government." This was in spite of the fact that Section 42 of the Channel Tunnel Bill prohibits the use of public money.

The link will not be ready until 1998, at least five years after the tunnel is due to be opened (→2/11).

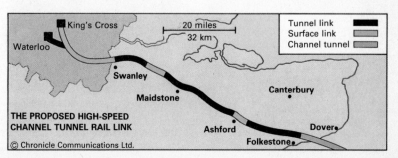

THE PROPOSED HIGH-SPEED CHANNEL TUNNEL RAIL LINK
© Chronicle Communications Ltd.

## 1989

| Su | Mo | Tu | We | Th | Fr | Sa |
|----|----|----|----|----|----|----|
|    |    |    | 1  | 2  | 3  | 4  |
| 5  | 6  | 7  | 8  | 9  | 10 | 11 |
| 12 | 13 | 14 | 15 | 16 | 17 | 18 |
| 19 | 20 | 21 | 22 | 23 | 24 | 25 |
| 26 | 27 | 28 | 29 | 30 | 31 |    |

**12.** W Germany: In the Hesse local elections, the neo-Nazi National Democrats make gains; the Christian Democrats lose Frankfurt (→13/4).

**12.** Romania: Six senior Communist Party figures sign an open letter to President Ceausescu criticizing his rule.

**12.** UK: Plans are revealed to exclude the government's chief medical officer from the new NHS policy board (→31).

**13.** Yugoslavia: Thousands of miners strike in Kosovo as the crackdown intensifies against ethnic Albanians (→15).

**13.** UK: Retail sales in February rose by 2.5 per cent over the previous month.

**13.** UK: The government launches a far-reaching plan to reform Scotland's legal system.

**14.** Greece: A senior minister, Agamemnon Koutsoyorgas, resigns in connection with the Bank of Crete scandal (→19/6).

**14.** Belfast: Eighteen Royal Ulster Constabulary officers linked with Armagh shootings in 1982 are reprimanded.

**15.** Spain: Police say that British intelligence knew that the IRA team shot dead in Gibraltar last year was not carrying arms or explosives at the time.

**15.** Yugoslavia: A liberal from Croatia, Ante Markovic, forms a new government (→24).

**16.** UK: Home Office figures show that violent crime and sex offences continued to increase in 1988.

**17.** USSR: The Communist Party establishment steps up its campaign to discredit Boris Yeltsin (→22).

**17.** UK: Opposition MPs seek an inquiry into alleged links between Pamella Bordes and a Libyan intelligence agent (→19).

**18.** El Salvador: Elections are marred by fighting between troops and guerrillas (→20).

### DEATHS

**14.** Zita, former empress of Austria (*9/5/1892).

**16.** Rev Marcus Morris, British churchman and founder of *Eagle* magazine (*25/5/16).

## No Moslem backing on Rushdie for Iran

**March 16.** Ayatollah Khomeini, the spiritual and political leader of Iran, failed to win support tonight from the 46-member Islamic Conference Organization (ICO) for his death sentence on the British writer Salman Rushdie.

In a declaration at the end of their four-day meeting in Riyadh, the ICO foreign ministers described the author of *The Satanic Verses* as an apostate and demanded the withdrawal of the book from sale, but they stopped short of endorsing the call for Rushdie's execution. The declaration said: "This publication transgresses all norms of civility and decency and is a deliberate attempt to malign Islam and the revered Islamic personalities."

It told member states to boycott publishers who did not withdraw the book and to ban future books insulting religion. British Moslem observers at the meeting claimed credit for the tone of moderation. Iran's attempt to make the affair the central issue in Riyadh was eclipsed by events in Afghanistan and the Palestine question (→20).

## Beirut sees worst fighting for years

**March 14.** Britain is considering the closure of its embassy in Beirut after the worst fighting between Moslems and Christians for four years. Foreign Office officials in London said it was only their desire not to worsen the situation and concern for British hostages in the city that stood in the way of a complete withdrawal.

At least 30 people died in the bombardment, most in Moslem west Beirut. Claiming that Syrian troops based in Lebanon were fighting on the Moslem side, Michel Aoun, the leader of the Christian government, said that the battle had begun to rid Lebanon of its "foreign occupiers" (→2/4).

## Manchester report on air disaster

**March 13.** The 55 people who died in the Manchester airport disaster may not have perished if the aircraft had been fitted with smoke hoods and sprinklers, according to the long-awaited Department of Transport report into the accident in August 1985.

Most of the victims were killed by lethal smoke and fumes from burning fittings in the British Airtours Boeing 737, which caught fire on the ground when a fuel tank ignited after an explosion caused by engine structural failure. Smoke hoods and sprinklers are among the report's 31 recommendations, most of which the Civil Aviation Authority has already implemented.

**Designers signal the end of the no-nonsense eighties in Britain's fashion week. The new season's styles are aggressively flamboyant. Left: the jewels and jeans effect by Ozbek. Right: leather and studs by Katharine Hamnett.**

## Desert Orchid wins Cheltenham gold

*Desert Orchid on his day of triumph.*

**March 16.** In defiance of atrociously heavy going, the 5-2 favourite Desert Orchid streaked past the post today the hugely popular winner of the Cheltenham Gold Cup.

Celebrations were marred by the fate of Ten Plus, who was leading the field when he fell and broke a leg three fences from home and had to be destroyed. The fall left Desert Orchid and Simon Sherwood in the lead. Two fences from home they were passed by Tom Morgan on Yahoo. Desert Orchid landed behind over the last, but in a brave final burst he edged past Yahoo to win by a length and a half.

## Cautious budget by Chancellor Lawson

**March 14.** In contrast to his usual style Nigel Lawson, the chancellor of the exchequer, introduced a cautious, even dull, budget. In one flash of his old exuberance, he told MPs he was still committed to achieving an income tax rate of 20 pence in the pound: "You don't have to reduce the basic rate in every single budget. There are other budgets to come."

The emphasis was on cutting inflation, now nearly eight per cent. Interest rates are to stay at 13 per cent and the only dramatic tax cut is that of tax on unleaded petrol. He hopes to cut the rise in consumer spending by more than half (→23).

# Court firm on Carl's three murderers

**March 17.** There were angry scenes in the appeal court today when the the conviction of three men for murdering newsboy Carl Bridgewater was upheld in a 238-page judgement that took almost six hours to read.

The decision was a particularly bitter blow for Ann Whelan, mother of Michael Hickey, one of the convicted men, who has conducted a ten-year campaign to prove her son's innocence. Despite doubts surrounding many of the witnesses and a lack of forensic evidence, the judges declared the convictions "safe and satisfactory". Afterwards Mrs Wheland said: "I am horrified. This is definitely not the end of the fight."

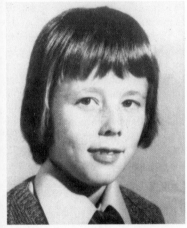

*Carl: are his murderers still free?*

# Pan Am admits it had bomb warnings

**March 16.** The Department of Transport is at the centre of an escalating row as more details emerge about alerts which went unheeded before last December's Lockerbie disaster, in which 270 people died.

Pan Am said today it had received a warning about bombs in cassette recorders – the type of device that blew up its flight 103 over Lockerbie – in November. But the airline did not see a letter from the Department of Transport explaining the mechanics of these bombs until mid-January. Although it was dated 19 December – two days before the disaster – the letter may not have been sent out until after Christmas.

Paul Channon, the transport secretary, also came under fire for dismissing a warning received by the US embassy in Helsinki as of "little credibility". A telephone call to the embassy stated that a Pan Am flight from Frankfurt to the US might be blown up in the fortnight after 5 December. The Department of Transport was informed of this warning, but decided that it did not merit stepping up airline or airport security. John Prescott, Labour's transport spokesman, asked why no one linked the Helsinki warning with those concerning cassette-recorder bombs. He is leading calls for a Commons statement and a public inquiry (→19).

# Thousands call for freedom in Budapest

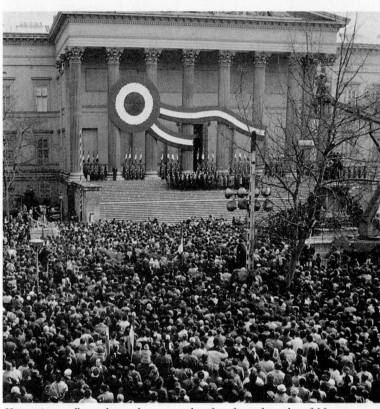

*Hungarians rally to demand a new order, free from the yoke of Moscow.*

**March 15.** Hungary's fast-moving political and social changes were underlined today when Hungarians marched through the streets of Budapest calling for freedom, democracy and an end to the presence of Soviet troops. The national day rally was held to mark the anniversary of the 1848 revolution against Austrian rule.

In fact there were two rallies – one held by the government and attended by some 30,000 people, and the second which drew more than 80,000 people to hear opposition speakers denounce the regime. Both passed off peacefully.

Budapest was turned into a sea of red, white and green, the country's national colours. There were very few police on the streets and the water cannons present on some previous anniversaries were kept well out of sight. Soviet troops were confined to barracks.

The opposition rally began in a festive atmosphere at the statue of Sandor Petofi, the poet whose words incited the Hungarians to revolt. But speakers also referred to the revolution of 1956, which still cannot be celebrated, and called for the disbanding of the Workers' Guard, the force set up by the Communist authorities after 1956 to prevent any further such trouble.

There were loud cheers for other calls for a free, neutral Hungary and self-determination for the peoples of Eastern Europe (→2/5).

# Pamella set to bring down government?

**March 16.** Pamella Bordes, the parliamentary researcher alleged last week by the *News of the World* to be a high-class call girl, claimed today that she could bring down the government with Christine Keeler-style revelations. "The City would grind to a standstill if I spoke out," she said. The reaction at Westminster, however, was sceptical.

Among the public figures linked to Ms Bordes have been Colin Moynihan, the sports minister, and two newspaper editors – Andrew Neil, editor of the *Sunday Times*, and his arch-rival Donald Trelford, editor of the *Observer* – both of whom have been seen holding hands with her in West End nightclubs (→17).

*All smiles: Pamella and Andrew.*

# England beaten and France keep crown

**March 18.** England's rugby players today failed again to beat Wales in Cardiff, and in losing the match they lost the chance to win the five nations' championship. Victory at Cardiff Arms Park would have given England the title, but victory is something they have not known there since 1963. And today, while England were losing by 12 points to nine against a Welsh side which had lost every other match this season, France were beating Scotland by 19 points to three at the Parc des Princes in Paris. The French victory was sufficient to give them the title, finishing with seven points to five for each of England and Scotland. Wales and Ireland each won two points.

| Su | Mo | Tu | We | Th | Fr | Sa |
|----|----|----|----|----|----|----|
|    |    |    | 1  | 2  | 3  | 4  |
| 5  | 6  | 7  | 8  | 9  | 10 | 11 |
| 12 | 13 | 14 | 15 | 16 | 17 | 18 |
| 19 | 20 | 21 | 22 | 23 | 24 | 25 |
| 26 | 27 | 28 | 29 | 30 | 31 |    |

**19.** Channel: Bad weather halts the search for a container of highly toxic lindane, lost when a ship sank last week. →

**19.** UK: Pamella Bordes is said to have received police clearance to work as a Tory researcher, despite her Libyan link (→21).

**19.** UK: The Department of Transport admits that a bomb warning from December last year was not posted until "early new year". →

**20.** Brussels: The European Community envoys to Iran, who were withdrawn a month ago, are to return (→29).

**20.** France: The victory of the left in municipal elections is seen as a personal triumph for the premier, Michel Rocard.

**21.** US: In the first sea-launched test of Trident-2, the missile explodes four seconds after launch.

**21.** UK: Security at the Commons is tightened; the two MPs who applied for Bordes's pass are exonerated.

**21.** Australia: The premier, Bob Hawke, weeps on TV after admitting marital infidelity.

**22.** USSR: The Academy of Sciences general assembly backs Andrei Sakharov's parliamentary candidacy (→20/4).

**22.** UK: £500 million government aid is pledged for an employee buy-out of Harland and Wolff's Belfast shipyards.

**22.** UK: A van packed with explosives blows up, devastating a Peterborough industrial estate and killing a fireman.

**23.** UK: Roy Garner, a former Scotland Yard informer, is jailed for 22 years for his part in a cocaine conspiracy.

**23.** UK: Inflation rises to 7.8 per cent.

**24.** US: Bush wins Congress's approval to give $41 million aid to the Contras in return for his support for Central American peace moves.

**24.** Yugoslavia: Constitutional changes surrender much of Kosovo's autonomy to the largest republic, Serbia (→28).

**25.** UK: Oxford wins the Boat Race.

# RUC officers shot in South Armagh were in unprotected car

**March 21.** Two senior Royal Ulster Constabulary officers were killed by the IRA yesterday as they drove back from a security meeting in the Irish Republic. Chief Superintendent Harry Breen and Superintendent Ken Buchanan were ambushed as they crossed the border on a country road in South Armagh. They wore plain clothes and were in an unmarked car. Breen – the most senior RUC officer yet to die in the troubles – was the South Armagh divisional commander and Buchanan had special responsibility for border security. The RUC has discounted suggestions that a Garda source tipped off the IRA.

*Harry Breen and Ken Buchanan.*

# Yeltsin supporters march in Moscow

*Fists raised in Moscow in support of Boris Yeltsin and a multi-party system.*

**March 22.** Boris Yeltsin, an ousted Kremlin radical, emerged today as a prominent opposition figure to the Soviet Communist Party leader, Mikhail Gorbachev. Defying a ban, thousands of Yeltsin's supporters marched through Moscow's centre, chanting his name and calling for a multi-party system.

Yeltsin was sacked 17 months ago from the ruling Politburo and from the leadership of the Moscow Communist Party for showing his impatience with the slow pace of Gorbachev's reforms.

The six-hour rally ended outside the Moscow City Soviet on Gorky Street. In the week before elections to the new Congress of People's Deputies, it has boosted Yeltsin's chances of winning a seat in the new parliament to continue his attacks on the party establishment for sabotaging the reforms (→28).

# La Gavroche cleared of hygiene charges

*Albert Roux at work in the gleaming kitchens of the three-star La Gavroche.*

**March 23.** The expensive Mayfair restaurant La Gavroche – one of Britain's only two holders of the Michelin Guide's coveted three stars – was cleared today of 15 charges relating to food hygiene and to health and safety at work. Health inspectors from Westminster Council had condemned conditions in the restaurant kitchen as "disgusting", but magistrates fully acquitted La Gavroche, and its owner, the master-chef Albert Roux. Roux, who was awarded the £100,000 costs, said he had been victimized.

# Cold nuclear fusion claim in question

**March 24.** Scientists have greeted with scepticism today's announcement in the US state of Utah of what could be one of the greatest scientific discoveries ever made.

Professor Stanley Pons of Utah University and Professor Martin Fleischmann of Southampton University in Britain claim they have produced nuclear fusion at room temperature. Nuclear fusion, the power behind the sun, is the process by which atomic nuclei are joined together, producing vast quantities of energy but very little radioactive waste. Hitherto, attempts to produce fusion have involved creating temperatures close to that of the sun, at huge expense, and useful fusion energy has been thought to be a long way off. If the new "cold fusion" is proved to work, it would be a source of clean, cheap and almost limitless energy.

# Channon survives row over Lockerbie

**March 21.** Heated criticism of his handling of airport security and the Lockerbie bomb investigation have failed to bow the transport secretary, Paul Channon – though his ability to survive the next government reshuffle is still in doubt.

Channon has been at the centre of a row since the Lockerbie inquiry revealed his department's apparently lax approach to security warnings. In a Commons debate today he refused to confirm allegations that he told journalists last week the police knew the identity and whereabouts of the Lockerbie bombers – a suggestion since criticized by the Scottish Lord Advocate as "wild, irresponsible speculation".

# Drums of pesticide lie on Channel bed

**March 22.** Britain is to mount an operation to recover 32 drums of toxic pesticides from the Channel bed. They were part of the cargo of the Panamanian-registered ship *Perintis*, which sank ten days ago 35 miles off the coast of Devon while en route from Antwerp to Jakarta.

The chemicals are permethrin and cypermethrin, both of which could kill and contaminate marine life over a large area if a leak occurred. Although more securely packed, they are much more toxic than the pesticide lindane, a container of which was dropped by the same ship near the French coast and has not yet been found (→25/4).

# Alaska hit by worst-ever US oil spill

*Salvage vessels with the damaged supertanker after she was refloated.*

*Seen from the air, the slick spreads.*

**March 25.** The captain and two crew members of an oil tanker have been subpoenaed by the US Coast Guard in Alaska following the worst oil spillage in US history.

The 987-foot supertanker *Exxon Valdez* ran aground on a reef yesterday, shortly after leaving the port of Valdez, the terminus of the Alaskan oil pipeline, causing 11 million gallons of crude oil to pour out into Prince William Sound, an area rich in marine wildlife and economically crucial to local fishing communities. According to an estimate by Alaska state authorities, the slick covers 50 square miles.

Officials are not yet able to identify the cause of the accident, but the US Coast Guard said today that it had subpoenaed the captain of the ship, Joseph Hazelwood, and two other crew members to be available to face federal investigators in to the disaster. Exxon Shipping, the owners of the *Exxon Valdez*, confirmed that the captain had been in his cabin, one deck below the bridge, at the time of the accident.

Exxon says that all possible resources are being used to clean up the huge spillage, and promises to take financial responsibility. But the company has come under fire from state sources for its allegedly slow response to the disaster (→27).

# Redundant senior keepers at the V&A vow to continue the fight

**March 23.** The Victoria and Albert Museum staff restructuring, which has cost eight of the nine department heads their jobs, was publicly criticized by the keepers who have been made redundant at a press conference today. They vowed to go on fighting, saying that the changes at the V & A were part of "a bigger attack on scholarship" that would be carried on at museums around the country.

Departments are being abolished and the keepers will be paid compensation from £300,000 saved on much-needed maintenance work at the museum. The chairman of the trustees, Lord Armstrong, admitted in the House of Lords that the government had advised them on the dismissals.

# Arafat talks with US were "positive"

*Arafat: satisfied with his US talks.*

**March 23.** Yasser Arafat, the chairman of the Palestine Liberation Organization, said today in Tunis that the first formal talks between the PLO and the new US administration had been "positive and bore the stamp of seriousness".

After a meeting between the US ambassador, Robert Pelletreau, and a member of the PLO's executive, Yasser Abed Rabbo, Arafat said: "The two sides have the firm will to pursue this dialogue to a fruitful conclusion." The US did not ask for an end to the uprising.

# Right wing scores El Salvador poll win

**March 20.** After an election campaign in which at least 38 people were killed and 150 government troops wounded in clashes with opposition guerrillas, the right-wing Arena Party is in power in El Salvador tonight. Alfredo Cristiani, the Arena leader, has won 53 per cent of the vote in a provisional count. The party founder, Roberto D'Aubuisson, was accused of involvement with death squads in the early 1980s.

**BAFTA award-winner Thora Hird, judged best TV actress.**

# March

## 1989

| Su | Mo | Tu | We | Th | Fr | Sa |
|----|----|----|----|----|----|----|
|    |    |    | 1  | 2  | 3  | 4  |
| 5  | 6  | 7  | 8  | 9  | 10 | 11 |
| 12 | 13 | 14 | 15 | 16 | 17 | 18 |
| 19 | 20 | 21 | 22 | 23 | 24 | 25 |
| 26 | 27 | 28 | 29 | 30 | 31 |    |

**26.** India: At least 20 people have died in two days of fighting between Sikhs and security forces in Punjab.

**26.** Turkey: The ruling Motherland Party suffers large defeats in local elections (→31).

**27.** US: Alaska is declared a disaster zone as the oil slick grows to 100 square miles.→

**27.** Morocco: Margaret Thatcher starts a tour of Africa with a visit to a harem.→

**27.** Japan: Hisashi Shinto, a prominent businessman, is charged with accepting bribes in the Recruit scandal (→31).

**28.** Yugoslavia: The death toll in clashes between police and demonstrators in Kosovo rises to 21 (→3/4).

**28.** Spain: Howard Marks, a Briton accused of a huge drugs scam, loses his fight against extradition to the US.

**29.** Brussels: In an attack linked to the Rushdie affair, Abdullah Ahdel, a Moslem leader, and his deputy are murdered in a mosque (→25/4).

**29.** Paris: President Mitterrand inaugurates a new glass pyramid at the Louvre.

**29.** UK: At an inquiry into the Purley rail crash, British Rail blames driver error.

**30.** Pretoria: Six black activists end a day-long sit-in at the British embassy, complaining of "inhuman treatment".

**30.** UK: The Home Office publishes plans under which parents may be held responsible for juvenile crime.

**30.** UK: Delegates to the first Scottish Constitutional Convention sign a claim in support of home rule for Scotland.

**31.** Japan: Noboru Takeshita, the prime minister, admits receiving 20 million yen from Recruit during his leadership campaign (→25/4).

**31.** US: A judge rules that Ronald Reagan, the former president, will not be forced to testify at the North trial (→7/4).

**31.** Turkey: Turgut Ozal, the premier, radically reshuffles his cabinet to counter charges of economic mismanagement and nepotism (→1/5).

## Exxon captain fired after alcohol test

**March 31.** The master of the oil tanker which caused the worst oil spillage in US history has been fired after investigators revealed he had twice the legal level of alcohol in his blood at the time of the accident.

Captain Joseph Hazelwood, until now employed by the oil company Exxon, put the tanker *Exxon Valdez* under the command of an unqualified third mate before going to his cabin, where he was when the ship ran aground off Alaska early last Friday. US coast guards apparently smelled alcohol on his breath when they went aboard, but he was only tested when they came ashore, about ten hours after the accident. Even then, his blood alcohol level was 0.06 to 0.09 per cent, compared with a US Coast Guard legal limit of 0.04 per cent. In addition to his dismissal, the ex-master could now face state and federal charges.

The scale of the ecological damage to this wildlife paradise is far worse than at first feared. High winds have thwarted efforts to mop up the 12 million gallons of oil which spilt from the tanker, and three days ago Alaska declared a state of emergency.

Exxon, which owns the tanker, has come under increasing attack for being evidently ill-prepared for such a spillage, and for playing down the extent of the disaster.

## Thatcher predicts the end of apartheid

*Margaret Thatcher agrees to disagree with President Mugabe of Zimbabwe.*

**March 31.** As the British prime minister ended a tour of Zimbabwe yesterday, President Robert Mugabe expressed grave doubts about her policy of trying to persuade South Africa to abandon apartheid. He said it would require a political magician to make apartheid disappear without more rigorous measures than she advocated.

At a state banquet two days ago, Mrs Thatcher said: "I think we shall get rid of apartheid without sanctions and without destroying the economy of South Africa." Her host argued, however, that the "political situation in South Africa shows no signs of improving" and that there was no peaceful alternative to sanctions.

During her visit to Zimbabwe, Mrs Thatcher also held talks with President Joaquim Chissano of Mozambique. She offered more military aid against the Renamo guerrilla movement, which is fighting the government. Renamo's backers are believed to include South Africa, although Pretoria denies it.

Today, on the last leg of her week-long tour of African states, Mrs Thatcher travels to Malawi, where she will visit Mozambican refugee camps and meet fugitives from one of Africa's cruellest wars.

## Brazilian Grand Prix victory for Mansell

**March 26.** Britain's Nigel Mansell confounded the critics and became the hero of Italy today when he won the Brazilian Grand Prix in his first outing as Ferrari's leading driver. "It's the best start I've ever had," said Mansell, who won by more than seven seconds from Alain Prost, driving one of the McLarens which were expected to continue last season's dominance of the Grand Prix circuit.

The second McLaren, driven by the Brazilian Ayrton Senna, who had never won his home Grand Prix, could finish only 11th after colliding with the second Ferrari driven by Gerhard Berger. It was a good day for Britain, with Johnny Herbert finishing fourth and Derek Warwick in fifth position.

*Prost congratulates victor Mansell.*

## GPs launch "SOS for NHS" campaign

**March 31.** Doctors have launched an unprecedented campaign to win support for their objections to some of the government's planned National Health Service reforms.

The British Medical Association has printed 11 million leaflets called "SOS for the NHS". Aimed primarily at patients, the leaflets target four key government proposals: limited drug budgets for doctors; incentives for GPs to take on more patients; "opting-out" of hospitals from local authority control; and greater cost-effectiveness of hospitals.

Kenneth Clarke, the health secretary, dismissed the campaign as "alarmist nonsense" (→15/4).

# Shock resignation by Khomeini heir

**March 27.** In a mounting purge of moderates, Ali Montazeri, the heir-apparent to Ayatollah Khomeini as spiritual leader of Iran's Islamic revolution, has announced his resignation. Ayatollah Montazeri's fate was sealed by his public admission of mistakes made by the revolutionary regime and his failure to back Khomeini over the Rushdie affair. His departure leaves in control of Iran a tight-knit group of hardline radicals, whose next target may be the parliamentary speaker, Ali Akbar Hashemi Rafsanjani.

*Boris Yeltsin – given an outstanding vote of confidence by the electorate.*

# America's Cup goes to New Zealand

**March 29.** A supreme court judge has shocked the San Diego Yacht Club with a ruling that New Zealand was the rightful winner of last year's America's Cup series. San Diego's Dennis Conner had sailed a 60-foot catamaran against the New Zealand monohull and won easily.

Justice Carmen Ciparick said the use of a catamaran had violated the 101-year-old deed of gift governing the race. "San Diego's clear goal was to retain the cup at all costs so that it could host a competition on its own terms," she said (→ 19/9).

# Soviet party bosses humiliated in polls

**March 28.** The Soviet people have gone to the polls to test out a new multi-candidate system – and have dealt a humiliating blow to the Communist Party and many of its candidates. Voters have bounced out dozens of provincial party barons all over the country, with reformers, among them Boris Yeltsin, scoring stunning victories.

The election was to return members to the Congress of People's Deputies, the cornerstone of what amounts to a new constitution. The Soviet Communist Party never had the slightest intention of losing its grip on power, so a quarter of the seats were uncontested and went to safe members of the old Communist establishment.

But in contested seats some 184 million voters used their first opportunity of a genuine ballot-box choice since 1918 to rebuff the party which rules in their name. Dozens of city party first secretaries and mayors were repudiated, as were many humbler district party bosses. The major casualties are strewn across the entire country, with the most jarring jolts to the system coming in the Ukraine and Leningrad. Yeltsin won 90 per cent of the votes in a constituency of seven million, to emerge as a clear symbol of the new alternative politics (→ 25/4).

# Observer publishes Harrods sale report

**March 30.** The long-running battle between "Tiny" Rowland and the Al-Fayed brothers for control of the department store Harrods took a dramatic turn today.

In an almost unprecedented move, the Sunday newspaper the *Observer* – owned by Rowland's company Lonrho – published a special mid-week edition devoted to a secret report by the Department of Trade and Industry (DTI).

For four years the *Observer* has conducted a ferocious campaign against the Al-Fayeds, following their successful purchase of the House of Fraser – owners of Harrods – in the teeth of a rival bid by Lonrho. The paper claims that the Al-Fayeds did not have the £615 million it took to buy the store, but were effectively acting as front men for the Sultan of Brunei, thereby breaking the law that requires statements made in connection with a bid to be truthful. The Al-Fayeds have always denied the charge.

The DTI set up an inquiry into the bid and it is that report – which the trade secretary, Lord Young, first said he would make public, but then declined to do so in case it prejudiced legal proceedings – that the *Observer* has published today. The government has won an injunction against the sale of the special edition (→ 4/4).

**March 30. "Rainman" wins four Oscars. Dustin Hoffman plays an autistic savant who stirs the finer feelings of his long-lost brother, Tom Cruise. It is a journey of discovery shared by a winner and a loser in today's US.**

# Bishop of Durham doubts the resurrection

**March 26.** The bishop of Durham, the Rt Rev David Jenkins, found himself in hot water again today. In an Easter address in Durham Cathedral, he said: "We really do not know what the resurrection of Jesus Christ from the dead means." In a TV interview he expanded on his remark, suggesting that the spiritual aspect was what mattered, not "the revival of a corpse".

By this evening eight MPs had called for his resignation. One Conservative, Sir Nicholas Fairbairn, said that Christ actually showed his disciples the wounds of the nails on the cross when they doubted: "If this is fiction, then the Christian religion is fiction." Sir Nicholas preferred to believe "the bishop of Durham is fiction".

*The doubting bishop David Jenkins.*

| Su | Mo | Tu | We | Th | Fr | Sa |
|----|----|----|----|----|----|----|
|    |    |    |    |    |    | 1  |
| 2  | 3  | 4  | 5  | 6  | 7  | 8  |
| 9  | 10 | 11 | 12 | 13 | 14 | 15 |
| 16 | 17 | 18 | 19 | 20 | 21 | 22 |
| 23 | 24 | 25 | 26 | 27 | 28 | 29 |
| 30 |    |    |    |    |    |    |

**1.** Namibia: Fighting breaks out between South African forces and Swapo guerrillas as Namibia's independence accord comes into effect (→4).

**1.** UK: Free eye tests end for 60 per cent of the population.

**2.** Ireland: Mikhail Gorbachev holds talks with the Irish premier, Charles Haughey (→5).

**2.** Haiti: An attempted coup against the Haitian leader, Prosper Avril, fails (→8).

**2.** London: Two people die when petrol is poured on them and set alight during the robbery of a Soho amusement arcade.

**3.** Yugoslavia: The Kosovo authorities order a huge purge affecting ethnic Albanian politicians and intellectuals.

**3.** UK: *The Channel 4 Daily*, a breakfast TV programme, goes on the air.

**4.** UK: Neil Kinnock launches Labour's campaign against the poll tax, stressing that he does not condone non-payment.

**4.** S Africa: The government threatens to suspend the Namibia peace plan unless the United Nations curbs Swapo.→

**5.** UK: Mikhail Gorbachev arrives in Britain after a three-day visit to Cuba.→

**5.** UK: David Gower is appointed captain of the England cricket team.

**6.** US: Bush holds his first meeting with the Israeli premier, Yitzhak Shamir.

**6:** UK: Housing costs for homebuyers are estimated to have risen by an average of 62.5 per cent in the past year.

**7.** US: Oliver North admits during his trial that he lied to Congress to cover up his role in the Iran-Contra affair (→4/5).

**7.** China: Chen Jun, one of China's most outspoken dissidents, is expelled.

**7.** Mediterranean: France sends a hospital ship and an oil tanker loaded with supplies to Lebanon.

**8.** Haiti: Rebel officers launch the second unsuccessful coup attempt in a week.

# Solidarity signs accord with Communists

**April 5.** The Communist authorities and the opposition in Poland have reached a stunning agreement in a last-ditch effort by both sides to save the country from spinning into an unending cycle of chaos and repression. After weeks of round-table negotiations, the government of Wojciech Jaruzelski has agreed to the re-legalization of the Solidarity trade union within the next few weeks and to hold democratic elections for 35 per cent of parliamentary seats in June.

At the closing ceremony, the interior minister, Czeslaw Kiszczak, shook the hand of Lech Walesa, the Solidarity leader, and spoke of the creation of a "new model of political culture". Walesa quoted his union's slogan – "there is no freedom without Solidarity" – but he added that "words were no longer enough".

The agreement also provides for a second fully democratic legislative senate and a presidency, prompting a Solidarity spokesman

*Lech Walesa at round-table talks.*

to comment that the "structure of a future democratic government is in place". Solidarity is now able to run an opposition newspaper, as well as smaller factory papers, and will have "some" access to radio and television (→17).

# Harrods report "disclosed wrongdoing"

**April 4.** Lord Young, the trade secretary, said on BBC radio today that his department's report on the 1985 sale of Harrods to the Al-Fayed brothers "clearly disclosed wrongdoing". Neil Kinnock, the Labour leader, said: "I think Lord Young has done exactly what he wanted everyone else not to do,

which was to make a judgement in public on the report." Last week Lord Young secured an injunction banning the media from revealing details of the report after the *Observer* newspaper published large extracts from it in a special edition. The report has been referred to the Serious Fraud Office.

**April 8:** Little Polveir wins the Grand National accompanied by the riderless Smart Tar. Two horses had to be destroyed after the race.

# Soviet nuclear sub sinks following fire

**April 8.** A Soviet nuclear-powered submarine, the *Komsomolets*, has caught fire and sunk, with the loss of 42 lives, in the Norwegian Sea. The Soviet government confirmed the accident after American and Norwegian reports.

The submarine, which had a Nato designation of Mike-1 and a crew of 95, went down some 118 miles south of Bear Island between Norway and Greenland. The Soviet navy rejected offers of foreign help, which drew some fierce complaints that safety was being sacrificed to secrecy. The Russians have denied that the nuclear propulsion system was involved in the fire.

# Brittan revives row over Westland leak

*Brittan: brought down by Westland.*

**April 5.** Sir Leon Brittan claimed tonight that Mrs Thatcher's private secretary, Charles Powell, and her press secretary, Bernard Ingham, authorized his leaking of a confidential letter during the Westland affair.

The leak was aimed at damaging Michael Heseltine, then defence secretary, who resigned from the cabinet during the fracas. Later Sir Leon was also forced to quit as trade and industry secretary. At one stage Mrs Thatcher feared that she too might have to go, on account of blatant and unsuccessful news management at No. 10.

# UN makes ceasefire proposals in Namibia

*UN forces move a wounded Swapo guerrilla while the fighting goes on.*

**April 6.** The United Nations has formulated a plan aimed at ending almost a week of fighting in northern Namibia between South African troops and guerrillas of Swapo (the South West African People's Organization), the territory's main opposition group.

The bloodshed erupted on April 1, the first day of a UN-supervised transition period to prepare the way for Namibia's independence from South Africa and free elections which Swapo is almost certain to win. About 1,400 Swapo guerrillas are believed to have been infiltrated across the border from their bases in Angola, apparently on the orders of Sam Nujoma, the exiled Swapo leader. Over 170 Swapo guerrillas and over 20 South Africans have died in five days of fighting which has threatened the entire transition process.

Both sides have been urging the United Nations Transition Assistance Group (Untag) to intervene and halt the violence, but the multinational force has as yet only 65 personnel in the northern frontier area. Under the peace formula announced today it is hoped that a ceasefire will be followed by a Swapo withdrawal into Angola via Untag-monitored camps on the Namibia-Angola border (→12).

# Vietnam announces Cambodia pull-out

**April 5.** The spectre of a return to power by the Khmer Rouge – who slaughtered over a million people during their ruthless regime – re-emerged in Cambodia today with the announcement by Vietnam that it would withdraw all its troops by September. Vietnam has occupied its neighbour for ten years, but now its puppet, the People's Republic of Kampuchea (PRK), is certain to be challenged by a resistance coalition – including the Khmer Rouge.

Yesterday's Hanoi statement urges other countries to call on Cambodian factions to meet. Hun Sen, the PRK leader, has said that his government is prepared to make "significant concessions" (→25/9).

# Fowler abolishes dock labour scheme

**April 6.** The abolition of the dock labour scheme, which 42 years ago ended work on a casual basis, was announced by Norman Fowler, the employment secretary, today.

Legislation to scrap what Tories call "jobs for life" will be rushed through parliament. Affronted union leaders talked of "wilful sabotage" and threatened strike action. The scheme covers 40 out of 75 of Britain's main ports and applies to one-third of the dockers.

The government will offer redundancy payments of up to £35,000 in order to slim down the dock labour force. It expects this to discourage any attempts at crippling industrial disruption (→19/5).

# Queen accepts invitation to Soviet Union

**April 7.** During a cordial lunch at Windsor Castle today, the Queen accepted an invitation from the Soviet leader, Mikhail Gorbachev, to visit Moscow.

No date was fixed and it could be two years away. She will be the first British monarch to go to Russia since the 1917 Communist revolution and the murder of her family's cousins, the Romanovs.

Mrs Thatcher said towards the end of a three-day visit to Britain by Mr Gorbachev that a turning-point had been reached in Anglo-Soviet relations. She told him: "You have provided us with an occasion we shall never forget and it is the start of something big."

The timing of the Queen's visit will depend on the progress of Gorbachev's policies of perestroika and glasnost. Mrs Thatcher is still advising caution.

Her press secretary annoyed the Queen's advisers at Buckingham Palace last year when he hinted that the prime minister might veto the

*An historic meeting at Windsor.*

trip which was then being tentatively mooted in Moscow. However, it was said in Downing Street tonight that the royal visit now has her full blessing. Mr Gorbachev has also invited the prime minister to Moscow again (→23/9).

# Cheap low-alcohol beer for lager louts

**April 5.** The curse of the "lager lout", typically a young man with too much to drink and too little to do, whose antics are increasingly wreaking mayhem in town and country alike, may be alleviated by the promotion of cheaper low-alcohol and even non-alcoholic beers. Today's Home Office report on "Drinking and Disorder" recommends staggering pub-closing hours, revamping the image of the pub as an all-male preserve, and encouraging weaker drinks.

# New ferocity in 14-year Beirut civil war

**April 2.** Christian areas in east Beirut today suffered one of their heaviest bombardments since the beginning of the Lebanese civil war in April 1975.

An indiscriminate hail of shells, rockets and mortar bombs struck apartments, schools and hospitals, starting a series of fires.

The attack provoked an immediate response from the Christians, who retaliated with a barrage on Syrian positions in Moslem west Beirut. At least seven people were killed and 20 wounded in the battle. Shells also struck several diplomatic residences. It was the worst fighting since the Christian leader, Michel Aoun, vowed three weeks ago to drive Syrian troops out of Lebanon (→16).

*More bombs for battered Lebanon.*

# April
## 1989

**9.** UK: Nottingham Forest win the Littlewoods Cup, beating Luton 3-1.

**9.** Namibia: South Africa and Namibia ratify a plan for a UN-monitored withdrawal of Swapo guerrillas to Angola.→

**9.** US: More than 300,000 people march in Washington against a threatened weakening of the right to abortion (→3/7).

**10.** France: A Fokker 27 crashes into a cliff near Valence, killing all 22 on board.

**11.** Portugal: Europe's football authority agrees to lift a ban from European competition on English first division clubs.

**11.** UK: Abbey National members vote to convert the society into a bank and float it on the Stock Exchange.

**12.** UK: Thousands of Heinz baby food jars are removed from sale after glass is found in a jar in Southampton (→25).

**13.** W Germany: Chancellor Kohl reshuffles his government to bolster his leadership (→21).

**13.** UK: 57-year-old Edward Adcock causes a security scare by lungeing at the Princess of Wales during a royal walkabout in Northumberland.

**13.** UK: Tony Maclean, the "Notting Hill rapist", is given three life jail sentences.

**14.** USSR: The Communist Party chief and prime minister in Georgia are replaced in a purge of local leaders (→18).

**14.** UK: Sales of unleaded fuel are reported to have doubled in the past three months.

**15.** UK: The Royal College of General Practitioners votes to reject the white paper on the health service reform (→4/5).

**15.** Italy: The third mass trial of the Mafia ends with 80 acquittals and 40 convictions.

### DEATHS

**12.** Sugar Ray Robinson, US boxer (*1922).

**12.** Abbie Hoffmann, US revolutionary activist and writer (*30/11/36).

**15.** Hu Yaobang, Chinese liberal reformer (*1915) (→22).

## Crisis in Georgia: Shevardnadze flies in

*The peaceful night-time demonstration in Tbilisi, before the police arrived.*

**April 10.** A night of peaceful protest has turned to terror in Tbilisi, the capital of Georgia, after troops and police fought with demonstrators calling for independence from the rule of Moscow. Up to 30 people have died. A curfew is in force and the Soviet foreign minister, Eduard Shevardnadze, flew to Tbilisi today to take control.

The people who died were involved in clashes in front of the main government building. Troops fired tear gas into the crowd, and then charged, using truncheons and shovels. A Soviet statement said the action was taken after the rally got out of control and nationalist and anti-Soviet slogans were shouted.

Discontent has been simmering in Georgia for years, much of it focused on demands for greater autonomy from Moscow, defence of the Georgian language and culture, and protection of the environment. But the latest trouble arose from an upsurge of nationalism in the tiny enclave of Abkhazia, which is seeking autonomy from Tbilisi and where there have been clashes between the two ethnic groups.

Georgia has been under Russian rule since 1800, except for a brief period after 1918 (→14).

## Swapo guerrillas shun UN camps

**April 12.** Almost a day and a half after UN camps opened near the Namibia-Angola border to receive Swapo guerrillas, only four troops have so far handed themselves over to UN troops supervising a ceasefire in the area. The camps were set up as part of a plan to end clashes which erupted last week between Swapo insurgents and South African troops. Swapo guerrillas had crossed the border from bases in Angola in contravention of agreements aimed at ensuring Namibia's smooth transition to independence from South Africa. Observers blame the guerrillas' reluctance to come forward on the conspicuous South African presence near the UN assembly camps.

**Britain's Nick Faldo makes clear his joy as he wins the US Masters Golf Championship in Augusta. "I feel ecstatic," he said later.**

## Israelis accused of village massacre

**April 13.** Israeli armed forces were accused of a massacre today when they apparently opened fire indiscriminately on Arab villagers who were returning from early-morning prayers.

At least four people died and 18 were wounded in the shooting at the village of Nahhalin on the West Bank. The incident, the bloodiest yet experienced during the Palestinian *intifada*, or uprising, sparked a wave of protests in which at least six Arabs were shot.

The Israeli army said that border police had opened fire against stone-throwers resisting a search and arrest operation (→7/5).

## Girl killed by two pet rottweilers

**April 14.** An 11-year-old girl was savaged to death today by the pair of rottweiler dogs that she was exercising on a Scottish beach.

Kelly Lynch was walking the dogs, owned by the father of her school friend Lorraine Simpson, on the seashore at Dunoon near the Firth of Clyde, when they launched their unprovoked attack.

A woman tried to pull off the dogs, but she too was mauled. Lorraine attempted to call her father, but before he could reach the spot Kelly was dead.

## Judges delay clash with government

**April 13.** Over 100 senior judges today called off "strike action" which they had threatened for next Monday. They will not after all close their courts in order to hold a protest meeting about the government's plans to overhaul the legal profession. Instead they will have a Saturday meeting next month. The move was described by Mrs Thatcher as "a very welcome change". It followed Whitehall hints of concessions to the judges and scornful charges by Labour MPs that the judiciary was indulging in "unlawful industrial action to protect their own bulging wallets".

# Horrific death for fans in Hillsborough disaster

**April 15.** A police officer ordered a gate to be opened at a football stadium today to allow in a tightly packed crowd of fans to watch an FA Cup semi-final. The result was the worst-ever disaster in Britain's sporting history.

Ninety-four people perished and 170 were injured when Liverpool supporters rushed on to the already crowded centre section of the west stand at Hillsborough in Sheffield, during a match between Liverpool and Nottingham Forest. Victims were crushed in the entrance tunnel, on the steps up to the terraces and against the perimeter fence.

In horrific, chaotic scenes, dead and badly injured supporters – most of them from Liverpool – were passed over the fence on to the pitch. Others scrambled to safety on to the balcony above. Within minutes, the match was abandoned and the pitch became like a battlefield, with police, ambulancemen and fans working frantically to revive the dying and cope with countless broken arms and legs.

Nottingham fans at the far end of the stadium initially jeered, unaware of the scale of the disaster and convinced that Liverpool fans were rampaging. With police struggling to keep the opposing factions apart, Liverpool manager Kenny Dalgish appealed for calm. "I think everyone knows there have been a few problems," he said over the stadium's public address system.

"Please try to be calm. We are doing our best for you."

As ambulances appeared on the pitch and fans ripped advertising hoardings from their mountings for use as makeshift stretchers, the crowd hushed and watched as the frantic efforts continued. A doctor appealed for a defibulator – a resuscitation device – to be told that none was available. An oxygen bottle was found to be empty.

One man was seen to be given mouth-to-mouth resuscitation as ambulancemen pumped his heart. The crowd applauded when he appeared to come to life, only to be stilled when his head sagged finally.

As the pitch was slowly cleared of the dead and injured, survivors talked of the horror of the crush. Wayne Adams, aged 17, was five rows from the front on the terrace. "It was mainly youngsters standing in front of me," he said. "I realized it was serious when I saw one of the lasses standing near me just turn blue in the face. She went down. She was dead. That was it."

Peter Wells, one of 30 St John Ambulance volunteers, told of helping a young girl in her twenties: "I was trying to hold her mouth through the wire mesh to keep her breathing going, but there was nothing we could do. She died."

Liverpool is in deep mourning tonight. Many of the dead are teenagers. Most are young. The youngest is a boy of ten (→ 18).

*Helpless supporters trapped at the perimeter fence as the tragedy unfolds.*

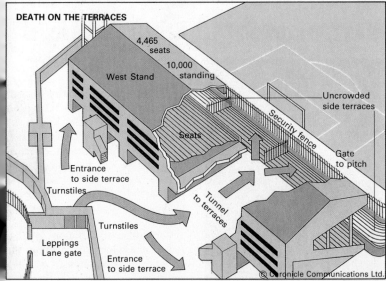

**DEATH ON THE TERRACES**

4,465 seats

10,000 standing

West Stand

Seats

Uncrowded side terraces

Security fence

Gate to pitch

Entrance to side terrace

Turnstiles

Turnstiles

Leppings Lane gate

Tunnel to terraces

Entrance to side terrace

© Chronicle Communications Ltd.

*Fans who poured through the Leppings Lane gate headed for the central tunnel; two side entrances would have led to less crowded parts of the stand.*

*Some of the lucky ones are hauled from the packed terraces to safety on the balcony while their rescuers stare in disbelief at scenes down by the fence.*

# April

### 1989

| Su | Mo | Tu | We | Th | Fr | Sa |
|----|----|----|----|----|----|----|
|    |    |    |    |    |    | 1  |
| 2  | 3  | 4  | 5  | 6  | 7  | 8  |
| 9  | 10 | 11 | 12 | 13 | 14 | 15 |
| 16 | 17 | 18 | 19 | 20 | 21 | 22 |
| 23 | 24 | 25 | 26 | 27 | 28 | 29 |
| 30 |    |    |    |    |    |    |

**16.** Sri Lanka: India decides to withdraw 7,000 of its peace-keeping troops.

**16.** Beirut: The Spanish envoy and two of his family are among 20 killed in Moslem-Christian fighting (→16/8).

**17.** UK: Nigel Lawson, the chancellor, rejects plans for European economic and monetary union.

**17.** UK: The West German company Bosch announces plans to build a £100 million car plant in South Wales.

**17.** UK: A new round of petrol price increases brings the average price rise this year to 24p per gallon.

**18.** USSR: The curfew is lifted in Tbilisi as calm returns to Georgia (→20).

**18.** UK: Hillsborough claims its 95th victim, 14-year-old Lee Nichol.→

**18.** UK: Toyota announces plans to build a £700 million car plant at Burnaston, near Derby, creating 6,000 jobs.

**19.** Beijing: Police put an end to a second night of pro-democracy demonstrations.→

**20.** USSR: Sakharov and other leading reformers are elected to the new parliament.

**20.** USSR: Police are said to have used toxic gas to break up the protest in Georgia, which cost 20 lives.

**20.** W Germany: A rise in interest rates prompts increases across Europe.

**20.** London: Unofficial action by tube drivers paralyses the network for the second time in a fortnight (→5/5).

**21.** UK: The Right of Reply Bill is talked out in the House of Commons.

**22.** UK: The oil platforms closed after the Cormorant Alpha explosion are set to stay closed until further notice.

**22.** France: A Bordeaux wine scandal inquiry reveals that six million bottles may have been sold under false pretences.

**DEATH**

**19.** Daphne du Maurier, British novelist (*13/5/07).→

# Anfield shrine is created

*A sea of flowers on the pitch at Anfield: a week of mourning is declared.*

**April 22.** The football-loving people of Liverpool are turning the Anfield stadium into a shrine, with thousands of supporters queuing to place bunches of flowers on the Kop end of the pitch and hang their red and white scarves on goalposts and fences. It will take more than the sweet smell of a million blooms to assuage the collective grief of this seaport city, however, as it prepares to bury the dead of Hillsborough.

The city's council has declared a week of official mourning and will cover the cost of every funeral. "This city will look after its own," declared the council leader, Keva Coombes. "No one will want for anything and certainly not money." As muffled church bells tolled throughout the day, thousands attended services at the Anglican and Catholic cathedrals. The city's footballer heroes drove to Sheffield to talk to injured spectators. Not since the Blitz has a British city been so united in its grief.

But Liverpool's grief is mingled with anger at the South Yorkshire police, who are blamed for causing the Hillsborough disaster; and some of whom in turn have accused the Liverpool fans of drunkenness both before the match and during the horror on the pitch.

Some fans claimed that police looked on "with utter contempt" as people escaped from the crush and failed to realize the extent of the disaster (→23).

## "Aspects of Love" delights the crowds

**April 18.** Multi-millionaire composer Andrew Lloyd Webber has confounded his critics and done it again with a radically different new musical. For weeks there have been rumours of impending disasters for *Aspects of Love*. Leading man Roger Moore resigned five weeks ago; preview audiences were said to find it too long and boring; stage crews were demanding extra pay for the 50 scene changes. But last night it had a rapturous reception at London's Prince of Wales theatre. Gone are the spectacular sets and lavish choruses; in their place is a tender, complex love story hinting at incest and lesbianism.

*The stars of Lloyd Webber's new hit: Michael Ball and Anne Crumb.*

# Safety reviewed as full inquiry begins

**April 22.** As Mr Justice Taylor interviewed injured survivors of the Hillsborough disaster in Sheffield today – at the start of a "full and intensive" inquiry – the home secretary, Douglas Hurd, told the House of Commons that all leading football clubs would be required to convert their grounds to seating only. The government is under strong pressure from both sides of the House to postpone its bill that will require every football supporter to carry an identity card.

Several football clubs are taking immediate safety measures. Derby County and Tottenham Hotspur are already removing perimeter security fencing – installed to prevent hooligans from flooding the pitches – and others have said that they will follow suit (→4/8).

*Taking down the perimeter fencing.*

# Britain faces legal action over water

**April 18.** Britain was today formally declared in breach of European Community laws on drinking water standards. Carlo Ripa da Meana, the European environment commissioner, gave the government two months to act to reduce nitrate and lead levels in British water before facing a European court on the issue.

With the privatization of the British water industry looming, the government is anxious to avoid a court confrontation, and there are indications that an agreement could still be reached with Brussels.

# Hu's funeral marked by peaceful demo

**April 22.** China's leaders watched from their walled compound today as thousands of students converged on Beijing's Tiananmen Square to mark the funeral of Hu Yaobang, the former Communist Party head. As police stood by at the edge of the square, student leaders climbed on to a stone obelisk – built to commemorate China's martyrs – and unfurled a huge banner which read: "China's soul! Forever remember Comrade Hu Yaobang!" It was the climax of several days of pro-democracy demonstrations.

A students' spokesman called for the government's resignation, an apology and for a full reassessment of Hu's role. The former leader was deposed by conservatives in the party two years ago (→27).

*Hu Yaobang: focus for discontent.*

# Solidarity legalized after eight-year ban

**April 17.** After eight years of underground existence, the Polish free trade union Solidarity has been declared once again legal.

When the decision was announced by a judge at the end of a court hearing in Warsaw several hundred Solidarity supporters cheered, gave the familiar "V" for victory sign and sang Poland's national anthem.

The Solidarity leadership will now need to organize the new union and prepare for the country's first experiment with democracy for some 60 years. Under a deal reached with the Communists after several weeks of round-table negotiations, democratic elections will be held for a third of seats in the Polish parliament. There will also be fully democratic elections to a new senate, and a new presidency.

Lech Walesa, the Solidarity leader, said simply: "I am happy that we have now returned to the road of democracy and freedom." (→5/6).

# Oil prices up after North Sea disaster

**April 19.** Fears that motorists could soon pay £2 for a gallon of petrol are growing after an explosion last night in the North Sea oilfields severely cut Britain's oil output and sparked a rise in the price of oil.

No one was hurt in the blast, which followed a gas leak at Shell Esso's Cormorant Alpha platform in the Brent oilfield. The platform is a key confluence for oil pipelines carrying 470,000 barrels of oil a day – about a quarter of Britain's oil output. Brent Blend crude is widely traded and the halt in Brent output – perhaps for three weeks – will squeeze the market and drive up prices. After the explosion a barrel of Brent Blend jumped about $1.50 to $21.55 a barrel (→22).

**Charlie Chaplin in a scene from "The Kid", now back on screen for the centenary of his birth.**

# Short-range missile talks proposed

**April 21.** West Germany called today for early negotiations between the USA and the Soviet Union to scrap all short-range nuclear weapons in Europe.

There was instant consternation in Whitehall and Washington, where the move was seen as a betrayal of trust by the Bonn government. Chancellor Kohl is sending two senior ministers to Washington immediately to explain that West German public opinion is now strongly against having nuclear weapons on German soil and his coalition government is shaky on that account.

They will get a frosty reception. President Bush and Mrs Thatcher consider that West Germany is threatening the cohesion of Nato, and that with soft talk Mr Gorbachev will exploit the crack appearing in the Western alliance.

Mrs Thatcher is going to Bonn in the next few days to try to convince Kohl of the continuing need for the West to avert this split. After that she will demand that Nato retains short-range missiles (→30).

# Explosion on US battleship kills 47

*Thick brown smoke billows out of the exploded gun turret on the "Iowa".*

**April 20.** A 16-inch gun turret blew up yesterday on the US battleship *Iowa*, killing 47 sailors. The explosion took place as the *Iowa* fired a broadside during exercises in the Atlantic 300 miles north-east of Puerto Rico.

The 58,000-ton battleship, built in 1943, is one of the biggest as well as the oldest battleships afloat. She was one of four capital ships taken out of mothballs by President Reagan in his drive to give the US a 600-ship navy. Although the *Iowa* can carry nuclear warheads on her cruise missiles, the explosion resulted from what a Pentagon spokesman today called "pre-World War II technology". "Some kind of spark" prematurely ignited one of the hundredweight silk bags of cordite used to propel the 16-inch shells, weighing one ton, up to 23 miles.

# Novelist Daphne du Maurier dies, aged 81

**April 19.** Daphne du Maurier, once one of the best-loved best-sellers of her age, died in her sleep today at her home in Cornwall, aged 81. Her fame rested on two novels of the thirties, *Jamaica Inn*, a smuggling yarn, and *Rebecca*, a modern gothic novel about the gloomy house of Manderley. Both made successful films, as did *Frenchman's Creek*. Two of her short stories were made into horror films, *The Birds* and *Don't Look Now*. She wrote a disenchanted biography of her father, the actor-manager Sir Gerald du Maurier.

# April

## 1989

| Su | Mo | Tu | We | Th | Fr | Sa |
|----|----|----|----|----|----|----|
|    |    |    |    |    |    | 1  |
| 2  | 3  | 4  | 5  | 6  | 7  | 8  |
| 9  | 10 | 11 | 12 | 13 | 14 | 15 |
| 16 | 17 | 18 | 19 | 20 | 21 | 22 |
| 23 | 24 | 25 | 26 | 27 | 28 | 29 |
| 30 |    |    |    |    |    |    |

**23.** UK: The Anfield gates are finally closed after an estimated two million mourners have filed into the stadium.

**24.** W Germany: Herbert von Karajan resigns as director of the Berlin Philharmonic.

**24.** UK: BBC unions hold a 24-hour strike over pay (→12/5).

**25.** Iran: The government expels 18 Britons in retaliation for the expulsion of 18 Iranians from Britain.

**25.** Channel: The search for the containers of lindane is called off; 28 of the 32 drums of pesticide lost last month have now been recovered.

**25.** UK: In the twelfth such incident recently, metal objects are found in a jar of Heinz baby food in Kent.

**26.** Europe: England, Scotland, Northern Ireland and Ireland all win their World Cup qualifying matches.

**27.** UK: Winston Silcott, jailed for the murder of a policeman, is elected honorary president of the London School of Economics students' union (→2/5).

**28.** France: Three South African diplomats are expelled following the recent arrests of Ulster loyalists.

**28.** UK: John Cannon is jailed for life for the murder of Shirley Banks, who disappeared in October 1987.

**29.** UK: Bath defeat Leicester 10-6 to win the first rugby union Pilkington Cup final.

**29.** UK: Wigan defeat St Helens 27-0 to win the final of rugby's Challenge Cup.

**30.** W Germany: Margaret Thatcher and Chancellor Kohl fail to reach compromise on Nato missile modernization (→30/5).

**30.** UK: A gunman goes on the rampage at Monkseaton, near Whitley Bay, killing one person and injuring 13.

### DEATHS

**26.** Lucille Ball, US comedienne (*6/8/11). →

**30.** Serge Leone, Italian film director (*3/1/29).

# Japan's PM steps down

**April 25.** Japan's prime minister of the past 18 months, Noboru Takeshita, has resigned in an attempt to end the corruption scandal that has rocked the country for the past nine months. He said on TV: "I have decided to step down to try to restore the public's faith in politics." He also spoke of the need to get the 1989 budget through parliament; opposition groups have made its passage conditional on the resignation of the Takeshita cabinet.

Pressure for Takeshita to resign grew from allegations that he took "political gifts" from beneficiaries of the Recruit Corporation, which ran a lucrative insider-trading scheme. He is said to have received 100 million yen (£440,000) from Recruit, whose chairman faces bribery charges. Twelve former Recruit executives and senior public servants are also under arrest. Takeshita's Liberal Democratic Party (LDP) is now pushing to get the budget through as quickly as possible. But opposition members

*Takeshita bows to the inevitable.*

are calling for a fuller investigation of the scandal. Mitsuhiro Kaneko, the head of the Communist Party secretariat, said: "The last thing the LDP should try to do is to trade Takeshita's resignation for a quick passage of the budget." (→17/5).

## Ulster loyalists' deal with South Africa

**April 24.** Undercover agents have foiled an attempt by Ulster loyalists to swap British defence secrets for South African arms. Three Irishmen were arrested in a Paris hotel last Friday as they gave parts of a Blowpipe anti-aircraft missile to a South African embassy official. It is thought the loyalists were attempting to pass off a display model recently stolen from the makers in Belfast as a working missile.

The South African ambassador was called to the Foreign Office to give an explanation, but the foreign secretary, Sir Geoffrey Howe, today rejected calls for his immediate expulsion (→28).

## Berger survives 180mph crash in San Marino Grand Prix

**April 23.** The racing driver Gerhard Berger had a miraculous escape at the San Marino Grand Prix today when his Ferrari burst into flames after crashing on the fourth lap. Berger's car caught fire after it went straight on at a fast left-hand corner; he was travelling at around 180mph at the time.

Marshals rushed to his rescue and within 15 seconds the flames had been doused. Berger was taken away on a stretcher and was reported to have no more than a fractured shoulder and rib plus second-degree burns. The race, which had been stopped, was later won by Ayrton Senna in a McLaren.

*Sheets of flame rise from Berger's Ferrari: his escape was miraculous.*

# Heysel fans jailed for manslaughter

**April 29.** Fourteen Liverpool football fans received jail terms today for their part in the Heysel stadium disaster in Brussels four years ago, in which 39 people, most of them Italians, died. Another ten British supporters were acquitted. Convicted of manslaughter by a Belgian court, the guilty men were each sentenced to three years' imprisonment, half of it suspended, and fined £1,000. All the fans were allowed to return to Britain, however, while their lawyers decide whether to appeal.

The tragedy occurred at the 1985 European Cup final between Liverpool and the Italian club Juventus, when a charge by British fans resulted in the fatal collapse of a wall.

While the verdict met a mixed reaction in Liverpool, it was condemned in Italy as "ridiculous".

*British fans after the Belgian trial.*

# Students control Beijing

*Students march into Tiananmen Square; vehicles could not stop them.*

**April 27.** Students were effectively in control of Beijing's Tiananmen Square tonight as police and troops allowed protesters to turn what could have been a bloody trial of strength into something approaching a carnival. Cheered by construction workers banging lunch-boxes with chopsticks and others along the route, a vast tide of students swept through the streets of the capital, forcing their way through lines of police ten-deep.

As the huge procession entered the Avenue of Eternal Peace, a major confrontation looked inevitable as army vehicles tried to block the students' path. They were unstoppable, however, surging through a gap in police lines to overrun the square for a second time in a week.

No blood was spilled, but the Chinese leadership must be becoming increasingly concerned about the way in which students seem to be rallying the Chinese people in their call for democratic reform. From their enclave facing the square can be seen a huge banner which reads: "Whoever has the backing of youth has the backing of the future." (→4/5)

# Gorbachev purges the Communist Party

**April 25.** Mikhail Gorbachev has pensioned off 110 former Soviet Politburo members, ministers and provincial Communist Party bosses in a surprise purge. The group was pushed into retirement at the end of a meeting of the policy-making central committee. Gorbachev's top ideologist, Vadim Medvedev, said the purge was a "major landmark in the history of *perestroika*".

Among those to go was Andrei Gromyko, the 79-year-old former foreign minister who was obliged to step down as head of state last September. Some were other stalwarts of the 18-year rule of the former Soviet leader Leonid Brezhnev, now officially called the "period of stagnation". All were seen as opposed to Gorbachev's reforms (→2/7).

*Andrei Gromyko: finally outsted.*

# Up to 1,000 die in Bangladesh tornado

**April 28.** Up to 1,000 people are thought to have died in a tornado which struck central Bangladesh earlier this week. It devastated an area of 60 square miles, flattening houses and destroying crops already severely affected by prolonged drought.

One eye-witness spoke of seeing 30 bodies lying mutilated and rotting in a rice field two days after the tornado had passed. More than 600 injured, many of them with severed limbs, were treated in just one hospital, and hundreds more were sent to military medical centres and hospitals in the Bangladesh capital, Dhaka. The Red Crescent said that it had treated 2,500 people and the health ministry appealed for blood donors.

Homes in at least 30 villages were destroyed, power-lines were torn down, corrugated iron roofs thrown into trees and trucks blown 500 yards off the road.

# Madcap TV comic Lucille Ball dies at 78

**April 26.** The American comedienne Lucille Ball, creator of the long-running *I Love Lucy* show and the first international star produced by television, died today in Los Angeles aged 78. Set on an acting career from the age of 15, she was given her first break in Hollywood by Ginger Rogers after meeting her mother at acting classes. A string of variable movies followed. Some, such as *Without Love* with Hepburn and Tracy, were a delight; while the wartime *Meet the People*, about a shipyard riveter, bombed terribly.

In 1940 she married a singing bongo player, Desi Arnaz, and in the early fifties they devised for television *The Lucy Show*, about a suburban husband and his zany wife, which ran for over 1,000 episodes.

*Lucille Ball: a zany energy for life.*

# Champion jockey rides 200 winners

**April 27.** A chance ride on the 10-1 horse Gay Moore in the early evening at Towcester today took jockey Peter Scudamore to a record 200 victories in a season. He is the first jockey for 37 years to reach this figure and the first ever to do so over the fences and hurdles of National Hunt racing.

Scudamore, at 30, has been champion jockey four times and has already rewritten the record book this season: the fastest ever to 50 and then 100 victories, he broke the previous National Hunt total of 149 victories by Jonjo O'Neill in February. Many of his winning rides have been saddled by the trainer Martin Pipe, who has also broken records this year.

**Veronique Marot (France) and Douglas Wakiihuri (Kenya) win the London Marathon; 22,406 runners finished, making it the world's largest marathon.**

# May

### 1989

| Su | Mo | Tu | We | Th | Fr | Sa |
|----|----|----|----|----|----|----|
|    | 1  | 2  | 3  | 4  | 5  | 6  |
| 7  | 8  | 9  | 10 | 11 | 12 | 13 |
| 14 | 15 | 16 | 17 | 18 | 19 | 20 |
| 21 | 22 | 23 | 24 | 25 | 26 | 27 |
| 28 | 29 | 30 | 31 |    |    |    |

**1. UK:** Police seal off Risley remand centre after two separate incidents. →

**1. UK:** The Low Pay Unit says that nearly half of adult employees in Britain earn wages below the European "decency threshold" (→11).

**1. S Africa:** David Webster, a white anti-apartheid activist, is shot dead in Johannesburg in an apparent political killing.

**2. China:** Thousands of students march in Shanghai in support of democracy (→3).

**2. Paraguay:** Initial election results give Andres Rodriguez, the ruling party candidate, 74 per cent of the vote, but opposition groups allege fraud.

**2. UK:** Students at the London School of Economics students fail to overturn Winston Silcott's election as their union president (→9).

**3. Afghanistan:** Afghan troops claim victory in a battle with mujahedin groups for control of the Salang Highway.

**3. UK:** Charges against six police officers involved in the 1986 Wapping dispute are dismissed by magistrates.

**3. China:** On the 70th anniversary of the first pro-democracy protests, thousands of students march in Beijing (→8).

**4. UK:** Family doctors' leaders reach a deal on their new contracts with the health secretary, K. Clarke (→21/6).

**4. US:** Oliver North found guilty on 3 minor charges in the Iran-Contra affair (→5/7).

**5. Geneva:** The World Health Organization says that reported global cases of Aids rose by 3.6 per cent in April to a total of 151,790.

**5. UK:** Rail unions call off a tube strike to comply with a high court injunction (→8).

**6. Canada:** John Turner, resigns as Liberal Party leader.

### DEATH

**1.** Sir John Boyd, British former trade union leader and Labour Party chairman (*8/10/17).

# Battles with police and mass violence mar Europe's May Day

## Prague: numerous arrests during rally

**May 1.** Czechoslovak police used force to break up anti-government demonstrations in Prague today to coincide with the official May Day parade. Scores of people were arrested, including a correspondent of the BBC, Misha Glenny, who was manhandled and detained for five hours. Britain has protested to the Czech government about the assault.

The protests began as the rally got underway in Wenceslas Square. When human rights campaigners raised banners demanding freedom for political prisoners, hundreds of uniformed and plain clothes police moved in. They tore up banners, encircled the protesters and began arresting them. At the end of the official parade, about 2,000 people gathered in the square shouting "Gorbachev is watching you" and demanding the release of the jailed playwright and dissident Vaclav Havel, who is serving a nine-month sentence for incitement and disturbing public order.

At the traditional rally tens of thousands of Czechs marched past the country's communist leaders carrying pictures of Marx, Lenin, and Mikhail Gorbachev (→17).

*Prague: May Day marchers protest.*

## Berlin: police hurt

**May 1.** May Day turned ugly in West Berlin when left-wing demonstrators battled with police in the city's worst riots for years. The riots took place after a rally in the Kreuzberg district, a hotbed of anarchist activity, where similar disturbances have occurred. More than 60 police were hurt after being showered by missiles, including stones and bottles. Cars were overturned, windows of banks and shops smashed, and there was some looting. In East Berlin the traditional communist parade passed off without trouble.

## Istanbul: defiant marchers fired on

**May 1.** Turkish policemen fired on protesters in Istanbul who had taken to the streets in defiance of a ban on May Day marches. At least 400 people were arrested, and dozens injured in what was seen as the country's worst street violence since the military coup of 1980.

Much of the trouble took place near the central square, where 37 people died 12 years ago, crushed after shots were fired over the heads of demonstrators and panic ensued. Today thousands of police and commandos, supported by armoured cars, blocked the square. The shooting broke out when the crowd approached them throwing stones and chanting workers' slogans.

The violence reflects mounting disillusion with the government of Turgut Ozal, which has allowed inflation to reach 75 per cent and has been accused of corruption. In the March elections his party won only 20 per cent of the vote, and lost control of all the main cities. Ozal personally ordered the May Day ban on marches.

Apart from its domestic impact, the unrest may impair Turkey's bid for full membership of the European Community.

# Pledge of fair treatment ends protest at Risley remand centre

**May 3.** The 54 prisoners who have been staging a protest at Risley remand centre in Cheshire since Sunday have tonight agreed to end their demonstration.

Before coming down off the roof, they lined up to sing the Liverpool football song "You'll never walk alone". A message made from prison sheets read: "RIP. Risley '89. Thank-U media."

The remand prisoners agreed to end the siege after speaking with the north-west regional director of prisons, Bill Driscoll, and obtaining his assurance that they would receive fair treatment.

The protest began with an apparently unimportant complaint over food. Ian Boon, the prison governor, then banned visitors from the jail until the disturbance could be

*Risley prisoners line up for the cameras before ending their roof-top protest.*

settled. But by Monday morning the men were out on the roof and had begun what prison officers described as wanton destruction of the centre. Robin Cook, the Labour

health spokesman, has already challenged ministers on conditions at Risley, drawing particular attention to the number of mental patients held there (→25/7).

# Biggest poll swing to Labour since 1935

**May 5.** Labour romped to victory in yesterday's Vale of Glamorgan by-election with an impressive 12.5 per cent voting swing away from the Tories – its best performance in any such contest since 1935.

The Tories had held the seat for 38 years and saw their last general election majority of 6,251 changed to a Labour one of 6,028. Cabinet ministers quickly shrugged off the result as "mid-term blues" and pointed to Tory gains in the county

council elections held on the same day. Labour jubilantly claimed: "We're on our way again."

Voters' anxieties over the future of the National Health Service and high interest rates were apparent throughout the campaign and must have cost the government candidate many votes. The result was humiliating for the former Alliance partners, the Democrats and the SDP. Between them they got ten per cent of the votes (→9).

# Britain ousts South African diplomats

**May 5.** Britain has given three South African envoys a week to leave the country, in the wake of allegations that Pretoria was involved in covert attempts to acquire British missile secrets.

The government said today that, although it did not suspect the three were directly involved in the operation, it had to express its "grave concern" to South Africa over the affair, which came to a head just over a week ago when three Northern Irish loyalists were found by French police in a Paris hotel with a South African diplomat and an arms dealer. A piece of missile made by Shorts of Belfast was also seized. Reliable sources in Belfast claim that South Africans sent arms to extreme loyalist groups in 1987.

# Rafsanjani calls for Westerners' deaths

**May 5.** The speaker of the Iranian parliament has called for the deaths of five Westerners for every Palestinian killed in Israeli-occupied territory. Ali Akbar Hashemi Rafsanjani said that if such action were taken "the Zionists would not long continue these wrongs". He also urged Palestinians to bomb western factories and hijack planes to further their campaign.

A spokesman from the British Foreign Office said the speech amounted to an incitement to murder and marked a further affront to the standards of international behaviour.

Observers suggested that Rafsanjani was adopting a more radical line to improve his chances in the forthcoming presidential elections, which he is expected to win (→7).

# Pollution row fells Dutch government

**May 2.** For the first time, a western government has fallen over an environmental issue. The Christian Democrat-led coalition in the Netherlands collapsed today over proposals to finance a 70 per cent reduction in pollution over the next 20 years.

After a day of tough political argument, the prime minister, Ruud Lubbers, told parliament he was resigning. He rejected demands from his coalition partners in the Liberal Party for the retention of tax concessions for car commuters. He said they must be cut to reduce pollution and traffic problems.

**May 2. Hungary starts to destroy its border fence with Austria, reducing the Iron Curtain to a mere heap of tangled wire (→8).**

# Thatcher celebrates ten years in power

**May 4.** Margaret Thatcher today completed ten years as prime minister. She celebrated the anniversary quietly. Her opponents said it was more a day for national mourning than rejoicing. According to the latest opinion poll, only one voter in three now thinks Britain is heading in the right direction.

The premier said that she was too busy for any fireworks. However, newspapers carried photographs of her on the doorstep of No. 10 Downing Street cuddling her first grandchild (Michael, the two-month-old son of Mark Thatcher). She had managed to stop work long enough for that.

Leader-writers have produced a variety of balance sheets for the Thatcher years. All agree that she has been a strong leader and that the nation is fundamentally changed. Some threw back at her as a broken promise, however, her words on the same doorstep before entering No. 10 as prime minister. On that day she quoted a prayer of St Francis of Assisi: "Where there

*Little boy blue and his grandmother.*

is discord, may we bring harmony ... where there is despair may we bring hope."

On one question Mrs Thatcher has nothing to say. It is about when she will retire. She seems to want to go on and on and on (→16).

# Davis wins sixth world championship

*Steve Davis in record-breaking form at the snooker world championship.*

**May 1.** Steve Davis has strolled to a record-breaking victory in the world snooker championship in Sheffield. It was his sixth victory and it was achieved by the biggest margin, Liverpool's John Parrott succumbing to Davis by 18 frames to three with an entire evening session to spare. "I played like a slow

puncture. I started badly and got progressively worse," said a rueful Parrott afterwards.

Some consolation might be his £63,000 cheque for finishing as runner-up. For Davis it was his third successive victory after, by his standards, a comparatively lean time this season.

# May

## 1989

| Su | Mo | Tu | We | Th | Fr | Sa |
|----|----|----|----|----|----|----|
|    | 1  | 2  | 3  | 4  | 5  | 6  |
| 7  | 8  | 9  | 10 | 11 | 12 | 13 |
| 14 | 15 | 16 | 17 | 18 | 19 | 20 |
| 21 | 22 | 23 | 24 | 25 | 26 | 27 |
| 28 | 29 | 30 | 31 |    |    |    |

**7.** Tunis: Yasser Arafat "totally rejects" Iran's call for the murder of Westerners.

**7.** Mexico City: The leader of a drug-smuggling voodoo cult that practised human sacrifice is killed in a shoot-out.

**8.** UK: BR decides to impose a seven per cent pay rise on its 100,000 workers (→15).

**8.** China: Zhao Ziyang, the Communist Party leader, promises political changes to meet protesters' demands (→14).

**9.** Australia: Andrew Peacock is chosen to lead the conservative opposition Liberal Party.

**9.** UK: The high court halts distribution of a "potentially misleading" government leaflet explaining the poll tax.

**9.** UK: Winston Silcott resigns as honorary president of the LSE students' union.

**10.** Iran: Rafsanjani says that he does not advocate the killing of Westerners (→29/7).

**10.** Europe: The air traffic controllers' federation says air travellers face another "disastrous" summer of chaos (→17/7).

**11.** US: President Bush orders 2,000 more troops into Panama to boost the 11,000-strong US garrison there.

**11.** US: The CIA says Iran hired the radical Popular Front for the Liberation of Palestine-General Command to plant the Lockerbie bomb.

**12.** USSR: In talks with US secretary of state, James Baker, Gorbachev offers to remove 500 Soviet short-range nuclear weapons from Europe (→30).

**12.** USSR: Some 400,000 people gather in the Armenian capital, Yerevan, to demand the annexation of Nagorny Karabakh from Azerbaijan.

**12.** UK: The Department of Health says there have been 62 victims of Legionnaires' disease this year; seven have died.

**13.** China: Chinese Moslems protest about a book on sexual customs, which they condemn as racist and blasphemous.

**13.** UK: On the last full day of the league season, a wave of violence hits football matches.

## Troops beat Panama election protesters

**May 10.** Demonstrators against vote-rigging in Panama were attacked today by paramilitary forces in the country's capital, Panama City. The opposition candidate in Sunday's presidential election, Guillermo Endara, was beaten repeatedly with iron bars and taken to hospital drenched in blood. He was later discharged.

The opposition's candidates for the post of vice-president were also attacked and journalists' lines of communication were cut. These latest incidents in a saga of violence can only intensify America's desire to oust General Manuel Noriega, its former ally, from power. The US has repeatedly asked other Latin American countries to intervene.

The election has thoroughly discredited Noriega's regime. Though results are still coming in, they are so widely disbelieved that not even the government television stations are bothering to report them (→11).

*Guillermo Endara manages a wave and a bloody smile on his way to hospital.*

## Battle of Britain pilot abducted in Beirut

**May 13.** A former Battle of Britain pilot kidnapped today in Beirut was always convinced he was not a hostage target. As a result, Squadron Leader Jack Mann, a 74-year-old Briton, maintained a daily routine. He was snatched as he made a regular trip between bank and supermarket. His captors, a previously unknown group who call themselves the Armed Struggle Cells, left a note demanding proof of the guilt of prisoners held for the murder of a Palestinian cartoonist in London – but no one has been charged with the killing.

## Poverty claim exaggerated, says minister

**May 11.** Spokesmen for Britain's poverty lobby have castigated John Moore, the secretary of state for social security, after he dismissed their claim that more than nine million Britons live on or below the poverty line.

"Not only are those with lower incomes not getting poorer," said Mr Moore, "they are substantially better off than they have ever been before." He accused campaigners of manipulating statistics, and said that to suggest that 30 per cent of the population was in dire need was "false and dangerous".

Chris Pond, the director of the Low Pay Unit, attacked what he called Moore's "insults"; while Robin Corbett, the Labour MP for Birmingham Erdington, said: "I will show him poverty and deprivation not seen since the 1930s."

Moore rebuffs his critics as politically motivated people who would "find poverty in paradise".

## Bush hints at a welcome to Moscow

**May 13.** In his long-awaited first speech on the subject of US-Soviet relations, President George Bush today proclaimed a "bold new goal". Speaking in Texas, he proposed that the US move "beyond containment" and "welcome the Soviet Union back into the world order".

The president's tone was stern, however, and his price steep. He spoke of his dream of a western hemisphere that was "no longer threatened by a Cuba or a Nicaragua armed by Moscow". Bush demanded that the Soviet Union cut its armed forces even further than already planned, drop the "Brezhnev doctrine" of support for revolutions and back self-determination in Eastern Europe.

## SDP scales down election ambitions

*David Owen: a leader with no party.*

**May 13.** The Social Democratic Party has bowed to the inevitable. With party membership slumped to 11,000 and after by-election humiliations, its national committee announced that it will only "fight selectively" at the next election.

Dr David Owen defiantly insisted that the SDP remains a national party. In reality he is now a leader without a party. "Come back home," both Labour and Democrats appealed to the SDP rump.

## Labour declares it is ready to govern

**May 9.** Labour's policy-making national executive committee (NEC) tonight broke with its past, dumped vote-losing policies and proclaimed the party fit and eager to govern again. By big majority votes the NEC jettisoned unilateral nuclear disarmament, soft-pedalled on nationalization, abandoned penal taxation of the rich, and proposed big pension increases. Another scheme is for a statutory minimum wage set at half average earnings for men.

This huge face-lift marks the end of Labour's two-year policy review. Heavily outnumbered party left-wingers protested against a sell-out of socialism. Mrs Thatcher described the policy changes as cosmetic and accused Neil Kinnock of sacrificing principles in search of power. Labour's leader – once an enthusiastic supporter of the Campaign for Nuclear Disarmament – made a soulful U-turn speech at the NEC meeting. He said: "We are living in radically changed circumstances. Unilateralism is not even comprehended by those who share our objectives in other countries."

Labour will shortly issue its comprehensive new policy statement, entitled "Meet the Challenge, Make the Change". With its so-called new realism the party is confident that it is now out of the wilderness (→18).

## Gaza curfew is too late to halt killings

*Palestinians in the Gaza Strip bewail another day of violence and death.*

**May 7.** A curfew imposed by the Israelis tonight on all eight Palestinian refugee camps in the Gaza Strip has come too late to prevent the worst day's fighting since the Palestinian uprising began.

The trouble began yesterday, when a violent confrontation at the An-Nuseirat camp sparked fighting further south. Four people died, including a man murdered by his own people for allegedly collaborating with the Israelis, and 343 were injured. Almost 150 of them had gunshot wounds after coming under Israeli army fire. Early this morning, as men were leaving the An-Nuseirat mosque and walking towards the cemetery – in accordance with the growing practice of visiting the graves of those killed in the uprising – a low-flying Israeli helicopter doused them with tear gas. Troops then moved into the camp. Some Palestinians began stoning the soldiers, and they responded by opening fire. Two men were killed at once and 40 injured.

An army spokesman said that the Israeli troops had reacted to violent provocation when residents sought a confrontation. One soldier had his jaw smashed and a police officer suffered a broken arm.

## Hungarian leader removed by party

**May 8.** The long political career of Hungary's venerated leader Janos Kadar ended today, when he lost his place on the Communist Party's policy-making central committee and was fired from the nominal post of party chairman because of his age and ill health. Kadar, aged 76, was ousted last May as the party general secretary in a move which has since generated major reforms. The central committee also decided to hold a special conference expected to give reformers a chance to remove other hardliners (→30).

*Janos Kadar: ousted by reformers.*

**The advertisements that have been puzzling people in the south-east of England over the past few weeks are revealed to herald a forthcoming tour of the country by the renowned American evangelist Billy Graham – apparently the only person wise enough to make sense of "LIFE." (→8/7).**

## BBC unions launch campaign of strikes

**May 12.** BBC viewers and listeners are likely to miss some important sporting and news events in the coming weeks, after the decision by BBC unions to mount a series of lightning stikes in support of a 16 per cent pay claim. Out of respect for the Hillsborough disaster victims, however, the FA Cup final on Saturday will not be disrupted.

The move comes in the wake of a 48-hour strike which severely affected radio and TV news programmes. Roger Bolton, a union spokesman, said: "We see this as a dispute which is going to take a little while to resolve." The BBC management said its seven per cent pay offer would not be raised.

## UK snubs Europe's language scheme

**May 12.** Lingua – an ambitious attempt by European Community countries to promote the learning of one another's languages, starting in primary school – risks foundering on strong opposition from a British government once again out of step with its European partners.

Kenneth Baker, the education secretary, is prepared to accept the provisions of Lingua aimed at the over-16s, but otherwise considers the £166 million programme too expensive. With Britain facing another European row over the proposed issuing of identity cards to senior citizens, the Community will have to decide if Britain's compromise merits discussion.

# May

## 1989

| Su | Mo | Tu | We | Th | Fr | Sa |
|----|----|----|----|----|----|----|
|    | 1  | 2  | 3  | 4  | 5  | 6  |
| 7  | 8  | 9  | 10 | 11 | 12 | 13 |
| 14 | 15 | 16 | 17 | 18 | 19 | 20 |
| 21 | 22 | 23 | 24 | 25 | 26 | 27 |
| 28 | 29 | 30 | 31 |    |    |    |

**14.** China: Protesters stage a huge all-night demonstration in Tiananmen Square.→

**14.** USSR: Baltic nationalists call for economic independence from Moscow by next year.

**14.** UK: Kenneth Clarke, the health secretary, drops plans to leave the chief medical officer off the new NHS policy board.

**15.** US: Rupert Murdoch sues the Walt Disney company for £1.5 billion for reneging on an agreement with Sky TV.

**16.** Beirut: A car bomb kills Sheikh Hassan Khaled, the Sunni grand mufti of Lebanon.

**16.** UK: Minorco withdraws a £3.5 billion bid for Consolidated Gold Fields (→4/7).

**16.** UK: The British Guardian Angels go on patrol on the London tube for the first time.

**17.** Prague: The playwright Vaclav Havel is freed on probation after serving four months in jail (→29/6).

**17.** Japan: Junya Yano, the leader of Clean Government, the second largest opposition party, resigns over Recruit.

**17.** Brussels: The European Community issues proposals for a Social Charter guaranteeing workers' rights (→27/6).

**18.** China: More than a million people march in Beijing for the second day running, as talks between students and the Chinese leadership fail (→20).

**18.** N Ireland: In local government polls, Ian Paisley's Democratic Unionists see a five per cent fall in support.

**18.** UK: Paul Channon, the transport secretary, announces new nationwide road-building schemes costing £12 billion.

**19.** UK: Inflation hits eight per cent; Thatcher blames Lawson, the chancellor (→24).

**19.** UK: Dockers vote by 3-1 in favour of a national strike (→11/7).

**20.** China: Martial law is declared in Beijing (→21).

**DEATH**

**20.** Sir John Hicks, the first Briton to win the Nobel Prize for Economics (*1904).

## Kinnock claims the middle ground with new policy launch

**May 18.** Under banners proclaiming moderation, Neil Kinnock marched his new-look Labour army on to the vacant middle ground of British politics.

He presented the party's new policy statement – an 88-page document – with much slick ballyhoo. With unilateral nuclear disarmament and old-style socialism now abandoned, his sermon focused on injecting social responsibility into a mixed economy.

Mr Kinnock was enthusiastic about Britain belonging to the Common Market. He said that the Labour Party had been and always would be better Europeans than Mrs Thatcher was. He went on: "She persists in trying to impose her free-market dogma on the rest of the European Community in seeking to thwart social progress."

On Labour's new defence policy he explained: "We have made it categorically clear. Our conference has repeatedly voted to remain in Nato, which we acknowledge to be a nuclear alliance." Within an hour the party's veteran left-winger Tony Benn announced plans to hold a conference of true socialists to challenge the direction in which Labour is going. He also hopes for mass demonstrations to bring down Thatcherism (→9/6).

## Peronist rules Argentina

*Victory for Peronist Carlos Menem, who promises a "government of unity".*

**May 15.** Jubilant crowds packed the Avenida 9 de Julio – the widest thoroughfare in the world – in the Argentine capital of Buenos Aires last night, waving blue and white Peronist banners, banging drums, blowing whistles and chanting songs of triumph. Their candidate, the slight and sideburned Carlos Menem, has won a sensational victory in Argentina's presidential election, with a 12-point lead over his radical opponent.

Menem owes his victory largely to the votes of millions of poorly paid industrial workers who have suffered badly from Argentina's economic chaos with hyperinflation which has put even basic foodstuffs beyond the reach of many.

For other people, however, the return of a Peronist president has revived memories of the previous regime of 15 years ago, when right-wing death squads often roamed the streets and left-wing revolutionaries brought the country close to civil war.

Menem was conciliatory last night. "I have spoken of forming a government of unity and I will call together all Argentines," he said. Before Menem takes over in December, President Alfonsin may be forced to introduce radical measures to combat inflation (→30).

## Liverpool beat Everton 3-2 after extra time to take FA Cup

*Ian Rush scores one of his two goals which brought Liverpool the FA Cup.*

**May 20.** Liverpool today won the FA Cup they had thought about quitting after the disaster at the Hillsborough semi-final. But there was drama to the end as their Merseyside rivals snatched a last-minute equalizer to force the game into extra time. Then two goals by substitute Ian Rush gave Liverpool the trophy by three goals to two. Now Liverpool go forward to their two remaining matches to try to win the league and cup double.

In Scotland there was also a cup final between local rivals – Rangers and Celtic of Glasgow. Celtic won a dull match 1-0 to deny Rangers the Scottish double. Joe Miller scored the winning goal after 41 minutes (→26/5).

# European monetary policy puts Howe at odds with Thatcher

**May 16.** It became clear tonight that deep divisions within the Tory Party over European Community policy extend to the highest reaches of the cabinet. Sir Geoffrey Howe, the foreign secretary, told the Confederation of British Industry that Britain would join the European exchange rate mechanism "when we judge that the time is right". He also stressed the need for a sharing of sovereignty and give and take. His line contradicts that of the prime minister, who is known to oppose sterling's entry into the mechanism at least before the end of the current parliament (→19).

# Actors campaign for Rose theatre

*Ian McKellen offers a Rose to the Bard, as Glenys Kinnock looks on.*

**May 15.** An all-night vigil and dawn protest by actors and archaeologists led by two dames, Peggy Ashcroft and Judi Dench, won a month's reprieve for the newly discovered site of the Elizabethan Rose theatre, south of London's Southwark Bridge. Three hundred protesters barred the way of builders' lorries due to start constructing an office block there. The developers offered to raise the block on pillars so the foundations of the theatre, which staged Shakespeare plays, can still be seen (→12/10).

# Beijing marchers upstage Gorbachev

**May 16.** In the austere vastness of the Great Hall of the People, Mikhail Gorbachev shook hands with the Chinese leader, Deng Xiaoping, today. It was a historic moment – but totally overshadowed by the extraordinary events taking place a few hundred yards away, with up to half a million students and supporters from every walk of life occupying Beijing's great Tiananmen Square calling for democracy.

The incredible has happened in a country where discipline and respect for authority are paramount. Throughout the day processions flowed into the square, the marchers carrying banners in support of the students. Many of their slogans openly defied the country's leaders. One aimed at Deng, until recently regarded as China's saviour, read: "Down with the emperor!"

Until now this has been an entirely peaceful demonstration. Police have stood back, many of them clearly sympathetic with the crowd. Events could take a more ominous turn, however, if any of 3,000 hunger-striking students should die. Already 500 have been taken to hospital and 12 lives are in danger.

The Chinese leadership appears impotent – and embarrassed in the presence of the Soviet leader – in the face of such protest. Zhao Ziyang, the head of the Communist Party, has promised to "enhance democracy, oppose corruption and expand openness" (→18).

*One man speaks for the massed ranks of protesters in Tiananmen Square.*

*Tea for two communist leaders.*

*Students insist they are here to stay.*

# Travel strikes bring chaos to London

**May 15.** London's bus and tube workers went on strike for 24 hours today and brought chaos to the capital as millions of commuters struggled to travel to and from their jobs. More than 90 per cent of London Regional Transport's employees failed to turn up for work.

The strike, the third in the present unofficial campaign by tube drivers – who want a £64 bonus for operating trains without guards – is the worst to date. Delays increased when an unofficial overtime ban on the Southern Region forced the cancellation of ten per cent of rush-hour services (→23).

# Britain fails to veto tobacco warnings

**May 17.** Smokers are to be challenged by new and more forceful health warnings, following a directive passed by the European Community. This requires tobacco manufacturers to inform the public that "Smoking causes fatal disease" – just one of 16 hard-hitting messages that must in future be printed on cigarette packets.

Kenneth Clarke, Britain's health secretary, opposed yesterday's decision, arguing that the Community had no "competence on public health matters". He was, however, the only one of the 12 ministers to vote against it.

**May 16. Helen Suzman, veteran anti-apartheid campaigner, is to retire as a South African MP.**

# May

## 1989

| Su | Mo | Tu | We | Th | Fr | Sa |
|----|----|----|----|----|----|----|
|    | 1  | 2  | 3  | 4  | 5  | 6  |
| 7  | 8  | 9  | 10 | 11 | 12 | 13 |
| 14 | 15 | 16 | 17 | 18 | 19 | 20 |
| 21 | 22 | 23 | 24 | 25 | 26 | 27 |
| 28 | 29 | 30 | 31 |    |    |    |

**21.** Hong Kong: A million march in support of China's pro-democracy movement. →

**22.** UK: The pound falls to $1.58, a two-year low.

**22.** USSR: The British diplomatic representation of 375 is ordered to be cut by half (→26).

**23.** UK: London tube workers stage their fourth unofficial strike in seven weeks (→12/6).

**24.** UK: Interest rates are raised to 14 per cent.

**24.** USSR: A deadline for the withdrawal of British envoys is dropped and a compromise proposed to settle the spy row (→26).

**25.** USSR: At the inaugural session of the new Soviet parliament, Mikhail Gorbachev is elected president.

**25.** UK: A radio outburst by Neil Kinnock sparks a row between the BBC and the Labour Party.

**26.** Czechoslovakia: Four Britons are expelled in return for the expulsions of four Czechs from Britain.

**27.** UK: An anti-Rushdie march by 20,000 Moslems ends in 101 arrests and violent clashes with police.

**28.** UK: Police "shut" the Lake District when it is overwhelmed by bank holiday traffic.

**29.** USSR: Boris Yeltsin is elected to the Supreme Soviet, following popular outrage at his being denied a seat.

**30.** UK: In two separate attacks, alsatian and rottweiler dogs attack and hurt children.

**31.** Spain: The British embassy admits that a key statement by Spanish police on last year's Gibraltar killings was never sent to the inquest.

**31.** UK: Sir John Hermon resigns as chief constable of the Royal Ulster Constabulary.

### DEATHS

**26.** Don Revie, former Leeds and England football manager (*10/7/27).

**30.** James "Ginger" Lacey, former Battle of Britain fighter pilot (*1/2/17).

## Anglo-Soviet relations upset by spy row

**May 21.** The latest spy row between Britain and the Soviet Union gathered pace today when the Russians kicked out eight British diplomats and three journalists. The Foreign Office promptly said the move was unjustified and a "mirror image" retaliation for Britain's decision to order out an identical number of Soviet citizens working in London and accused of espionage.

The incident is the most serious of its kind since 1985, when each side sent home a total of 31 diplomats and journalists after the defection of a senior KGB officer. It is only six weeks since the Russian leader, Mikhail Gorbachev, visited London and there was a significant improvement in Anglo-Soviet relations. In recent months, however, British ministers have complained to Moscow about the increase in Soviet espionage activity.

When their objections were ignored, they decided to act, while bracing themselves for Moscow to match the expulsions. At the same time, the Foreign Office tried to avoid creating a full-scale diplomatic row by initially keeping the expulsions secret.

The Russians are also demanding a reduction in the quota of British representatives and their Soviet staff working in Moscow (→22).

## Over 1,000 arrests in Argentine food riots

*Armed police round up hungry looters in the Argentine capital, Buenos Aires.*

**May 30.** Buenos Aires, the Argentine capital, and the city of Rosario erupted into an orgy of rioting, bombing and looting last night after President Alfonsin declared a financial state of siege to cope with the country's chaotic inflation. As banks opened after ten days of government-enforced closure and a new £180 note appeared in the shops, shutters slammed down on supermarkets as thousands began to loot. There was no sign of an end to the disorder today. Four people are reported dead and 54 injured. More than 1,000 have been arrested and police are threatening to open fire on looters (→30/6).

## "Statue of liberty" erected in Beijing

*The towering Goddess of Freedom.*

**May 30.** Throughout the night, hundreds of Beijing's art students toiled to present the Chinese leadership with the most dramatic symbol yet of their democracy movement: a 30-feet-high plaster and fibreglass statue based on the Statue of Liberty. The statue – the "Goddess of Democracy and Freedom" – stands in Tiananmen Square, close to the towering Monument to Revolutionary Heroes.

As the movement for democracy continues to spread through China, with demonstrations in Shanghai, Canton and other major cities, Beijing itself appears to be firmly in the hands of the people. The leadership is clearly divided on how to handle the mass defiance. The premier, Li Peng, has ordered troops in; but the People's Liberation Army is remaining in Beijing's suburbs while the politicians dither (→4/6).

## Hungary admits that former PM Nagy was show-trial victim

**May 30.** Imre Nagy – a former prime minister whose execution in 1957 has haunted Hungary's postwar history – was officially declared today to have been the victim of a political show trial. The Communist Party's central committee decided that Nagy, who was executed for treason after the 1956 uprising, should not have been shot. A statement said his trial was "judicially unlawful".

Nagy became prime minister in June 1953 and proposed the creation of a Popular People's Front, a second party in all but name. During the uprising he was pushed onto the balcony to quieten the crowds, and was arrested when the Soviet tanks and troops entered Budapest. Nagy is coming to be seen as one of the nation's immortals and he will be given an official reburial, with five others, next month (→16/6).

44

# Nato summit salutes Bush arms initiative

*Mrs Thatcher has the last word as the Nato summit draws to a close.*

**May 30.** Nato's 40th-birthday summit in Bonn drew to a close today in harmony and with general applause for President Bush's arms control initiative.

In a speech in Brussels yesterday, the American president proposed to the Soviet Union and its allies in the Warsaw Pact what he described as "a revolutionary arms control agreement".

He called for a 20 per cent cut in US combat troops in Europe, a ceiling of 275,000 Soviet and American troops and sharp reductions in the numbers of aircraft, tanks and artillery on either side. Most of the Nato allies were delighted when Bush proclaimed that "the United States and its allies share a vision of a less militarized Europe". The euphoria of the Bonn summit concealed a diplomatic defeat for the British prime minister, Margaret Thatcher, however.

Although she claimed that she was "very satisfied" with the outcome, both the US position and the agreed communique came closer to the position of the West German chancellor, Helmut Kohl, who wants negotiations with the Soviet Union on short-range nuclear weapons, than to that of Mrs Thatcher, who does not.

Kohl said the agreement was "an excellent birthday present" for Nato. Mrs Thatcher said it was "entirely satisfactory". Eduard Shevardnadze, the Soviet foreign minister, called it "a serious step in the right direction" (→18/7).

# Lawson stands firm against policy shift

**May 28.** Professor Milton Friedman today called on Mrs Thatcher to tell her chancellor of the exchequer to let the pound slide and concentrate on keeping inflation down. Speaking on a BBC radio programme, Friedman, the archpriest of monetarism, was urging a return to pure monetarism.

Whitehall observers say, however, that Mrs Thatcher and Sir Alan Walters, her economic adviser, have already been urging such a change on Nigel Lawson. He has stood firm. Last week he raised the base rate to 14 per cent and told the Bank of England to support the pound (→12/6).

# Last-minute goal puts Arsenal on top

**May 26.** In the final minute of the English football league season Arsenal snatched the league title from Liverpool at Anfield tonight by the narrowest possible margin. The London team needed to win by at least two goals; that would make the sides level on points and goal difference, but give the title to Arsenal because they had scored more goals. As Liverpool fans prepared to celebrate a league championship to add to the FA Cup won last week, Michael Thomas ran through to score the crucial goal to give Arsenal victory by 2-0.

# "Eye" libel nets big sum for Ripper wife

**May 24.** There were gasps in court today when a jury awarded Sonia Sutcliffe, the wife of the "Yorkshire Ripper", Peter Sutcliffe, £600,000 damages for a libel by the satirical magazine *Private Eye*, which claimed she had sold the story of her life with the mass killer for £250,000. The libel sum is £100,000 higher than the record damages awarded to the novelist Jeffrey Archer. A flabbergasted Ian Hislop, editor of the *Eye*, said that the award was 100 times higher than any single sum received by families of the Ripper's murder victims: "If this is justice, I am a banana." The magazine plans to appeal (→19/10).

*The "Eye" announces its appeal.*

# Mackay suspension splits Presbyterians

**May 27.** At least one-third of the 3,000 members of the Free Presbyterian Church of Scotland are expected to resign and form a new church, to be called Associated Presbyterian Churches. They have been shocked by the decision of their synod to suspend Lord Mackay of Clashfern for attending a Roman Catholic requiem mass. Worse still, the synod said that the suspension would be lifted when he repents. Lord Mackay believes that he has done nothing wrong and that his job as lord chancellor requires him to go to such services in order to pay his respects to former colleagues.

*The lord chancellor: no repentance.*

# US speaker resigns in corruption row

**May 31.** Jim Wright – as speaker of the House of Representatives, the third-ranking elected official in the US and the top Democrat – resigned today after charges of financial corruption. He is the first speaker in US history to be forced out of office. Sobbing with emotion, Wright denied any intentional wrongdoing in his acceptance of gifts from a friend. The Democratic party's whip, Tony Coelho, resigned after similar charges on Friday. The Democratic majority leader, Tom Foley of Washington state, is expected to succeed as speaker.

**May 31.** Following his defeat by Jim McDonnell, featherweight Barry McGuigan announced his retirement from boxing tonight.

# June

## 1989

| Su | Mo | Tu | We | Th | Fr | Sa |
|----|----|----|----|----|----|----|
|    |    |    |    | 1  | 2  | 3  |
| 4  | 5  | 6  | 7  | 8  | 9  | 10 |
| 11 | 12 | 13 | 14 | 15 | 16 | 17 |
| 18 | 19 | 20 | 21 | 22 | 23 | 24 |
| 25 | 26 | 27 | 28 | 29 | 30 |    |

**1.** Belfast: Alex Murphy and Harry Maguire are jailed for life for the murders of two British army corporals at an IRA funeral last year.

**1.** UK: University lecturers accept a six per cent pay offer, ending a five-month dispute.

**2.** UK: William Waldegrave, a minister, repudiates a BBC report on Labour MPs "blackmailed" by Soviet spies, of which he is the alleged source.

**2.** Japan: Sosuke Uno is sworn in as prime minister (→25).

**2.** UK: Gerard Kelly, a convicted IRA bomber, is freed after serving a fraction of his numerous sentences.

**3.** UK: The Soviet ambassador protests to the Foreign Office after the discovery of listening bugs in diplomatic quarters.

**4.** UK: Nick Faldo wins the British Masters golf championship; last week he won the PGA championship.

**5.** USSR: More than 460 are now estimated to have been killed in yesterday's rail crash.

**5.** UK: The government refuses to offer a haven for the 3.25 million British passport-holders living in Hong Kong.→

**6.** UK: The Home Office imposes visa controls on Turks to prevent further Kurdish refugees from entering the UK (→19/10).

**7.** Hungary: Communist Party reformists led by Imre Pozsgay launch the Movement for a Democratic Hungary (→16).

**8.** London: The Arts Council chairman wins redevelopment approval for a City site involving the demolition of eight listed buildings.

**9.** UK: A Gallup poll gives Labour a seven-point lead over the Conservatives (→16).

**10.** Spain: Arantxa Sanchez of Spain beats Steffi Graf of West Germany to win the French Open tennis championship.

### DEATHS

**4.** Ruhollah Khomeini, leader of Iran (*1902).→

**4.** Cecil Collins, British painter (*23/3/08).

# Khomeini's funeral sparks hysteria

**June 6.** Iran today bade farewell to Ayatollah Ruhollah Khomeini in much the same way as it greeted him ten years ago, when he returned from exile to lead the country's Islamic revolution: with unfettered hysteria.

Such was the outburst of grief and religious fervour among the mourners who turned out to pay their last respects to the ayatollah, who died two days ago at the age of 86, that a first attempt to bury the late *imam*, or spiritual leader, had to be abandoned. The ayatollah's body was to have been paraded for 15 miles from the prayer ground where it had been lying in state, through Tehran to the burial site at Behesht Zahra, a cemetery south of the capital for "martyrs of the revolution". However, Iran's clerical leaders decided to scrap this plan as it became clear that around two million black-clad mourners, weeping and beating their heads and chests in grief, had swarmed the streets of the city soon after daybreak.

Instead, the body was flown to the cemetery by helicopter, which, after a perilous landing in the crowd, was beset by tens of thousands of mourners. In the ensuing melee the ayatollah's bier was jostled so much that his body was half exposed, as frantic mourners tore pieces off the shroud. Guards eventually got the ayatollah back into the helicopter and the funeral was abandoned until late afternoon.

This time the body was in a metal

*Mourners reach out to touch the dais where Ayatollah Khomeini's coffin stood.*

coffin and the immediate graveside had been cleared of all except Revolutionary Guards and officials, who included Iran's president, Ayatollah Ali Khamenei, appointed the country's new spiritual leader yesterday, and Ali Akbar Hashemi Rafsanjani, the speaker of the Iranian parliament, who is tipped to succeed Khamenei as president later this year.

Except for an outburst of grief among the guards themselves, who rushed to be near the coffin, the burial went reasonably smoothly, and, as the sun was setting over Tehran, the man who ousted the Iranian monarchy and transformed Iran into a strict, theocratic republic was finally laid to rest (→29/7).

*Ali Khamenei: taking over from Khomeini as spiritual leader of Iran.*

# Solidarity poised to form a government after crushing Polish Communists in polls

**June 5.** Solidarity has inflicted a crushing defeat on the discredited Communist Party in Poland's first contested election for 40 years. The Soviet bloc's first free trade union could now find itself forming a government. Although only 62 per cent of the electorate voted, it showed unequivocally that it was behind Solidarity and despised the government of Wojciech Jaruzelski.

The 35 government-sponsored candidates were all defeated when they failed to gain the 50 per cent of votes necessary to enter the new parliament. Meanwhile, Solidarity

won 80 per cent of the vote in many areas. Among those failing to win seats were Miecyzlaw Rakowski, the prime minister, and seven other members of the ruling politburo.

The government has conceded defeat and called for Solidarity to join a coalition. But the union, which was only re-legalized in April, may have ideas of its own about how Poland should be ruled, and the pace and direction of reforms. Having won every seat it contested, Solidarity may be thinking of forming a government in its own right (→19).

**Rain Man becomes a West End Shylock: Dustin Hoffman stars in "The Merchant of Venice".**

# Troops massacre protesters in Tiananmen Square

*Students carry away a victim of the night when Chinese troops – hailed as their "brothers and comrades" – unleashed their guns on fellow countrymen.*

**June 4.** In a brutal and horrific show of force, the Chinese government vented its fury and frustration on student dissidents and their supporters today. Up to 2,600 people are thought to have been killed and 10,000 injured when the People's Liberation Army appeared in the streets of Beijing, advancing on Tiananmen Square, firing indiscriminately on demonstrators.

No one on the streets really believed that the army – hailed only yesterday as "brothers and comrades" – could turn on their own people. When they did, it was with a cold savagery that spilt Chinese blood on the Avenue of Eternal Peace after the advancing troops met a hail of stones and petrol bombs. Twenty-six people died in the first encounter; but the real savagery was yet to come as thousands

manned flimsy barriers, pleading with the soldiers to "Go home, go home" – only to face fusillades of bullets.

Now it was the turn of students gathered in the vast Tiananmen Square. As the first armoured vehicles smashed their way through a ring of burning buses into the

square itself, the student occupiers began to fight. The first troop carrier jammed on a barricade; and quickly the crowd swarmed over it, pulling the crew out and beating them senseless before setting the vehicle alight.

By now, Beijing was in a state of siege, with fires burning across the

city and the streets ringing with the sound of tricycle bells – few ambulances were able to move safely in Beijing last night. Screams of agony rang out as hundreds of injured were carried through the streets by frantic riders to hospitals, many of which were filled to overflowing with dead, dying and wounded.

It was after one o'clock this morning when the troops lined up for their final assault on the great square, in which, until a few hours earlier, a near-carnival atmosphere had reigned. It took them 40 minutes to prepare. Then they began to march forward towards the students, shooting at will, climbing over bodies and still shooting.

Then came the tanks, which had no difficulty in flattening the students' tents or their occupants.

It was all over (→9).

## Beijing's countdown to mass slaughter

**APRIL 15.** Hu Yaobang dies.
**18.** Thousands of students call on the government to resign.
**22.** After four days of pro-democracy marches, 100,000 students mark Hu's funeral.
**MAY 15.** A day-long demo by 200,000 disrupts start of first Sino-Soviet summit in 30 years.

**17.** A million march in support of 3,000 student hunger strikers.
**18.** Talks between students and Chinese leaders fail as more than a million march for second day.
**20.** Martial law declared.
**30.** "Statue of liberty" erected.
**JUNE 3.** People's Liberation Army ordered into 'tiaction.

# China orders round-up of dissidents

*One man who stopped the tanks: his name is unknown, but his brave act of defiance won admiration around the world.*

**June 9.** Now comes the savage crackdown as China humiliates its young rebels and drags them, cowed, handcuffed and bruised, their heads shaven and bowed at rifle point, to the people's courts. The police show no mercy to these "counter-revolutionaries", who are being rounded up in their hundreds from their homes and colleges throughout China with other alleged "traitors to the people".

The Chinese leadership, unseen during the days of protest, is emerging to praise the troops who put down the demonstrations in Beijing and elsewhere with such brutality. The prime minister, Li Peng – who brought in martial law – has appeared on television; and so, too, has the aged leader Deng Xiaoping – whom many believed dead – to make an hour-long speech defending the role of the People's Liberation Army in "this incident".

The students who protested so joyfully and peacefully until the massacre in Tiananmen Square five days ago are now officially renegades and enemies of the people. It is they who are accused of the murder of soldiers who mowed down hundreds of their comrades on that night of terror. Many have confessed at rifle point; many more have gone underground, set on spreading the word through villages, factories and schools throughout China.

Some leading dissidents, such as the astrophysicist Fang Lizhi, have taken refuge in the US embassy. The authorities have issued a warrant for the arrest of Mr Fang and his wife, with unnamed workers demanding on television that the state should take "forceful measures to prevent this traitor from escaping" (→22).

## Shanghai streets fill with demonstrators

**June 6.** Confusion reigned in the streets of Shanghai – the very birthplace of Chinese communism – as thousands of bewildered demonstrators milled in all directions, building barricades of hijacked cars and buses and challenging authority at every point.

Local television stations warned that "all cliques and plotters must stop your attempts to disrupt the city of Shanghai – or you will be crushed". Rumours flowed freely through the turbulent streets. One wall-poster claimed the death of Deng Xiaoping; another reported a shooting incident involving the prime minister.

Whether or not the hardline authorities of Shanghai will adopt the same tactics as those used in Beijing remains to be seen. There is not even a policeman on the streets of this city tonight.

## Hong Kong reacts

**June 9.** Shares crashed on the Hong Kong stock exchange today as students and schoolchildren marched to the governor's office demanding a "strong response" to events in Beijing. What kind of response can be forthcoming from this colony – which will be part of China in 1997 – is not certain. The massacre in China's capital has renewed fears in Hong Kong's population, despite Chinese assurances (→25).

# Gas explosion kills hundreds on trans-Siberian rail route

**June 4.** Children setting out on their summer holidays are among the victims of what is probably the worst rail disaster in Soviet history.

Shortly after one o'clock this morning two passing trains on the Trans-Siberian Railway, both brimful of passengers, were destroyed by an explosion of gas from a leaking pipeline. The death toll could be more than 800. The alarm was raised by the driver of one of the trains, who, in spite of severe burns, crawled some miles to the nearest village.

Mikhail Gorbachev, wasting no time, has travelled the 750 miles from Moscow to the scene of the debacle, in the eastern Urals. After visiting survivors in hospital he said that human error was to blame.

Reports suggest that hours before the disaster a smell of leaking gas was noticed up to five miles from the pipeline. Instead of looking for the leak, an employee turned up the pressure of the liquefied gas. The crossing of the trains kindled the catastrophe.

As flags fly at half-mast all over the Soviet Union, pictures of severely burnt survivors have moved hundreds of people to donate blood. The president has confirmed that a top-level investigation into the explosion will include the services of the KGB (→5).

**June 7: Willie Carson celebrates a clear-cut victory in the Epsom Derby on the favourite, Nashwan.**

# June

## 1989

| Su | Mo | Tu | We | Th | Fr | Sa |
|----|----|----|----|----|----|----|
|    |    |    |    | 1  | 2  | 3  |
| 4  | 5  | 6  | 7  | 8  | 9  | 10 |
| 11 | 12 | 13 | 14 | 15 | 16 | 17 |
| 18 | 19 | 20 | 21 | 22 | 23 | 24 |
| 25 | 26 | 27 | 28 | 29 | 30 |    |

**11.** France: Michael Chang (USA) wins the French Open tennis title, beating Stefan Edberg of Sweden.

**12.** UK: Nigel Lawson, the chancellor, concedes that the UK should not become a full member of the European Monetary System before 1990 (→14).

**12.** UK: Workers on British Rail and the London tube vote decisively for industrial action (→26).

**13.** UK: Australia win the first test, at Headingley, beating England by 210 runs (→24).

**13.** Canada: The athlete Ben Johnson accepts full blame for drug-taking and asks for the chance to run again.

**13.** Atlantic: The wreck of the German ship *Bismarck*, which was sunk in 1941, has been found 600 miles west of Brest.

**14.** UK: Thatcher mounts a strong defence of her economic adviser, Sir Alan Walters, and repudiates an apparent truce with Lawson (→15).

**14.** UK: The Queen bestows a knighthood on Ronald Reagan.

**15.** W Germany: Gorbachev tells the West Germans that the Berlin Wall could one day disappear.

**15.** UK: The total number of people who have contracted botulism from hazelnut yoghurt rises to 22 (→26).

**15.** UK: Inflation rises to 8.3 per cent (→23).

**16.** Hungary: Five executed leaders of Hungary's uprising in 1956, including Imre Nagy, are reburied (→24).

**16.** UK: Labour wins the Vauxhall and Glasgow Central by-elections and achieves its best result in local elections for ten years (→19).

**17.** Paris: The centenary of the Eiffel Tower is celebrated.

### DEATHS

**11.** Robin Howard, founder of the London Contemporary Dance Theatre (*17/5/24).

**17.** Ray McAnally, Irish actor (*30/3/26).

## Turkish exodus from Bulgaria intensifies

*Cultural refugees from Bulgaria find a temporary home in a Turkish camp.*

**June 12.** Tens of thousands of Turks are leaving Bulgaria for Turkey in one of the largest population movements in Europe since the late 1940s. The exodus of the ethnic Turks is the outcome of a four-year campaign by the communist authorities in Sofia to persuade the 1.5 million Turks in their country to assume Slavic names and become "reborn Bulgarians". The Turkish language is banned, along with aspects of Moslem Turkish culture ranging from religious holidays to funeral rights. The dispute has now blown up into a major diplomatic row between Bulgaria and Turkey, who are ancient enemies (→2/7).

## Fianna Fail loses seats in Irish elections

**June 16.** An attempt by Charles Haughey's Fianna Fail party to win an outright majority in the Irish parliament at the fifth attempt appears to have failed. Haughey called yesterday's general election with the express aim of winning an overall majority, but early returns indicate that he may suffer a net loss of seats in the Dail, the Irish parliament. Fianna Fail held 81 at the dissolution and need 83 for an absolute majority, but they are now predicted to win only 78. Haughey is nevertheless expected to lead the next government (→29).

## Botulism spread by hazelnut yoghurt

**June 13.** Five children and five adults have been hospitalized in the first outbreak of botulism in Britain for ten years. The poison has been traced to a puree used to flavour hazelnut yoghurt produced by a food processing company called Young's Fruit in Kent, but the Department of Health has warned shoppers to avoid all brands of the yoghurt until tests are completed.

Botulism, a potentially fatal form of food poisoning, causes respiratory and heart failure. Several of the patients have been put on life-support machines (→15).

## "Gorbymania" hits new heights during West German tour

**June 13.** President Gorbachev – voted the most popular politician among West Germans – has joined Chancellor Kohl in signing a Bonn Declaration putting Soviet-German relations on a new plane. During a four-day visit to West Germany, in which "Gorbymania" reached new heights, the Soviet leader offered peace and reconciliation in Europe in exchange for the economic assistance his reforms so desperately need.

Gorbachev's visit coincided with an opinion poll showing 90 per cent of the population trusting him, as against 58 per cent for President Bush. West Germans also favoured neutrality for their country and the removal of foreign troops.

The Soviet leader has been given an extraordinary welcome; his reception by 7,000 Dortmund steelworkers chanting "Gor-By, Gor-By" was typical. At the same time in Bonn's market square there were Berliners waving a banner which urged him to "make love not walls" – a reference to the division of Berlin which Gorbachev has said he does not see as a "problem".

Gorbachev's visit has marked a new stage in a diplomatic relationship which could hold the key to the future of Europe. German economic power can help the Soviet Union and Eastern Europe reform their economies (→15).

## Ethnic violence escalates in Uzbekistan

**June 12.** Bloody ethnic violence is spreading in the Soviet Central Asian republic of Uzbekistan, and some reports say that at least 100 people have died. The rioting broke out ten days ago when Uzbeks in the Fergina region attacked homes in villages inhabited by Meskhetians. A 160,000-strong Turkish minority, the Meshketians were deported by Stalin in 1944 from their homeland in Georgia.

At least 1,000 people are said to have been injured, and troops from the Soviet ministry of the interior are being rushed to the area. Several thousand Meshketians are being evacuated to other regions.

*First aid in the aftermath of riots.*

# June

## 1989

| Su | Mo | Tu | We | Th | Fr | Sa |
|----|----|----|----|----|----|----|
|    |    |    |    | 1  | 2  | 3  |
| 4  | 5  | 6  | 7  | 8  | 9  | 10 |
| 11 | 12 | 13 | 14 | 15 | 16 | 17 |
| 18 | 19 | 20 | 21 | 22 | 23 | 24 |
| 25 | 26 | 27 | 28 | 29 | 30 |    |

**18.** UK: Tory members of the European Parliament blame Thatcher for a negative Tory European election campaign.→

**19.** W Germany: Terrorists are disturbed while planting bombs at a British army barracks at Osnabruck (→2/7).

**19.** Poland: Solidarity wins 99 seats in the new 100-seat senate (10/7).

**19.** UK: Kenneth Baker, the education secretary, announces details of proposed "top-up" loans for students.

**20.** USSR: Hundreds of immigrants are evacuated and a curfew imposed on the Kazakhstan oil town of Novy Uzen after fatal rioting.

**20.** US: Bush suspends all high-level exchanges between US and Chinese officials.

**20.** Arctic: The Soviet cruise liner *Maxim Gorky* hits an iceberg deep inside the Arctic Circle; 990 people are rescued.

**20.** UK: Thatcher tells MPs that the basic state pension was never intended to cater for all the needs of life.

**21.** UK: A GPs' conference throws out the contract agreed between their leaders and the health secretary, Kenneth Clarke (→20/7).

**21.** Afghanistan: The siege of Jalalabad by mujahedin guerrillas has ended after 15 weeks.

**21.** UK: Police arrest 250 people in a huge operation to stop "hippies" celebrating the summer solstice at Stonehenge.

**22.** UK: The Lords vote to end a two-year freeze on child benefit, inflicting a major defeat on the government.

**23.** Brussels: In advance of the Madrid summit, Jacques Delors, the president of the European Commission, attacks the British "ayatollahs".

**24.** UK: David Gower, the England cricket captain, walks out of a press conference at Lord's after his team's bad performance (→27).

**24.** Hungary: A four-member ruling praesidium is elected, ending Karoly Grosz's 13-month undisputed leadership (→11/9).

# Strikes freeze transport

*A lone passenger waits in vain at King's Cross while the trains stay silent.*

**June 22.** A 24-hour strike by British Rail workers – coinciding in London for the first time since 1926 with stoppages on tubes and buses – paralysed the country's public transport system yesterday, but the expected traffic chaos failed to materialize. Between a third and a half of London office workers stayed at home and, although the morning and evening rush-hours started two hours earlier than usual, the traffic was lighter than on an average day; many walked or cycled. Elsewhere in the country, most people managed to get to work.

Britain's summer of transport strikes is set to continue, however. The National Union of Railwaymen (NUR) has ordered two more 24-hour stoppages on British Rail and London Transport in the next two weeks. Unions and management are due to hold more talks tomorrow, but neither sounds optimistic for a settlement. The NUR has rejected BR's plan to impose a seven per cent pay hike and there is argument between the two sides about the bargaining procedure itself. Jimmy Knapp, the NUR general secretary, is confident the "magnificent support" of his members will remain solid (→28).

**June 18: Luciano Pavarotti hits a high note in his first concert at the London Arena, a new arts and sports hall in the former docklands of east London. Pavarotti drew 12,000 fans – and caused record traffic jams.**

# Papandreou loses elections in Greece

**June 19.** Andreas Papandreou, Greece's socialist prime minister, has offered his resignation following his party's election defeat on Sunday. President Sartzetakis has asked him to organize a caretaker government until a new administration can be sworn in.

Constantine Mitsotakis, leader of the New Democracy party, which took most seats but failed to win a majority, will now attempt to form a government by reaching some sort of compromise with the Coalition of the Left. The first priority then will be *katharsis* – a thorough purge of the Bank of Crete financial scandal that has dogged Papandreou's Pasok government in recent months. But the election result may also reflect public disquiet about recent events in Papandreou's private life (→2/7).

*Exit: Papandreou and friend.*

# Ferry line charged with manslaughter

**June 22.** Two years after the sinking of the *Herald of Free Enterprise* at Zeebrugge, seven employees of the ferry's owners, Townsend Thoresen – three senior officials and four crewmen – have been charged with corporate manslaughter. P&O, the owners of Townsend Thoresen, are similarly charged. If convicted, the men face possible life sentences and unlimited fines.

# Greens and Left triumph in Euro polls

## Monetary harmony urged by top Tories

**June 23.** Two former Tory cabinet ministers have called on the prime minister to make a firm commitment at next week's Madrid summit of the European Commission to joining the European Monetary System (EMS). Michael Heseltine and Leon Brittan were on opposite sides during the 1988 Westland affair, which ended in both their resignations.

Today they spoke with one voice, Mr Heseltine in a Portsmouth speech and Mr Brittan in an interview in *The Times*. Nigel Lawson, the chancellor of the exchequer, is thought to agree with them. But he heeded party calls not to rock the boat and did not mention the issue in his speech to Welsh Tories today. Mrs Thatcher, on the other hand, has to stress the snags she sees in EMS membership (→27).

## Strange wins US open championship

**June 18.** Curtis Strange held off a strong late challenge from Ian Woosnam of Wales and two fellow Americans today to win the US Open golf championship for the second successive year. His victory at the Oak Hill country club in Rochester, New York, makes him the first player to retain the title since Ben Hogan in 1950 and 1951. Last year he defeated Britain's Nick Faldo in a play-off.

*Strange: driving into record books.*

## First national win for Labour in years

**June 19.** Labour has won 45 of Britain's 78 constituencies in the elections to the European Parliament and the Tories got 32. Thirteen seats changed hands in this massive swing to the left. Scottish Nationalists kept their one place.

The result has secured Labour its first victory in a national poll since 1974. When the final figures were declared tonight, Neil Kinnock crowed: "This is a rehearsal for things to come." Sir Geoffrey Howe, the foreign secretary, retorted that the outcome was freakish: "like a by-election on a national scale". The Tories have paid dearly for running a lacklustre campaign and appearing divided about the future of Europe.

Most remarkable feature of the poll was the success of the Green Party in collecting 2.3 million votes (15 per cent of the total) in their first full-scale effort – although they failed to win a single seat. This was achieved largely at the expense of the Social and Liberal Democrats and the Social Democratic Party, whose support withered disastrously. "Greenery" is firmly planted on the political agenda. All parties must now treat environmental issues more seriously.

## Chinese death toll continues to mount

**June 22.** No effort is being spared by the Chinese government in its ruthless clampdown on the former student "heroes" of the democracy campaign. The heroes of a few days ago are being sat in front of television cameras, their hands bound, their eyes glassy and unseeing, their heads bowed, each held by stone-faced prison guards.

Many face death by shooting – a single bullet in the back of the head is the traditional method. Seven are reported to have died today in Beijing, and newspapers in Shandong province report the executions of a further 17 "common criminals" (→25).

*Neil Kinnock: savouring the delights of success after Labour's lean years.*

## Greens may hold European power balance

**June 19.** Left-wing parties will have a working majority in the new European Parliament providing they successfully woo an assortment of Greens, who have doubled in strength and could now hold the balance of power. This was the position as the final European election results were declared tonight. The Socialists are again the biggest single party, with Britain's Labour contingent as its strongest national group.

The final seats tally is: Socialists 181, European People's Party 123, Liberals 44, Communists and allies 41, Greens 39, Democrats 34, European Right 22, Democratic Alliance 19, and Independents 15.

Ultra-right populists led by a former Waffen-SS member took 750,000 votes in West Germany.

## Sakharov cautions West about Gorbachev

**June 21.** Andrei Sakharov, the Soviet physicist and former dissident, has urged the West to treat his country's leadership with caution.

Speaking yesterday during his first visit to Britain, Sakharov – whose outspoken advocacy of human rights during the Brezhnev years led to internal exile in Gorky – described the Soviet Union as "the last empire on the planet" and called it "the country of the enmity of peoples". Although he praised Mikhail Gorbachev for *perestroika*, he reminded his audience of the Soviet leader's rise to power through Communist Party ranks. Sakharov, who looked frail and was helped in his speech by his wife, now sits in the Soviet parliament.

*Sakharov: free to speak at last.*

# June

## 1989

| Su | Mo | Tu | We | Th | Fr | Sa |
|----|----|----|----|----|----|----|
|    |    |    |    | 1  | 2  | 3  |
| 4  | 5  | 6  | 7  | 8  | 9  | 10 |
| 11 | 12 | 13 | 14 | 15 | 16 | 17 |
| 18 | 19 | 20 | 21 | 22 | 23 | 24 |
| 25 | 26 | 27 | 28 | 29 | 30 |    |

**25. China:** Zhao Ziyang and other leading reformers are stripped of their posts, and a purge by hardliners is extended to ordinary party members.

**25. India:** Sikh extremists shoot dead 24 Hindus in a public park in Punjab.

**26. UK:** A ban is lifted on sales of hazelnut yoghurt after the worst botulism outbreak for 60 years affected 27 people.

**26. Norwegian Sea:** In the third such incident in two months, a Soviet nuclear submarine is forced to close down its main reactor.

**27. Madrid:** Thatcher is alone among European Community leaders in refusing to approve the proposed Social Charter.→

**27. UK:** Nalgo, the local government union, calls its first national strike (→18/7).

**27. UK:** The Transport and General Workers' Union votes against Neil Kinnock's "flexible" approach to defence.

**28. UK:** The second national one-day rail strike again coincides with a virtual shutdown of the London underground (→30).

**28. Yugoslavia:** In a show of Serbian nationalism, a million Serbs mark the 600th anniversary of a landmark battle.

**29. UK:** People in eight London boroughs are warned that worms up to an inch long could be found in their tap water for several days.

**29. UK:** Plans are announced to put the first Briton in space in 1991.

**29. US:** Some White House officials are linked with a homosexual prostitution ring.

**30. Sudan:** A military coup topples the elected government of Sadiq el Mahdi.

**30. Argentina:** Amid raging inflation and rising unemployment, Raul Alfonsin resigns as president (→8/7).

**30. UK:** Jimmy Knapp, the NUR leader, rebuffs BR's offer of peace talks (→6/7).

**DEATH**

**27.** A J Ayer, British philosopher (*29/10/10).→

---

# Hong Kong overwhelmed by boat people

*Behind the wire: Vietnamese refugees wait for freedom in Hong Kong.*

**June 27.** Few in Hong Kong notice the boat people directly any more. The storm-battered, foul-smelling wooden craft that arrive in the British colony almost daily are shunted to separate docks – away from the tourist liners – by the harbour police. Their occupants are packed into buses and taken immediately to refugee camps, where they are left very much to fend for themselves and rot with 45,000 of their fellow Vietnamese citizens.

Hong Kong claims that it is doing its best for the boat people, with United Nations help. But there are growing fears in the colony of disease through overcrowding and the danger of civil disorder.

Most boat people know before they leave their homes – to risk typhoons, pirates and leaking boats – that they face the ordeal of Hong Kong's internment camps, with little chance of resettlement. So what drives them to do it?

The answer is to be found in Vietnam itself, the country which brought the US army to its knees. Vietnam is desperately poor; with an annual average income of £85 per head, it is worse off even than Bangladesh. For boat people, any life might be better (→25/10).

# Britain turns down pleas for a haven

**June 25.** The British government has given a cold reply to a plea by Hong Kong's 3.25 million British nationals who are seeking a haven in the UK when their colony reverts to China in 1997. Since the events in Beijing and elsewhere, Hong Kong's residents have become increasingly insecure.

Mrs Thatcher has told MPs that three million refugees would, at a stroke, double the ethnic population in Britain. The foreign secretary, Sir Geoffrey Howe, has said he will speed up direct elections to an assembly in the colony to ensure a democratic structure before China takes over (→4/7).

# Great thinker Ayer meets a logical end

**June 27.** The much admired philosopher A J Ayer died today, aged 78. His great intellectual abilities became evident when, in his twenties, he published his first book, *Language, Truth and Logic*. In it he expounded the theory which, although modified, was to remain central: that thought had to be guaranteed by its formal or logical coherence or by the evidence of the senses. All other types of thought – religion, ethics, astrology, metaphysics – Ayer saw as nonsense.

# Australia have Ashes in sight as England slump to Lord's defeat

**June 27.** England slumped to their second successive defeat in the test series against Australia at Lord's today, losing by six wickets after a fine bowling spell by Neil Foster briefly stirred hopes of an unlikely victory. But the target of 118 runs was too small and it was Steve Waugh, undefeated centurymaker in Australia's first innings total of 528, who hit the winning boundary.

David Gower, with a captain's century in England's second innings, supported by Robin Smith's valiant 96, restored some pride, but England has only once ever come back from a 2-0 deficit even to square a series, let alone to win. England's hold on the Ashes is therefore looking vulnerable.

*Captain's innings: Australian skipper Allan Border steps up the attack.*

# Haughey resigns as premier of Ireland

**June 29.** Charles Haughey has resigned as prime minister of Ireland after failing to secure re-election in the Dail, the Irish parliament. He will spend the next few days attempting to negotiate pacts with other parties to establish a working majority. The resignation comes after the failure of his party, Fianna Fail, to win an overall majority in the 15 June election.

Opposition parties, wary of a public backlash, are unlikely to force another election so soon after the last one, and Mr Haughey is expected to enter coalition talks with the centre-right Progressive Democrats (→2/7).

# Prince attacks low teaching standards

**June 28.** "English is taught so bloody badly," the Prince of Wales said yesterday, that his own staff cannot write or speak it properly. The prince, who was addressing a meeting of senior executives seeking closer links between industry and schools, complained that he personally has to correct all the letters sent from his office. Concerned that the present system is incapable of producing literate writers for the future, he favours drilling and other more structured teaching methods.

*All smiles for the camera as European leaders patch up their differences.*

# Monetary union comes closer in Madrid

**June 27.** Mrs Thatcher reaffirmed today that Britain wants closer economic and monetary union in Europe. She also signalled greater readiness to join the European Monetary System – but still did not say when.

The prime minister redefined her attitude at a summit meeting of European Community leaders in Madrid. They accepted that she is willing for a compromise deal. This would not involve acceptance of plans for a common currency. But it would include a fixed exchange rate regime built around the German mark.

In adopting a more conciliatory stance and abandoning the idea of a floating pound, Mrs Thatcher appears to have yielded to pressure from Sir Geoffrey Howe, the foreign secretary, and Nigel Lawson, the chancellor of the exchequer.

She has backed away from confrontation with Britain's partners and agreed to further negotiations for closer integration – even if the other European leaders still suspect her of adopting delaying tactics.

On the face of it, this shift should end the war between No. 10 Downing Street and the Treasury (with Foreign Office backing) which has rumbled on and disturbed the Tory Party for many months. A spokesman at No. 10 claimed: "It's all been speculation." (→25/7).

# New petition issued by Czech dissidents

**June 29.** A new anti-government campaign has been launched in Prague with a petition calling for urgent political reforms, including freedom of religion and of the press. The petition, which has been signed by 1,800 people – many from outside traditional opposition circles – is expected to be rejected by the Czechoslovak authorities. It is being seen as the most important political petition in the country for a decade. The campaign, whose leaders include the playwright Vaclav Havel, includes demands for freedom of association, improved environmental protection and discussion of the 1968 "Prague Spring".

*Vaclav Havel: dissident playwright who was recently released from jail.*

# Geisha girl apologizes on television to Japanese prime minister

**June 25.** Mitsuko Nakanishi chose a Buddhist temple as a backdrop for her candid television revelations about life as a former geisha girl and mistress of Japan's prime minister, Sosuke Uno.

While apologizing for the pain caused to him and his family by her publicizing of the affair – for which Uno is alleged to have paid her £15,000 – she portrayed a man who liked to humiliate underlings, such as the manageress of a restaurant whom he addressed as an "old woman".

Miss Nakanishi's disclosures are in contravention of the geisha code of silence, but she maintains that "he is a public figure and people have the right to know" (→24/7).

**Indiana meets 007: Harrison Ford is joined by Sean Connery in the new Indiana Jones film.**

*Telling all: Mitsuko Nakanishi, the geisha girl who broke her silence.*

# July

## 1989

| Su | Mo | Tu | We | Th | Fr | Sa |
|----|----|----|----|----|----|----|
|    |    |    |    |    |    | 1  |
| 2  | 3  | 4  | 5  | 6  | 7  | 8  |
| 9  | 10 | 11 | 12 | 13 | 14 | 15 |
| 16 | 17 | 18 | 19 | 20 | 21 | 22 |
| 23 | 24 | 25 | 26 | 27 | 28 | 29 |
| 30 | 31 |    |    |    |    |    |

**1. USSR:** On Soviet TV, Gorbachev says that he will not tolerate separatism (→6).

**2. Greece:** Tzannis Tzannetakis is sworn in as interim premier, heading a communist-conservative coalition (→28/9).

**2. Bulgaria:** More than 100,000 Turks are reported to have been expelled.

**2. Ireland:** The Dail votes to adjourn again after the failure of Fianna Fail to reach a power-sharing agreement (→12).

**3. UK:** The bill abolishing the 40-year-old dock labour scheme receives the Royal Assent (→7).

**3. Egypt:** Abdullah al-Mashad, a leading Islamic scholar, says that all Aids victims should be killed.

**4. UK:** Consolidated Gold Fields agrees to a £3.5 billion takeover by Hanson.

**5. US:** Oliver North is given a suspended prison sentence and fined $150,000 for his part in the Iran-Contra affair.

**6. Strasbourg:** In a speech to the Council of Europe, Gorbachev sets out his vision of a "common European home".

**6. UK:** Aslef, the train drivers' union, votes 7-1 in favour of an overtime ban in support of a pay claim (→10).

**6. Israel:** Fourteen Israelis die when a Palestinian grabs the steering wheel of a bus in which they are travelling and sends it into a ravine.

**7. UK:** Dock workers vote by 3-1 for an all-out strike (→11).

**7. UK:** Nicholas Ridley, the environment secretary, gives the go-ahead for the building of Foxley Wood, a new town in Hampshire (→4/10).

**8. Argentina:** Carlos Menem is inaugurated as president.

**8. UK:** The US evangelist Billy Graham ends his Mission '89 crusade to Britain.

### DEATHS

**2.** Andrei Gromyko, former Soviet defence minister (*18/7/09).→

**6.** Janos Kadar, Hungarian leader (*26/6/12).→

# Botha has met Mandela

*Mandela: in jail for over 26 years.*

*Botha: outgoing South African boss.*

**July 8.** There has been a mixed reaction in South Africa to today's official announcement that the outgoing president, P W Botha, had a meeting with Nelson Mandela, the jailed African National Congress (ANC) leader, three days ago.

Leaders of the main opposition groups were surprised by the brief government statement on the meeting, which took place at Tuynhuys, the presidential offices in Cape Town. There was no advance press notice of the "courtesy visit" and its significance is uncertain. Some activists see it as a prelude to Mandela's release, and think it means that the government effectively recognizes his role and that of the ANC in future talks between Pretoria and the anti-apartheid opposition.

Although this possibility has delighted white liberal groups, other groups such as the South African Council of Churches and the liberal Democratic Party are more muted in their response; while radicals such as Mandela's wife, Winnie, see the 45-minute meeting as some sort of set-up. The far-right Conservative Party said it was proof that the government is planning a "sellout" to black extremists.

# Right to abortion threatened in US

**July 3.** American women's constitutional right to abortion has been seriously challenged by a ruling of the US supreme court. The increasingly conservative court has upheld a Missouri law which states that life begins at conception, grants rights to the foetus at 20 weeks and forbids public funding of abortions and abortion counselling.

The right to abortion rests on the 1973 *Roe* v. *Wade* ruling, which was not affected directly by today's judgement but which many believe may soon be overturned. "This is a very dark day for women," declared Kate Mitchelman, executive director of the National Abortion Rights Action League.

# Water bill passed

**July 8.** The government benches at the House of Lords were unusually full last night as peers voted in the measure that paves the way for the £7 billion privatization of the water industry in England and Wales.

An opposition attempt to force the new water companies to submit investment plans on the promised clean-up of the water supply was defeated by 168 votes to 114. The Tory whips, recoiling from a defeat over the electricity sell-off, played safe with this vote (→25/8).

# Two giants of communist rule die in Moscow and Budapest

## Andrei Gromyko

**July 2.** Andrei Gromyko, Russia's stony-faced foreign minister for nearly 30 years, died in Moscow today, aged 79. For three years – until he was sacked by Gorbachev, whom he had sponsored as Soviet leader – he also held the post of president of the Supreme Soviet.

Gromyko, the son of peasants, was educated and raised to the heights solely by the Communist Party, and he gave it total loyalty in return. At the age of 34 he was Soviet ambassador to Washington. He went on to repeat the word *nyet* at the United Nations more times than anyone can count, and to earn the nickname "Grim Grom".

*Gromyko lies in state in Moscow; Gorbachev will not be at his funeral.*

## Janos Kadar

**July 6.** Janos Kadar, the ruler of Hungary for 32 years, died in Budapest today at the age of 77. Kadar lost his post as party leader in May last year, and was forced into full retirement last month after a mental and physical decline.

Kadar was called many things in his long political career – including the "Butcher of Budapest" after helping the Russians suppress the 1956 uprising, and the "Chief Chef of Goulash Communism" for masterminding the country's prosperity in the 1960s. But he won genuine popularity for giving Hungarians the most liberal and open society in the Soviet bloc.

# Hong Kong passport-holders boo Howe

**July 4.** Sir Geoffrey Howe, the normally urbane and unflappable British foreign secretary, was shocked to find himself booed on arrival in Hong Kong yesterday.

The ugly scenes at the airport followed his refusal to accept a petition signed by 600,000 people urging the British government to grant more than five million Hong Kong residents – with or without British nationality – the right to live in the UK. Last night 400 protesters were still chanting outside Government House, where he is staying. Hong Kong has lost confidence since the massacre of demonstrators in China last month.

At a meeting with the press, Sir Geoffrey issued a brief statement – which did not mention the nationality issue – saying he was in Hong Kong "to listen as well as to explain". As protesters became more vociferous, he agreed to meet a local deputation tomorrow.

In the meantime, an independent report by British university economists suggests that mass migration

*Hong Kong protesters in full cry.*

from the colony could be of advantage to Britain. The country's balance of payments would improve; and a building boom would result from the demand for new homes. The costs of such a move would not be excessive.

# The acid party's off: police clamp down

**July 1.** Traditional rivalries between pleasure-seeking young people and the police were exacerbated tonight as the authorities combed London and the home counties in an attempt to shut down at least a dozen versions of this summer's latest craze: the "acid house party". Once a preserve of the truly chic, who launched them on the island of Ibiza, these invitation-only parties, fuelled by the drug "Ecstasy" (or "acid") – some of which have up to 5,000 guests – have spread to the suburbs. Urged on by a vociferous media, the police are determined to stamp out these mass-market get-togethers.

**Chris Evert leaves Wimbledon for the last time: beaten by Steffi Graf in the semi-finals of a tournament she won three times and had graced for 17 years. Graf won the match, but it was Evert who won the cheers.**

# Car bomb kills British soldier in Hanover

**July 2.** A British soldier was killed and his wife and four children were injured today when a booby-trap bomb exploded in their car in West Germany. The IRA are thought to have planted the device in the car of Corporal Steven Smith in a residential street in Hanover.

The bomb exploded immediately after the corporal opened the door of his Mercedes. He died almost instantly and his wife was severely burnt. Their children required treatment in hospital for splinter injuries. People in the street, many of them from service families, were evacuated as other cars in the area were searched.

Another device was found under a British-registered Datsun and later defused by bomb-disposal experts.

A British military spokesman commented that the "callousness of the attack involving children just defies description". It fuels concern that the IRA has launched a new terrorist campaign against British military personnel on the continent of Europe.

# Tension mounts in summer of discontent

*Hyde Park becomes a parking lot – and one man does some advertising.*

**July 5.** As rail workers staged their third one-day strike today, and leaders of two million engineering workers announced plans to target top firms for indefinite disruption, Britain's industrial relations reached their lowest ebb since the miners' strike of 1984-5. Local government workers have already struck and trouble is brewing in the docks. Pessimists are predicting a "summer of discontent" to rival 1979's winter chaos that undermined the Labour government. But ministers are united in their resolve to fight off what they see as a direct challenge to their determination to keep spending and inflation down (→7).

# Pilotless Soviet MiG crashes in Belgium

**July 4.** An 18-year-old man was killed in a village in western Belgium today when a Soviet MiG-23 fighter plane without a pilot crashed into his parents' house.

The jet had flown hundreds of miles across Europe from Poland before it ran out of fuel and came down in the village of Bellegem. It had been escorted by two American F-15 fighter planes from the moment it entered West German airspace, but their orders to shoot it down were withdrawn when they reported that it had no pilot. They were, however, told to destroy it if it threatened a populated area.

The Soviets will be under pressure to explain why they issued no warning about the jet, whose pilot had bailed out during exercises because of technical problems.

# July

## 1989

| Su | Mo | Tu | We | Th | Fr | Sa |
|----|----|----|----|----|----|----|
|    |    |    |    |    |    | 1  |
| 2  | 3  | 4  | 5  | 6  | 7  | 8  |
| 9  | 10 | 11 | 12 | 13 | 14 | 15 |
| 16 | 17 | 18 | 19 | 20 | 21 | 22 |
| 23 | 24 | 25 | 26 | 27 | 28 | 29 |
| 30 | 31 |    |    |    |    |    |

**9. Poland:** George Bush, the US president, begins a tour of Europe (→18).

**10. UK:** BR offers the rail unions talks at Acas (→11).

**10. UK:** The government is forced to back down over proposals to break the big brewers' hold on pubs.

**10. Poland:** Solidarity says it is ready to form a government under certain conditions (→14).

**11. UK:** Talks to end the rail dispute break down after BR offers an 8.8 per pay rise but attaches strings (→12).

**11. UK:** Sir James Goldsmith, Jacob Rothschild and Kerry Packer launch a £13 billion takeover bid for BAT, the UK's third biggest company.

**12. UK:** The fourth one-day rail strike brings the worst traffic jams seen so far (→13).

**12. France:** Christian Dornier, a farmworker, shoots dead 14 people, including most of his own family, at the village of Luxiol, near Besancon.

**13. UK:** BR lifts conditions on its latest pay offer (→17).

**13. UK:** The Japanese company Honda announces plans to open a car plant at Swindon, creating 1,300 jobs.

**13. UK:** The government signals the end of ship-building in Sunderland.

**14. Poland:** Lech Walesa, the Solidarity leader, says the union will accept Wojciech Jaruzelski as president (→19).

**14. USSR:** Miners go on strike in seven Siberian cities (→16).

**15. UK:** Nottinghamshire defeat Essex to win the Benson and Hedges Cup cricket final.

**15. USSR:** Eleven people are killed and 127 hurt in fights between Georgians and Abkhazians in Abkhazia, an enclave of Georgia (→17).

## DEATHS

**10.** Tommy Trinder, British comedian (*24/3/09).→

**10.** Mel Blanc, US actor (*1908).

**11.** Lord (Laurence) Olivier, British actor (*22/5/07).→

# Haughey returns to power in Ireland

*Back in power: Charles Haughey celebrates his re-election as premier.*

**July 12.** Charles Haughey has retained his hold on the Irish premiership after concluding a last-minute power-sharing deal with the right-of-centre Progressive Democrat (PD) party.

His Fianna Fail party, which holds 78 of the seats in the Dail, the Irish parliament, gave two cabinet places to the PDs, who have just six members of parliament. The determination of the PDs' leader, Des O'Malley, to hold out for cabinet representation finally wore down Haughey's resistance to sharing power. O'Malley takes the industry and commerce portfolio and his colleague, Bobby Molloy, will become energy minister. The PDs won pol-

icy changes, including a faster move towards a standard income tax rate of 25p.

In addition, £115 million will be spent to cut hospital waiting lists and reopen wards shut through cutbacks. There will also be a £11 million programme for treatment of haemophiliacs with the Aids virus. The issue of compensation for patients infected by blood products led to the defeat of the government and helped precipitate the election.

The resolution of the month-long political crisis came only an hour before the Dail voted on a motion to elect Haughey as premier. With the support of the six PD members, he won by 84 votes to 79.

# Rangers sign up Catholic Johnston

**July 10.** Glasgow Rangers made football history today when they paid £1.5 million for Maurice Johnston, a Scottish striker now with the French club Nantes. The price is not unusual, but Johnston's religion is: he is a Catholic and for a century Rangers have fielded only Protestants. Sectarian passions will be stirred still further by the fact that until today Johnston had been expected to return to Rangers' great rivals, Celtic, traditionally the Catholic club. How fans will react is hard to forecast; policemen were last night guarding the Rangers ground as Protestants protested.

**July 10: Tommy Trinder dies, aged 80, a star of two eras – music hall and television.**

# Wimbledon double taken by Germany

**July 9.** The green, green grass of Wimbledon belongs to Germany this weekend after Boris Becker won the men's singles title to complete a West German double. His compatriot, Steffi Graf, had earlier retained her women's singles title by defeating Martina Navratilova in three sets, 6-2, 6-7, 6-1.

Becker's victory was even more comprehensive, powering to a third title against the defending champion, Stefan Edberg of Sweden, who lost in straight sets – 6-0, 7-6, 6-4. Becker, who is 21, grew up six miles from the 20-year-old Steffi Graf, near Heidelberg.

*German double: Graf and Becker.*

# Nationwide dock strike begins in UK

**July 11.** Britain's dockers began a national strike today in protest at the abolition of the dock labour scheme, halting work at 42 ports. Ron Todd, the leader of the Transport and General Workers' Union, said that 96 per cent of the country's registered dockers had joined the walkout. But the National Association of Port Employers said that the union is badly divided, many workers are not striking and large numbers are accepting redundancy payoffs. Todd rejects such talk as "the brave music of a distant drum" and calls upon all dockers to join the industrial action (→31).

## The supreme actor takes his final bow

*Early days with Vivien Leigh.*

**July 11.** Surrounded by his family, Laurence Olivier, the grand old man of the stage, died in his sleep early today, aged 82. This evening, London's theatres dimmed their lights for him. At the National, of which he was the first director, audiences stood in silent tribute.

Olivier was judged the greatest actor of his time. In Shakespeare he triumphed, from his legendary wartime Richard III at the Old Vic and his celebrated filmed Henry V to his television performance as King Lear in 1983. He was one of the last actor-managers, working at the St James's theatre with his second wife Vivien Leigh. He founded and led the National Theatre company from 1963-73 and was the first actor to be created a peer. He made some 60 films, including *The ˌtainer* with his third wife, ˌ Plowright.

*Final Act: as King Lear on TV.*

# France indulges in Revolution fever

**July 15.** The celebrations ordered by President Mitterrand to mark the 200th anniversary of the French Revolution reached a festive climax in Paris yesterday. An especially grand version of the traditional Bastille Day military parade was followed last night by a lavish pageant through the French capital.

The pageant embraced "national" displays from around the world, including, appropriately and movingly in this homage to democracy, Chinese students with bicycles. Britain was represented by military bands bearing regimental colours (largely won in battles against the French), and by dancers in rain supplied by Kent fire engines.

The idea of pouring water on Britain's display was appropriate revenge, many French observers might say, for Mrs Thatcher's attempt to dampen the festivities with remarks she made last week on French television.

The prime minister, in Paris for a summit conference of the world's seven leading economic powers timed to coincide with the bicentenary, upset her hosts by denying either that the Revolution still had a universal message ("It heralded the reign of terror, and then came Napoleon") or that the idea of human rights sprang from it ("Good heavens, no. We had the Magna Carta in 1215. The notion of human rights goes back to ancient Greece"). Not surprisingly, per-

*International fireworks: France celebrates, Mrs Thatcher has her doubts.*

haps, Mrs Thatcher was jeered at a commemoration of the Declaration of the Rights of Man on 13 July, and French premier Michel Rocard yesterday referred to the British government's "trend towards social cruelty". One French MP remarked that ancient Greek human rights included a belief in slavery; he also pointed out that the Greeks firmly excluded women from political power.

## Solidarity says it is prepared for power

**July 10.** Solidarity signalled today that it is prepared to form the Soviet bloc's first non-communist government for 40 years. A spokesman for the movement, which crushed the Communist Party in elections last month, said Solidarity would form a government if the Soviet Union agreed and Western countries offered significant economic aid. Solidarity is expected, however, to form a coalition with other, smaller parties in the *Sejm*, or parliament, and the likelihood that the Polish Communist Party will insist on retaining some key posts has not been ruled out (→14).

## Victory for British Lions in Australia

**July 15.** The British Lions snatched a one-point victory over Australia in the third and decisive rugby international at Sydney today to win the series by two matches to one. It was the first time this century that the Lions have won a series after losing the opening test.

Ironically, it was Australia's greatest player, David Campese, who turned out to be the villain. Running the ball out of defence instead of kicking into touch, he then made a hash of a pass, allowing Ieuan Evans to score the Lions' only try. It was not converted, but five penalties by Gavin Hastings were enough to give victory by 19 points to 18.

*Lions on their way to glory.*

| Su | Mo | Tu | We | Th | Fr | Sa |
|----|----|----|----|----|----|----|
|    |    |    |    |    |    | 1  |
| 2  | 3  | 4  | 5  | 6  | 7  | 8  |
| 9  | 10 | 11 | 12 | 13 | 14 | 15 |
| 16 | 17 | 18 | 19 | 20 | 21 | 22 |
| 23 | 24 | 25 | 26 | 27 | 28 | 29 |
| 30 | 31 |    |    |    |    |    |

**16.** UK: Alain Prost of France wins the British Grand Prix, taking a 20-point lead in the world drivers' championship.

**16.** USSR: Tens of thousands demonstrate in Prokopyevsk in Siberia, in support of 100,000 striking miners (→17).

**17.** UK: The National Union of Railwaymen rejects a peace formula – accepted by other rail unions – to end their month-long dispute with BR (→27).

**17.** USSR: Strikes spread to the Donbass coal-mining region in the Ukraine.→

**17.** Iran: Six senior Iranian army officers are said to have been executed for plotting to overthrow the Islamic republic.

**17.** USSR: Violence between Georgians and Abkhazians has now claimed fourteen lives.

**18.** N Ireland: The body of John McAnulty, a businessman abducted yesterday, is found; the IRA admits killing him.

**18.** UK: Local government workers start a three-day strike.

**18.** Paris: A group of fugitive Chinese dissidents sets up a movement to overthrow the Chinese regime non-violently.

**19.** Poland: Jaruzelski is elected to the new post of executive president by the narrowest possible margin (→31).

**19.** UK: BBC's *Panorama* accuses Lady Porter, the Tory leader of Westminster City Council, of gerrymandering (→26).

**20.** UK: Family doctors reject their new contracts by 3-1 (→16/10).

**21.** Malaysia: Derrick Gregory, a convicted British drug trafficker, is hanged.

**22.** UK: A £208,000 pay rise for Lord King, the chairman of BA, is revealed to be only one of a number of huge pay awards to top directors.

### DEATHS

**16.** Herbert von Karajan, Austrian conductor (*5/4/08).

**20.** Harry Worth, British comedian (*20/11/18).

## Europe tour boosts image of US president

**July 18.** President Bush flew back to Washington from the Netherlands today after a highly successful tour in which he visited Poland and Hungary as well as five West European countries.

While he has not offered arms cuts as deep as those proposed by Mikhail Gorbachev, Mr Bush has shown himself as willing as the Soviet leader to move the process of arms control ahead.

He has made it plain that he considers the maintenance of close relations with President Mitterrand of France and the West German chancellor, Helmut Kohl, at least as important as his relationship with the British prime minister. The intimate ties between London and Washington of President Reagan's day are over.

It is clear that Mr Bush, a Texas conservative who started by responding warily to political change in Eastern Europe, has now had his imagination truly touched by what

*Bush in Poland with Lech Walesa.*

is happening there. He was especially moved by visiting the Warsaw ghetto and the Gdansk shipyard and is giving Poland a $100 million "enterprise fund".

## DC10 airliner crashes in flames in Iowa

**July 20.** A United Airlines DC-10 on its way from Denver to Chicago crashed and exploded yesterday while making an emergency landing at Sioux City, Iowa. The death toll is believed to be 107, while 186 are known to have survived. The first messages of trouble from the

pilot indicated one engine out of action and then, a few minutes later, total hydraulic failure. Experts said that the likely cause of the crash was malfunctioning of the auxiliary power unit, which suggests that the plane was flying with maintenance incomplete.

## Hottest summer in Britain since 1976

**July 22.** Weather experts forecast no let-up in the scorching temperatures that have all but dried up water supplies to 500,000 people in south-east London and Kent. While 100,000 have been without water completely for nearly a week, all residents in the area are being advised to boil drinking water because of fears of contamination. Six million people across the country are watching their lawns turn brown and their plants die as the hosepipe ban continues. Today temperatures reached levels not seen since 1976, with 93F (34C) recorded at Heathrow. Mediterranean resorts are having a mild summer in comparison with Britain (→29).

## Ken Dodd cleared of all tax charges

**July 21.** Clutching a paper cup of champagne, a tearful Ken Dodd yelled to the cheering crowd outside Liverpool crown court today: "What a beautiful day it is to say: Thank God it's all over." The comedian was celebrating his acquittal on charges of defrauding the Inland Revenue "on a grand scale". The court had heard how he kept £336,000 in cash in his attic as a "nest egg".

## British flights delayed by French air traffic control strikes

**July 17.** Long delays, in some cases overnight, hit thousands of travellers from Britain's airports this weekend. The chief cause of the disruption is a strike by air-traffic controllers in France. The dispute caused waits of up to eight hours for 1,500 passengers at Gatwick on Saturday. Delays at Cardiff, Leeds, Bradford and Liverpool averaged about three hours, while Luton experienced three to six-hour hold-ups. Although the strike is due to end tomorrow, its effects may persist for two or three days. The waiting was worse for people booked with the Spanish airline Hispania. It closed yesterday, hitting passengers at Cardiff and several northern airports and stranding some in Majorca and the Canaries (→30).

*Holidaymakers at Gatwick hoping to get away despite the controllers' strike.*

# Conductor Herbert von Karajan dies

*Herbert von Karajan: the maestro conducting the Berlin Philharmonic.*

**July 16.** Herbert von Karajan, the brilliant, stormy and dictatorial conductor, died today at his home near his native Salzburg, in Austria. He was 81. For over 30 years von Karajan was a towering figure on the world musical scene, his name associated especially with the Berlin Philharmonic Orchestra, of which he was conductor-for-life until earlier this year, and with Salzburg, where he founded an Easter Festival. His decision to give up his Berlin post – he had held it for 34 years – was partly for health reasons and partly the culmination of years of a relationship which some compared to a marriage: mainly loving and affectionate, but at times moody and tempestuous.

Karajan's Nazi past made life difficult for him immediately after the last war, although he claimed he had to join the Nazi Party in 1934 to take up a job in Aachen. Controversial or not, von Karajan was still one of the greatest conductors of the century, even if some found his technically superb music-making so polished as to be at times machine-like and unfeeling. But with von Karajan's death, as one Berlin Philharmonic violinist put it today, "a musical era has ended".

**July 18. Kenya's president, Daniel arap Moi, sets alight 12 tons of ivory tusks, worth an estimated $3 million, in a ceremony in Nairobi to mark the country's commitment to the preservation of the African elephant.**

# Soviet miners end fortnight of strikes

*A woman joins grim-faced striking miners at Makeevka in the Ukraine.*

**July 21.** Tens of thousands of Soviet coal miners were streaming back to work today at the end of a damaging and unprecedented strike which has left the Soviet leadership badly shaken. The miners have been offered improved pay and conditions.

For nearly two weeks major Soviet coalfields have been idle with over 300,000 miners on strike. About 100,000 workers in other industries downed tools in sympathy. Some 700 million roubles are said to have been lost in output.

The strike began in Siberia and quickly developed into the most serious outbreak of industrial unrest since Mikhail Gorbachev came to power four years ago. Among the strikers' demands were greater political and economic independence for the mines, and a 40 per cent pay rise for night shifts.

The strikes spread quickly to dozens of mines in the Ukraine, Kazakhstan, and to the north-east corner of Europe above the Arctic Circle. Miners were also demanding soap to wash themselves, and milk for their families (→2/11).

# Radical plans for law shake-up published

**July 19.** Government plans for the radical reform of the legal profession were published today in spite of passionate objections from judges and barristers. A white paper envisages limited new rights for solicitors to appear in crown and high courts. Banks and building societies will be allowed to do conveyancing work. Barristers continued to squeal. The solicitors were unsure what to say.

# July

## 1989

| Su | Mo | Tu | We | Th | Fr | Sa |
|----|----|----|----|----|----|----|
|    |    |    |    |    |    | 1  |
| 2  | 3  | 4  | 5  | 6  | 7  | 8  |
| 9  | 10 | 11 | 12 | 13 | 14 | 15 |
| 16 | 17 | 18 | 19 | 20 | 21 | 22 |
| 23 | 24 | 25 | 26 | 27 | 28 | 29 |
| 30 | 31 |    |    |    |    |    |

**23.** Italy: The country's 49th postwar government is sworn in, with Giulio Andreotti as premier for the sixth time.

**24.** UK: Thatcher extensively reshuffles her government. →

**25.** UK: The closure of the male remand section at Risley centre is announced.

**26.** USSR: Thousands of pro-independence demonstrators march in Tbilisi, the capital of Georgia.

**26.** UK: Lady Porter survives a no-confidence vote at a Westminster council meeting.

**27.** Libya: A South Korean DC-10 crashes at Tripoli airport, killing 78 people.

**27.** Beirut: At least 28 people are killed and 80 wounded during a battle between Syrian and Christian forces.

**28.** Lebanon: Israelis abduct Sheikh Abduk Karim Obeid, a leading Shia Moslem (→ 30).

**28.** USSR: The newspaper *Pravda* attacks Gorbachev's reforms in an editorial.

**29.** Sri Lanka: India begins withdrawal of its 45,000 peacekeeping troops.

**29.** UK: The London Weather Centre says this is Britain's sunniest summer of the century so far.

**30.** Lebanon: The captors of the US hostage William Higgins threaten to kill him within 24 hours unless the Israelis free Sheikh Obeid. →

**30.** USSR: In Kishinev, the capital of Moldavia, 20,000 march for an end to second-class status for Moldavians (→ 29/8).

**30.** UK: Tens of thousands of holidaymakers are delayed at airports.

**31.** Dockers at Hull and Southampton return to work after several dockers' groups voted to end strikes (→ 1/8).

**31.** Poland: Czeslaw Kiszczak is named as the Communist Party's candidate for prime minister (→ 17/8).

**DEATH**

**23.** Donald Barthelme, US writer (*7/4/31).

# US hostage "hanged"

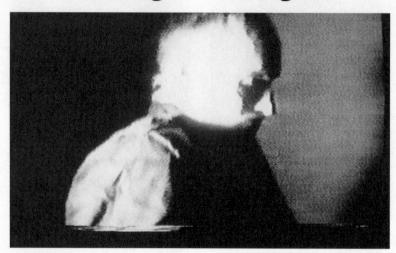

*A still from the video the kidnappers claim is of Lt-Col Higgins's hanging.*

*Abdul Karim Obeid: still a prisoner.*

**July 31.** An Arab terrorist group claims to have hanged a senior US marine officer in retaliation for the kidnapping of a pro-Iranian guerrilla leader by the Israelis. Lt-Col William Higgins is said to have been executed after a deadline for the release of Sheikh Abdul Karim Obeid passed without the Israelis letting him go. A video purporting to show Lt-Col Higgins's hanging was released by his captors, who call themselves the Organization of the Oppressed of the World. They seized him in February 1988 as he carried out his duties for the United Nations peace-keeping forces in Lebanon.

Sheikh Obeid was captured by the Israelis, along with two of his relatives, during a raid on their base in a village near Tyre three days before the alleged execution. An Israeli communique said that the sheikh had confessed under interrogation to organizing the kidnapping of Lt-Col Higgins.

The execution was immediately condemned by President Bush, who cut short a speaking tour of Chicago to return to the White House. He spoke of his outrage at "this kind of brutality, this uncalled-for terrorism".

News of Higgins's death was swiftly followed by a threat to kill another US hostage, Joseph Cicippio, unless Sheikh Obeid was freed. Cicippio, an accountant at the American University in Beirut, was seized in September 1986 (→ 3/8).

## NatWest boss resigns over Blue Arrow

**July 25.** Lord Boardman, the chairman of Britain's largest bank, National Westminster, today became the latest casualty in the Blue Arrow affair. Last week's report from the Department of Trade and Industry (DTI) said that County NatWest, the group's investment banking arm, had misled the market in its 1987 documents on behalf of the Blue Arrow employment agency. The Serious Fraud Office and police are now investigating.

The DTI criticized three main board NatWest directors who have since resigned. Lord Boardman was not himself criticized but felt that as head of the bank he should resign with his colleagues, whom he believes have been harshly treated.

## Rail unions call off strike campaign

**July 27.** The 24-hour strikes that brought chaos to British Rail travellers this summer are over. The National Union of Railwaymen (NUR) voted tonight to accept the employers' offer of an 8.8 per cent pay rise. One government minister said: "It's game, set and match to Jimmy Knapp." Mr Knapp, general secretary of the NUR, claimed victory for his men, saying that the strikes had changed the rail industry for ever: "Railway workers have won the right to be treated with dignity and respect."

BR welcome the end of the dispute, but called on the NUR to stop indulging in "insults and vilification". A major reshuffle is now predicted for BR managers.

*Knapp: game, set and match.*

## Salmonella illness affects 400 people

**July 31.** Nearly 400 Britons are now ill with salmonella poisoning. Three people have died in Chester and north Wales, where a total of 316 cases have been reported. This outbreak is apparently unconnected with that in County Durham which has so far affected 80 people.

Both outbreaks have been traced to cooked meats from different sources. Tests are also being done in a nursing home in Flint, where staff and patients are suffering from diarrhoea, and in Lluesty Hospital in Holywell.

# Row blows up over cabinet reshuffle

**July 25.** Mrs Thatcher is tonight embroiled in the most unseemly row of her whole premiership. Her most controversial cabinet reshuffle has left wounded senior colleagues accusing her of behaving with disgraceful pettiness. Yesterday the prime minister fired Sir Geoffrey Howe, the foreign secretary, and replaced him with John Major, the number-two treasury minister.

She offered Howe the Home Office. He turned that job down, but agreed to be leader of the House of Commons provided he had the title of deputy prime minister. Douglas Hurd, the home secretary, indirectly discovered that Mrs Thatcher had offered his job to Sir Geoffrey. The fat was in the fire.

Next Mrs Thatcher's press secretary rubbished the idea that deputy premiership means anything. Then Sir Geoffrey's friends were accused of leaking the fact that he had been offered Mr Hurd's job.

Mrs Thatcher has taken her revenge on Sir Geoffrey for having joined with Nigel Lawson, the chancellor, in forcing her to change her tune at the recent Madrid meeting of Common Market leaders on the question of European monetary union. The prime minister evidently felt that it would be too risky for her to remove both men from their jobs and Sir Geoffrey was the more expendable of the two.

*John Major: surprise promotion.*

*Geoffrey Howe: rudely debunked.*

## Japanese PM resigns as ruling party falls

**July 24.** The first defeat in 30 years for the ruling Liberal Democratic Party (LDP), in elections to the upper house of the Japanese parliament, has forced the resignation of the prime minister, Sosuke Uno.

Uno, who came in to clean up the LDP's image after the Recruit scandal brought down his predecessor, found his own reputation besmirched after last month's revelations by his former mistress. The election is a triumph for the Socialist Party, although burdened with ideological splits, and Takako Doi, its charismatic leader.

With Miss Doi expected to be voted leader of the upper house, the disgraced Uno has accepted total blame for the defeat. "My mind," he said as he rose to leave, "is now clear as a mirror."

**July 23. Greg Lemond races ahead in the 86th Tour de France. The American beat his closest rival, Laurent Fignon, by just eight seconds. Lemond covered the distance at 33.8mph, the fastest tour speed ever.**

## Drug addict jailed for murder of PM

**July 27.** An alcoholic and drug addict, Christer Pettersson, has been convicted of the assassination of Swedish prime minister Olof Palme three years ago, and sentenced to life imprisonment. But the conviction was carried by the vote of six lay assessors, while the court's two judges voted for Pettersson's acquittal. Judge Geijerstam said: "The high level of uncertainty presented during the trial makes it impossible to reach a guilty verdict." The case will now go to a higher court where judges are in the majority.

Pettersson, who has often been seen in an inebriated condition outside state alcohol stores, has no motive for the murder and has consistently pleaded his innocence.

## Calcavecchia is Open champion

## Rafsanjani secures landslide in Iran

**July 29.** The speaker of the Iranian parliament, Ali Akbar Hashemi Rafsanjani, has won the presidential election with a landslide majority. Rafsanjani, who is 55, is regarded in the West as a moderate among the fundamentalist Iranian revolutionary leadership. He was imprisoned by the shah and was active in the campaign which led to the 1979 revolution and the return of Ayatollah Khomeini.

## All Magnox power stations stay public

**July 24.** To Labour jeers, Cecil Parkinson, the energy secretary, announced in the House of Commons today that the Magnox nuclear power stations will not be sold off but will be kept in public ownership. This humiliating blow to the government's electricity privatization programme follows the realization – "literally in the last few weeks" – that the cost of decommissioning the ageing stations could reach £7.5 billion.

*Mark Calcavecchia with his trophy.*

**July 23.** Mark Calcavecchia of the United States won golf's Open Championship at Royal Troon today after the first-ever triple play-off. He had finished level with two Australians, Greg Norman and long-time leader Wayne Grady. Norman, who had set a course record 64 earlier in the day, was the favourite in a play-off over four extra holes. But after Norman drove out of bounds at the final extra hole Calcavecchia won by three strokes. It was his first victory in one of golf's four "majors".

# August

## 1989

| Su | Mo | Tu | We | Th | Fr | Sa |
|----|----|----|----|----|----|----|
|    |    | 1  | 2  | 3  | 4  | 5  |
| 6  | 7  | 8  | 9  | 10 | 11 | 12 |
| 13 | 14 | 15 | 16 | 17 | 18 | 19 |
| 20 | 21 | 22 | 23 | 24 | 25 | 26 |
| 27 | 28 | 29 | 30 | 31 |    |    |

**1. Israel:** A second deadline for the release of Sheikh Obeid, set by the captors of Joseph Cicippio, is ignored. →

**1. US:** The Bush administration makes contact with Syrian and Iranian leaders in a effort to defuse the hostage crisis. →

**1. Hong Kong:** Police take several hours to quell a riot among Vietnamese boat people in refugee camps (→10/9).

**1. UK:** Baroness Susan de Stempel is cleared of battering her former husband to death.

**2. France:** Fires in south-east France and Corsica reach catastrophic proportions.

**2. S Africa:** In an anti-apartheid protest, black patients are wheeled into whites-only hospitals (→1/9).

**2. UK:** The Midland Bank makes a first-half loss of £500 million because of debts from the third world.

**2. Argentina:** Trade restrictions with Britain are lifted for the first time since the 1982 Falklands war (→19/10).

**3.** The *Voyager II* space probe discovers three new moons around Neptune (→25/8).

**3. Iran:** Ali Akbar Hashemi Rafsanjani is sworn in as president.

**4. UK:** A Lebanese extremist group confirms that the London hotel bomber was preparing to kill Rushdie.

**4. UK:** John Ward, a British businessman, flies to Kenya for the inquest on his daughter, Julie, who died on a game reserve last year (→4/9).

**4. Indonesia:** The death toll from an earthquake earlier this week reaches 97.

**4. Japan:** At his first news conference, Emperor Akihito defends people's right to accuse his father, Hirohito, of war atrocities.

**5. UK:** British male athletes score five individual wins at the European Cup meeting in Gateshead (→6).

**DEATH**

**1.** John Ogdon, British pianist (*27/1/37).→

## Police blamed for Hillsborough tragedy

**Aug 4.** The police officer in charge at Hillsborough stadium on the day when 95 people died and 400 were injured at an FA Cup semi-final between Liverpool and Nottingham Forest has been suspended on full pay. The suspension follows an interim report on the disaster by Lord Justice Taylor which places the blame firmly on the shoulders of the South Yorkshire police.

David Duckenfield, aged 44, who was promoted to chief superintendent 21 days before the match, is accused in the report of lacking leadership and "lying in the aftermath of the disaster". The chief constable of South Yorkshire, Peter Wright, has offered his resignation.

Of Mr Duckenfield, Lord Justice Taylor said that, when another officer asked for permission to open an emergency gate because of the build-up of fans, his "capacity to take decisions and give orders seemed to collapse".

Sheffield Wednesday football club, which owns Hillsborough, and the local city council are also criticized in the report (→14).

## Mystery man blows himself up in hotel

**Aug 3.** A man was blown to pieces and two floors ripped out of a London hotel in a mysterious explosion today. Police have confirmed that the accident was caused by "an improvised explosive device". They believe that the man, who was of Middle Eastern origin, may have been priming the device when it went off. Having stayed at the Beverley House hotel, Paddington, for some days, the dead man was due to leave today. There is speculation that he may have been preparing to carry out the death sentence passed on the British author Salman Rushdie for his novel *The Satanic Verses* (→4).

## What, no hat! Portrait surprises public

**Aug 4.** The Queen Mother's 89th birthday was marked by two pictures: the official photograph by Norman Parkinson, showing her smiling in her garden at the Castle of Mey under a big hat; and a portrait, hatless and almost severe, unveiled at the National Portrait Gallery. Alison Watt, a 23-year-old Glasgow painter who won the John Player portrait award and chose this as her winning commission, calls it "an honest portrait". She said: "I wanted to make her look solid and bring out her very strong character. I'm pleased with it and so is the Queen Mother." Other viewers were stunned.

*"An honest portrait": Alison Watt and her painting of the Queen Mother.*

## Dockers ordered to give up their strike

**Aug 1.** The three-week-old national dock strike, already threatened by an accelerating collapse in support, ended abruptly last night when Ron Todd, the general secretary of the Transport and General Workers' Union, ordered an immediate return to work.

The union's executive voted 18-12 to accept the replacement of the national dock labour scheme – abolished by the government last month – with local-level talks on future employment negotiations.

While some dockers resent what they condemn as a union climb-down, Todd told them that they had to "face reality". Accusing the employers of "gangster tactics", he said: "I was not going to allow my union to have its head put on the block."

## Pianist John Ogdon dies of pneumonia

*The brilliant pianist John Ogdon.*

**Aug 1.** John Ogdon, the piano virtuoso, has died of pneumonia aged 52. His brilliant early career began with a sensational Proms debut at 21. He won the Tchaikovsky prize jointly with Vladimir Ashkenazy at 25, but ten years later he collapsed with schizophrenia. Since 1981 he had been making a comeback. He and his wife, the pianist Brenda Lucas, lived in separate flats in the same house, but appeared together on the platform.

# Eleventh-hour reprieve for US hostage

*American hostage Joseph Cicippio pleads for his life on video.*

**Aug 3.** Less than an hour before the appointed time, pro-Iranian terrorists have lifted their threat to kill Joseph Cicippio, a US hostage held in Lebanon. His captors, the Revolutionary Justice Organization, said in a statement passed to a Beirut newspaper that the reprieve had come after diplomatic efforts.

The US president, George Bush, has been exerting pressure on Iran's new president, Ali Akbar Hashemi Rafsanjani, through the Swiss ambassador in Tehran, saying that he holds Iran responsible for the safety of all US hostages in Lebanon. He has also concentrated a massive array of naval power in the region, including two aircraft-carriers.

Cicippio, who worked at the American University in Beirut, was kidnapped in September 1986. His captors say they will exchange him for Sheikh Abdul Karim Obeid, the pro-Iranian Hizbollah cleric who was seized by the Israelis last week. Another American, William Higgins, is alleged to have been killed after the failure to release Obeid. Israel says it will free the sheikh only on the release of all Western hostages and Israeli soldiers held in Lebanon (→7).

# Greenham missiles go: women celebrate

*The beginning of the end of eight years' work: watching as the missiles go.*

**Aug 1.** Today was a day of celebration for the women who have maintained an anti-nuclear vigil outside the Greenham Common air base for the past eight years. As they have done so many times before in a different spirit, they lined the fence and watched 16 cruise missiles being loaded on to a US air force transport carrier which was to fly them to Arizona.

The missiles' departure is part of the first phase of the decommission-ing of Nato's intermediate nuclear forces as agreed in the treaty signed by Ronald Reagan and Mikhail Gorbachev in December 1987. The missiles removed today are said to be the first of 96 kept at the base, and it will be two years before the last one leaves. The women intend to stay until then. Though they were celebrating, they also pointed out that the weapons could be recycled for another use such as in the Lance battlefield nuclear system.

# Rebel cricketers confirm South Africa tour

*The Australians, as David Boon scores the run to win the test and the Ashes.*

**Aug 1.** Sixteen English cricketers, headed by former test captain Mike Gatting, today announced that they would tour South Africa next winter. The news coincided with England's comprehensive defeat in the Fourth Test at Old Trafford, which saw Australia regain the Ashes.

The South African tourists will all face a five-year ban from international cricket under the terms of an agreement hammered out in January to try to end the divisions over South Africa. For most of the rebel tourists it is effectively the end of their test careers. Many had faded from the test scene, but two – Neil Foster and John Emburey – were on duty at Old Trafford yesterday as England tumbled to another defeat by the Australians, who now lead 3-0.

Mike Gatting was the surprise name to head the rebel tourists. He had a controversial tenure as England captain, but was respected by

*Protesters outside Lord's tonight.*

his players and is a player of undoubted international class and bulldog spirit whom many saw as the man to lead England out of their present doldrums.

# Public billions poured into water sell-off

**Aug 2.** The cabinet has approved a complete write-off of the water authorities' £5 billion of debt ahead of their privatization. In addition, the Treasury will provide another £1 billion "green dowry" for environmental schemes. Government ministers believe that this guarantees the successful stock market flotation of the water companies this coming November. Labour leaders have protested that taxpayers' money is being tossed around to entice City investors and to keep water price rises within politically acceptable limits after privatization.

Michael Howard, the environment minister, said today that the new water companies will be allowed to increase their prices on average by five per cent above inflation in the first five years after privatization and by 3.7 per cent for the next five years. "Scandalous," said the Labour opposition (→25).

# August

## 1989

| Su | Mo | Tu | We | Th | Fr | Sa |
|----|----|----|----|----|----|----|
|    |    | 1  | 2  | 3  | 4  | 5  |
| 6  | 7  | 8  | 9  | 10 | 11 | 12 |
| 13 | 14 | 15 | 16 | 17 | 18 | 19 |
| 20 | 21 | 22 | 23 | 24 | 25 | 26 |
| 27 | 28 | 29 | 30 | 31 |    |    |

**6.** Bolivia: Jaime Paz Zamora, a former left-wing revolutionary, is sworn in as president.

**6.** UK: Eight people are hurt when an express train jumps the tracks outside West Ealing station after hitting a heavy object placed on the line.

**7.** UK: A four-mile-wide tide of algae appears off Cornwall.

**7.** Ireland: The warning of a bomb on the track closes the Dublin-Belfast rail line.

**8.** US: The San Francisco area is rocked by an earthquake measuring 5.2 on the Richter scale (→19/10).

**8.** US: The government rejects an Iranian offer to help free hostages in return for the unfreezing of $12 billion of Iranian assets in the US.

**8.** Geneva: The latest round of US-Soviet arms talks ends without the hoped-for accord on nuclear-test monitoring.

**8.** New Zealand: Geoffrey Palmer is chosen to succeed David Lange as premier.

**9.** USSR: In Estonia 20,000 workers strike in protest at discriminatory amendments to Estonian electoral laws (→18).

**9.** Belfast: Seamus Duffy, aged 15, dies from a plastic-bullet wound during riots.→

**10.** Mexico: A train plunges into a rain-swollen river, killing 100.

**10.** Japan: Toshiki Kaifu is sworn in as prime minister.

**10.** UK: Bristol joins Tilbury and Liverpool in turning away a ship loaded with PCBs (→24).

**11.** UK: HP food producers say that glass has been found in seven cans of baked beans withdrawn from the shops.

**11.** UK: About 250 people are evacuated when a fire at a Lancashire toiletries factory produces a toxic gas cloud.

**12.** UK: Oliver Tambo, the president of the ANC, is treated in London after suffering a stroke.

**DEATH**

**9.** Audrey Russell, BBC war correspondent in the Second World War (*29/6/06).

## Toxic PCBs turned away by British ports

**Aug 9.** The port of Liverpool has banned the import of polychlorinated biphenyls (PCBs), highly toxic industrial waste products which can be destroyed only by burning at very high temperatures. The decision will affect a deal agreed by the company ReChem to import and incinerate in South Wales 1,500 tons of contaminated electrical equipment from Canada over the next three months. Already the first shipload has left Montreal, but now it may have to turn back.

The ban – which resulted from a dockers' vote not to handle PCBs and calls from environmentalists – follows a refusal by the port of Tilbury to allow the entry of a separate consignment of PCBs, also from Canada but aboard a Russian ship, on the grounds that the ship's papers were not in order.

Liverpool's decision is the latest challenge to a fast-growing industry. Britain disposes of about 8,000 tons of PCBs every year, of which about 1,000 tons are imported, but pressure is growing for these chemicals to be disposed of in their country of origin. Environmentalists say the possibility of accidents makes transporting them dangerous and are opposed to incineration. The companies involved say they are improving the environment (→10).

## Central America to disband Contras

**Aug 8.** After eight years of guerrilla warfare, the Contras – the 12,000-strong group backed by the US – are to be demobilized. Five Central American presidents have agreed to begin the process within 30 days and to close the Contra bases in Honduras. The decision is seen as a snub for President Bush, who pleaded with the presidents to delay signing their agreement. President Daniel Ortega of Nicaragua was delighted. The Contras were formed during the Reagan years to counter left-wing "subversion" by his government (→28/10).

## Batman flies again but Joker steals the limelight in new film

*Michael Keaton plays Batman.*

**Aug 12.** The most hyped film of the year, *Batman* – which cost $35 million to make and took $200 million in US cinemas – opened to a mixed reception in Britain. The general consensus was that Batman himself, with a lady photographer in tow instead of Robin, was no match for the Joker, a satanic ghoul whose chalk-white face is set in a scarlet grin of permanent glee by surgery.

Played by Jack Nicholson, the Joker steals the scenes, terrorizing Gotham City with deadly cosmetics, an acid-squirting buttonhole and an electrocuting handshake. At his most outrageous, he defaces a gallery of Old Masters but spares Francis Bacon. "Cultural garbage" and "a Batmess" said some.

*Jack Nicholson with his satanic grin.*

## New Zealand PM resigns over colleague

**Aug 7.** New Zealand's larger-than-life prime minister, David Lange, resigned today, just four days after the return of a former finance minister to his Labour cabinet. Lange, who is 47, insisted he had resigned partly on medical advice and had considered stepping down for months. But he criticized the decision last week of a government caucus to restore Roger Douglas, a former finance minister on the right of the party, to the cabinet. The present finance minister, David Caygill, presented a budget last month which was well received, and Lange said today that there was "no room" for Douglas's policies (→8).

*Lange announces his resignation.*

## Minister stands up for British history

**Aug 10.** John MacGregor, the education secretary, told his advisers today that British history should be given more space in the national curriculum.

Mr MacGregor said that the interim report published by the working party on history gave too much space to European and world history at the expense of British. He also insisted that dates, events and people should be at the heart of history syllabuses. This emphasis on historical facts is a far cry from the more creative demands of the new GCSE exam.

# Tube and town hall strikes called off

**Aug 11.** The strike on the London Underground, which has bedevilled the capital's transport system throughout the summer, has been called off. All 3,500 tube drivers have accepted a pay boost of up to £42 a week, as recommended by a mediation panel. Drivers will receive an additional lump sum to wipe out pay losses from their 13 one-day strikes.

A parallel dispute in Britain's town halls has also been settled: 740,000 Nalgo members, local government's white-collar workforce, are to receive a pay rise of 8.6 per cent. The union welcomed the deal, but employers warned that the pay increase, which will add 8.8 per cent to council salary bills, will only fuel an inflationary wage spiral and promote job losses.

# Britain regains the Admiral's Cup

*Britain's winner: the "Jamarella".*

**Aug 10.** It had been plain sailing, with frequent calms, all the way from Plymouth to the Fastnet; but as Admiral's Cup crews rounded the gaunt rock off the Irish coast, the wind lashed to a sail-popping gale force. For land lubbers, and some sailors, there were fears of a repeat of the 1979 race in which 15 people were lost. No one was; in a nail-biting, warp-chewing finish, Britain took the cup over Denmark.

# Plastic-bullet victim buried in Belfast

*Mourners attend the coffin of Seamus Duffy at his funeral in Belfast.*

**Aug 11.** The 17th person to be killed by a plastic bullet in Northern Ireland was buried today in Belfast. More than 1,000 people followed the funeral cortege of 15-year-old Seamus Duffy through the streets of the city. Among the mourners was Gerry Adams, the Sinn Fein MP for the area. The route was festooned with black flags, hanging from lamp-posts and windows.

At the graveside the boy's uncle, Paul Cassidy, appealed for the Irish prime minister, Charles Haughey, to bring the issue of plastic bullets before the European Court of Human Rights. Troops and police – anxious to avoid conflict and aware of possible further trouble next week on the 20th anniversary of the arrival of British troops in Northern Ireland – kept their distance.

A senior police officer has been appointed to investigate the incident, which happened three days ago, during demonstrations to mark the 18th anniversary of the introduction of internment in the province.

The Royal Ulster Constabulary said that there was serious rioting at the time of Duffy's death, with several officers attacked and injured. But friends of Seamus said there was no trouble at the moment he was hit by a round allegedly fired from a police Land-Rover (→13).

# Hopes dashed for release of hostages

**Aug 7.** The faint hope that Western hostages in Lebanon might be close to freedom was dashed today when the kidnappers made it clear that they would not negotiate the release of three Israeli prisoners.

The pro-Iranian group Hizbollah had hinted at a deal under which the hostages could be released in exchange for Sheikh Abdul Karim Obeid and 450 Arab prisoners. Israel agreed to negotiate, but Hussein Mousawi of Islamic Amal said that there could be no question of freeing Israeli prisoners. The Israeli defence minister, Yitzhak Rabin, insisted: "Our first priority is the Israelis." (→8).

# Europe plans labels for green products

**Aug 7.** "Green" labels – standardized throughout the European Community – could soon replace the confusing, and sometimes misleading, "environment-friendly" product labelling at present in use. Virginia Bottomley, a junior environment minister, launched a discussion paper on the scheme today, saying: "The green consumer is on the warpath, which we believe is a force for good. We are concerned to see they have the information that they need."

# British athletes storm to victory in European Cup in Gateshead

**Aug 6.** Britain's male athletes swept to an unlikely victory in the European Cup final at Gateshead this weekend. They now qualify for the World Cup final in Spain next month. Despite its array of individual stars, Britain had never finished higher than third in previous competitions and victory was secured only in the final event of the two-day competition – the 4 x 400 metres relay.

Five individual successes on the track, two in field events and the two relays saw Britain finish seven points ahead of Russia and pushing East Germany out of next month's finals. Britain's women fared less well, finishing third and missing their place in the finals (→9/9).

*Linford Christie and the British male athletes' team: victorious at Gateshead.*

# August

## 1989

| Su | Mo | Tu | We | Th | Fr | Sa |
|----|----|----|----|----|----|----|
|    |    | 1  | 2  | 3  | 4  | 5  |
| 6  | 7  | 8  | 9  | 10 | 11 | 12 |
| 13 | 14 | 15 | 16 | 17 | 18 | 19 |
| 20 | 21 | 22 | 23 | 24 | 25 | 26 |
| 27 | 28 | 29 | 30 | 31 |    |    |

**13.** Australia: A balloon crash near Alice Springs kills 13.

**13.** E Berlin: Some arrests follow a 50-strong protest at the Brandenburg gate (→20).

**14.** UK: The South Yorkshire police authority rejects Peter Wright's offer to resign as chief constable (→16).

**14.** S Africa: P W Botha resigns as president, ending a long struggle within the ruling National Party (→14/9).

**14.** India: Up to 100,000 people have fled their homes in Assam, after a massacre of the Bodo tribe, in which 200 died.

**15.** N Ireland: Martin Galvin, a banned director of Noraid, the US-based IRA-fundraising organization, is arrested.

**16.** UK: A full criminal inquiry is ordered into the Hillsborough disaster.

**17.** Sri Lanka: Tamil militants kill 24 Indian soldiers.

**17.** UK: The number of people who have fallen behind on mortgage repayments is said to have risen dramatically.

**17.** UK: Kenneth Grob and Ian Posgate, former leading figures in the Lloyd's insurance market, are cleared of fraud.

**18.** Colombia: Luis Carlos Galan, a presidential candidate, is assassinated (→27).

**18.** Zambia: The ANC is expelled from Zambia.

**18.** USSR: Russian workers in Estonia end their ten-day strike over new electoral laws.

**18.** Hungary: Two million workers strike in protest at planned price increases.

**18.** UK: Victor Cracknell, a Surrey businessman, is freed after a five-day kidnap and the payment of a ransom.

**18.** UK: BA services are disrupted by a 24-hour strike over a stewardess's sacking.

**19.** S Africa: The multi-racial Mass Democratic Movement holds a demonstration on a whites-only beach (→16/11).

**DEATH**

**17.** Harry Corbett, British entertainer (*1918). →

# Uneasy calm holds in deserted Beirut

*Aoun: Lebanese Christian leader.*

**Aug 16.** An uneasy calm has settled over Beirut following the ceasefire agreed early this afternoon between the Lebanese army, led by the Christian general Michel Aoun, and the Syrians and their Moslem militia allies.

The ceasefire ended five months of warfare, which began when General Aoun declared his intention of driving the Syrians out of Lebanon. In the course of the fighting, Beirut came under constant shellfire and many of its inhabitants fled for the relative safety of makeshift homes

*The night sky is lit up by gunfire: a common sight in war-torn Beirut.*

in the countryside north and south of the city. Beirut's population of 1.5 million has fallen to about 150,000.

Much of the fighting has centred on the hill-town of Soukh el Gharb, south-east of Beirut. Long abandoned by its civilian population, the town has become a major Christian stronghold, which General Aoun defended against an all-out Syrian

tank assault. The repulse severely embarrassed the Syrians, who immediately called on support from the various Moslem militias, in return for relaxations on their movements around Beirut.

It was at this point that the United Nations Security Council responded to appeals for intervention by passing a resolution calling for a halt to the fighting (→20).

## Protesters die in Azerbaijani riots

**Aug 14.** The Soviet Union's worst ethnic conflict in recent memory claimed more lives today when Nagorny Karabakh again erupted into violence. In spite of thousands of troops patrolling the area, there have been more bloody clashes between Armenians and Azeris, which have added to the death toll of more than 100.

Unrest in the mountain region deep in the Transcaucasus, with a population of fewer than 200,000, has precipitated a delicate constitutional crisis for Mikhail Gorbachev. Although part of Azerbaijan, Nagorny Karabakh has a population largely of Armenians. Armenia seeks to run the enclave, but Azerbaijan refuses to let it go.

Meanwhile, tens of thousands of Azeris have been demonstrating in Azerbaijan over the issue, and are preventing food and oil supplies reaching Armenia (→29).

## Mutant giant trees surround Chernobyl

**Aug 15.** Trees are reported to be shooting up to giant heights and sprouting huge leaves in the forests around the Chernobyl nuclear power plant, where an explosion

three years ago killed 31 people and caused 115,000 to be evacuated. Pine needles ten times their normal size have been found. Scientists are marking out the area for study.

## West Country faces rationing of water

**Aug 18.** As the hot summer continues, emergency measures could soon be introduced in Devon and Cornwall, where reservoirs have virtually dried up. Standpipes are due to be installed, and water tankers have been arranged for the Cornish resort of Bude, where there has been almost no rainfall since April after a dry winter. The public have been asked to cut consumption by 50 per cent, but warnings have gone largely unheeded. Not even last week's torrential downpours, which caused flooding in border areas, have alleviated the situation.

**Aug 17: Harry Corbett, the entertainer and inventor of the much-loved Sooty glove puppet, dies.**

# Anniversary violence averted in Ulster

*A suspected petrol bomber is dragged away by police in Londonderry.*

**Aug 13.** The security forces in Northern Ireland claim to have averted a number of potentially dangerous incidents intended to coincide with the 20th anniversary of the arrival of British troops in the province. In Londonderry police prevented the detonation of a bomb, and although a second did explode the area had already been cleared. In Belfast a bomb was defused after being dis-covered close to the route of a republican march. Police sealed off some nationalist areas to prevent loyalists attacking the marchers. Throughout the province, seven suspects were detained. Hugh Annesley, the Royal Ulster Constabulary's chief constable, praised the good sense of the community and the diligence of the police and the army.

# West Midlands police squad disbanded

**Aug 14.** In a dramatic move, 50 detectives from the West Midlands CID have been transferred or suspended after repeated allegations that the force has been guilty of fabricating confessions. The purge covers 39 present and former officers in the serious crimes squad and the CID senior command.

This most wide-ranging attack on police corruption since Sir Robert Mark purged the Metropolitan Police in the early 1970s was instigated by Geoffrey Dear, the West Midlands chief constable, who said he was prepared to be "quite ruthless". Dear has ordered an inquiry into the practices of the serious crimes squad, but says that in the meantime the entire section has been disbanded.

The trigger for the purge came on Friday night, when it was discovered that the confessions of two unnamed prisoners were missing. Until then, Dear believed that the actions of some officers had been

*Dear: a black day for the police.*

"cavalier and sloppy" but not criminal. This was in spite of the fact that ten cases involving the squad have been dropped or thrown out by the courts in the past two years.

# Solidarity stands on the brink of power

**Aug 17.** Poland's free trade union, Solidarity, was one step from power today. In talks with President Jaruzelski, Lech Walesa, the Solidarity leader, set in motion the process that could lead to the appointment of the first non-communist prime minister in Eastern Europe since the early post-war years. Walesa also had talks with the leaders of two smaller parties likely to take part in a coalition government.

The moves follow the surprising resignation of General Czeslaw Kiszczak, who was prime minister for two weeks, and who played a major role in crushing Solidarity under martial law. Kiszczak was unable to persuade enough senior figures, communist or otherwise, to serve under him.

Walesa came to Warsaw from Gdansk and stormed parliament, asserting that he personally would take charge and assemble a cabinet under the familiar banner of Solidarity. The Communist Party says it is against a coalition (→24).

# Attempts to save Hipparcos satellite fail

*"Hipparcos", the satellite that looks unlikely to chart the stars as intended.*

**Aug 17.** European scientists have failed in their fourth attempt to dislodge the European Space Agency (ESA) satellite Hipparcos from the wrong orbit.

The £200 million satellite has been in the wrong orbit since soon after launch on Tuesday of last week. It failed to shift into a correct orbit when a motor malfunctioned and is now on a course where it may be damaged by radiation from solar particles. Hipparcos's mission was to chart the stars more accurately than ever before, over three years. Now it may work for only four months. ESA scientists at Darmstadt, West Germany, will try again next week to right the satellite, but hopes are fading.

# Massive Mersey oil leak threatens birds

**Aug 19.** Thousand of migrating birds are under threat from a 13-mile-long oil slick in the Mersey estuary following the leakage of 150 tons of crude oil from a Shell pipeline. Already 67 oil-fouled birds have been recovered and more are expected.

A spokesman for Shell said that a "mechanical fault" rather than vandalism was suspected as the cause. "This is the worst spillage we have experienced here and we are taking it very seriously," he said. A clean-up operation has already begun.

The spill is threatening an important feeding ground for migrating birds, and John Armitage of the Royal Society for the Protection of Birds is anxiously awaiting expected westerly gales. "So far we have been lucky," he said, "but all it needs is a change in the weather."

# August

## 1989

| Su | Mo | Tu | We | Th | Fr | Sa |
|----|----|----|----|----|----|----|
|    |    | 1  | 2  | 3  | 4  | 5  |
| 6  | 7  | 8  | 9  | 10 | 11 | 12 |
| 13 | 14 | 15 | 16 | 17 | 18 | 19 |
| 20 | 21 | 22 | 23 | 24 | 25 | 26 |
| 27 | 28 | 29 | 30 | 31 |    |    |

**20.** W Germany: About 900 East Germans enter the country via Hungary and Austria in the biggest exodus since the Berlin Wall was built (→24).

**20.** Lebanon: A French peace initiative is denounced by Moslem groups.

**21.** Colombia: More than 12,000 people are reported to have been arrested in a cocaine-trafficking crackdown (→24).

**21.** Prague: Police break up a protest by several thousand to mark 21st anniversary of the Soviet-led invasion (→17/11).

**22.** UK: An inquiry is ordered into claims that microwave ovens fail to kill listeria.

**23.** UK: The death toll in the Thames disaster is now believed to be 55.

**24.** Colombia: The drug barons declare "total war" on the government (→31).

**24.** W Germany: More than 100 East Germans who took refuge in Bonn's embassy in Budapest arrive in the West (→31).

**24.** Canada: Ignoring an injunction, a Soviet freighter carrying PCBs back from Liverpool offloads containers.

**24.** UK: The brewer Bass announces plans to buy the US Holiday Inns chain, becoming the world's largest hotelier.

**25.** UK: At the Edinburgh international TV festival, Rupert Murdoch makes a bitter attack on British TV.

**26.** UK: Police fail to stop thousands of young people attending an acid house party at a remote Surrey farm.

### DEATHS

**21.** George Adamson, Kenyan conservationist (*1906).→

**21.** Diana Vreeland, US fashion writer (*c.1903).→

**22.** Lord (Charles) Hill, British former Tory cabinet minister and chairman of both the BBC and ITA (*15/1/04).

**23.** R D Laing, British psychiatrist (*7/10/27).

**24.** Feliks Topolski, Polish-born artist (*1907).

# Neptune's moon astounds scientists

**Aug 25.** Seasoned space scientists gasped in amazement today as they watched the latest pictures from the planet Neptune, beamed to earth by the spacecraft *Voyager 2*. This time it is the planet's moon Triton which is causing so much excitement. A spokesman at the National Space Agency's laboratory at Pasadena in California, which is monitoring *Voyager 2*'s mission, said: "Triton is incredible, incredible. It's out of this world in every sense. It has things we have never seen on another satellite."

Triton has hitherto been thought remarkable for two reasons: first, it has an atmosphere – like only one other planetary moon in the solar system; secondly, it orbits Neptune in a different direction from the planet's other seven moons, six of them discovered by Voyager.

The moon's thin methane and nitrogen atmosphere has been confirmed, but Triton (which is smaller than the Earth's moon) is now known to have no clouds and *Voyager* has sent back extraordinarily clear pictures of its surface. This is not made up of great nitrogen oceans, as expected, but is largely covered with pink glaciers, probably of methane, with white ice around the equator. There are few signs of impact craters caused by collision with other cosmic matter,

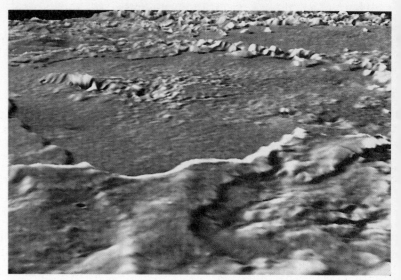

*A computer-generated perspective of one of the caldera-like cavities on Triton.*

suggesting that the surface is in a state of flux. *Voyager 2* has taken 12 years to get to Neptune, and what it has revealed in the last week is beyond all expectations.

Observers now know that Neptune itself is a busy, dynamic place, with great storms and 400 mph jet-streams, and with five rings rather than three. Its clouds throw shadows; the only other planet where this is known to occur is the Earth. *Voyager 2* has failed to live up to its promise in one respect. It passed Neptune behind schedule – by 1.4 seconds.

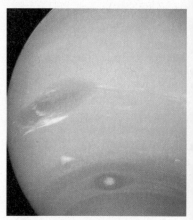

*Voyager 2's view of Neptune itself.*

**Aug 21. The colourful US fashion writer Diana Vreeland, a former editor of "Harper's Bazaar" and American "Vogue", died today.**

# Bandits shoot conservationist Adamson

**Aug 20.** George Adamson – the lion-loving conservationist who was married to Joy Adamson – was murdered today near his home in a remote camp in Kenya by armed bandits. Adamson, who was 83, and two of his workers were trying to protect a guest from the robbers when they were fatally gunned down.

Adamson and his wife became internationally famous with the book and film *Born Free*, the first of a trilogy Joy wrote about their work returning captive lions to the wild. Last year Adamson published his autobiography, *My Pride and Joy*. He and Joy were separated, but both continuing their work of protecting and encouraging Kenya's wildlife, when she was murdered by a member of her camp staff in 1980.

*Adamson with two of his charges.*

# Poland elects first non-communist head in Soviet bloc

**Aug 24.** Poland today became the first country in the Soviet bloc to appoint a non-communist prime minister. By a huge majority the parliament voted for Tadeusz Mazowiecki – a Catholic editor and adviser to Lech Walesa, the Solidarity leader – who was interned for a year by the communist authorities under martial law. After the vote the prime minister sat with his head bowed as he received a standing ovation. Fellow deputies embraced him, while others simply gazed and smiled in disbelief.

Lech Walesa, who had paved the way for Mazowiecki's election, said from his home in Gdansk: "Hopes are turning in the direction of a man who has devoted all his life to the struggle for Poland." Solidarity and the communists were at pains to emphasize today that they could work together (→12/9).

*Mazowiecki: Poland's new leader.*

# Thames boat sinks: revellers drown

*A diver comes up from inspecting the inside of the pleasure cruiser "Marchioness" after it was raised.*

**Aug 20.** Up to 150 fashionable young party-goers were dancing the night away and admiring the view from a Thames pleasure boat early this morning when a violent blow ran through the vessel, causing it to keel over and sink within seconds. Seventy-six people are known to have survived, and so far 26 bodies have been recovered. However, the exact figure of those on board is not known and the final death toll could be more than 60.

The pleasure boat, the 90-ton *Marchioness*, had been hit from behind by a 1,880-ton ocean-going dredger, the *Bowbelle*. "It was like a tank running over a Mini," said Ken Dwan, a director of Tidal Cruises, owners of the *Marchioness*. One of the survivors, Eric Wilson, a waiter, described what happened just before 2am: "The boat had just sailed under Blackfriars bridge when there was a massive jolt. The boat, facing downstream, swivelled to the left and tipped sharply on its side. People were screaming and shouting "Jump into the water! Jump into the water!". I jumped. I saw the ship that hit us sailing away, a great dark hulk, something out of a horror movie."

The party was to celebrate the 26th birthday of Antonio de Vasconcellos, a popular and extrovert figure with friends in photography, modelling and the City (→23).

*Relatives lay wreaths for the victims.*

# Trade deficit soars

**Aug 23.** City analysts were shocked today when the July figures were issued showing a deficit of £2.06 billion in Britain's trade with the rest of the world – nearly as bad as last October's record worst. Ministers said the figures were a freak caused by the investment boom and the dock strike. But Bryan Gould, the Labour trade spokesman, said that they prove the chancellor's strategy is in ruins.

# Nazi pact is marked by human chain

**Aug 23.** Russia's Baltic states today marked the 50th anniversary of the Soviet-Nazi pact which led to their incorporation into the Soviet empire by forming a 180-mile human chain for freedom. An estimated one million people held hands in Estonia, Latvia and Lithuania after staging rallies and demonstrations aimed at gaining independence.

All three Baltic republics have formed popular fronts which have effectively eclipsed the official local communist parties as the driving force in their affairs. They are also calling for much greater economic and political independence, and the human chain is a symbolic protest at the Molotov-Ribbentrop deal which led to their occupation by the Red Army in 1940. In Moscow a small demonstration to back the Baltic states' drive for freedom was broken up by police (→29).

# Money down drain?

**Aug 25.** The ten water authorities in England and Wales have said they are spending £21.8 million on a major advertising campaign. They deny that this is linked with the coming water privatization, before which the government plans to spend a further £20 million on advertisements. Labour's environment spokesman said there would be bitter public resentment, calling it "money down the plughole".

## August
### 1989

| Su | Mo | Tu | We | Th | Fr | Sa |
|----|----|----|----|----|----|----|
|    |    | 1  | 2  | 3  | 4  | 5  |
| 6  | 7  | 8  | 9  | 10 | 11 | 12 |
| 13 | 14 | 15 | 16 | 17 | 18 | 19 |
| 20 | 21 | 22 | 23 | 24 | 25 | 26 |
| 27 | 28 | 29 | 30 | 31 |    |    |

**27.** USSR: A 300,000-strong march takes place in Kishinev, the capital of Moldavia, in support of making Moldavian the official language.→

**27.** UK: Lancashire win the Refuge Assurance League cricket championship.→

**27.** Colombia: The justice minister, Monica de Greiff, is said to have resigned after learning of a plot to kill her.→

**28.** W Germany: A British serviceman foils an attempted bomb attack on British army living quarters in Hanover (→8/9).

**28.** UK: The British Medical Association launches a new advertising campaign against planned health reforms (→15/10).

**28.** UK: It is reported that 700 cases of food poisoning a month were being confirmed at the start of August.

**29.** UK: The Sixth Test in the Ashes series ends in a draw. Australia won the series 4-0.

**29.** Colombia: An intelligence report implicates British mercenaries in the training of assassins for cocaine gangs.→

**30.** Paris: A 19-nation peace conference on Cambodia breaks down; all signs point to a resumption of the civil war in Cambodia (→26/9).

**30.** Geneva: The US and USSR agree on key elements of a chemical weapons ban.

**30.** UK: Thomson Holidays, Britain's biggest tour operator, cuts half a million holidays from next year's programme and raises prices.

**30.** US: Leona Helmsley, New York's self-styled hotel queen, is found guilty of evading more than $1 million worth of taxes.

**31.** USSR: The Moldavian parliament passes a law making Moldavian the official language of the republic.

**31.** UK: The government announces new rules for Thames navigation.

**DEATH**

**29.** Sir Peter Scott, British naturalist and painter (*14/9/09).→

## East Germans head west via Hungary

**Aug 31.** Having demolished its own Iron Curtain with Austria, the new Hungary went a stage further today and approved the immediate exodus of 20,000 East Germans to the West. Budapest's move effectively holds out the prospect that any of East Germany's 16 million people may soon be free to settle in West Germany.

In the past few weeks thousands of East Germans have arrived in Hungary "on holiday" – in fact relying on Hungary's relaxation of frontier controls to give them the chance to reach the West (→4/9).

## Worcestershire win county cricket title

**Aug 31.** Worcestershire today retained cricket's premier domestic trophy when victory over their local rivals Gloucestershire secured them the county championship. They won by 131 runs and with a day to spare, leaving their closest challengers, Essex, to rue the 25 points deducted for what was officially classed as a "sub-standard" pitch. For the Worcestershire skipper, Phil Neale, today's victory more than compensates for finishing second to Lancashire in the Sunday league last weekend.

## Trouble flares at Notting Hill carnival

*Carnival colours before the trouble.*

**Aug 29.** Narrow streets surrounding Portobello Road were the scene of a violent confrontation last night between police and stone-throwing youths, ending what had until then been a trouble-free Notting Hill carnival. Innocent bystanders were among those injured.

The police decided to bring in mounted officers and riot squad reinforcements after having bottles hurled at them while they tried to arrest a man. However, one witness claimed that they engineered the initial provocation by blocking off roads with their vans, which prevented people from leaving.

In sharp contrast, the police and organizers had agreed a few hours earlier that this year's carnival had been the most peaceful ever.

# Cocaine warfare hots up

*Monica de Greiff: in fear of her life.*

*A victim of the Colombian drug war.*

**Aug 31.** Gun battles and bombings in Colombia today raised the temperature in an intensifying war between the government and the cocaine barons. The fighting centred on Medellin, the base of the leading cartel, where a rocket attack on a paint factory injured eight people.

Explosions echoed through the city for much of the day, and a country club used by government officials was bombed this evening. Five members of a paramilitary group connected to drug cartels were reportedly shot dead by troops. More than 500 people have been arrested for violating a night curfew in Medellin and the surrounding area.

The US government is sending military advisers and $65 million worth of military equipment to Colombia. It has denied reports that the Colombian justice minister, Monica de Greiff, intends to resign in the face of murder threats from drug traffickers. Earlier this week, US authorities broke up a money-laundering operation that was channelling $50 million a year in drug profits from New York to the Medellin cartel (→4/9).

## Kaunda meets de Klerk in Zambia

**Aug 28.** Talks between President F W de Klerk of South Africa and President Kenneth Kaunda of Zambia ended today with more of a whimper than a bang.

It was widely hoped that the two leaders, who met at Livingstone in Zambia, would discuss proposals by the African National Congress for negotiations on the future of South Africa. They did not. Instead, de Klerk's cordiality towards a veteran front-line black leader was probably aimed at voters in next week's South African white election. "South Africa is going to break out of the cycle of conflict" was typical of his optimistic – but suitably vague – comments (→7/9).

# Loyalists claim leaks by security forces

**Aug 30.** Loyalist paramilitaries in Northern Ireland have claimed that they regularly receive material on republican suspects from the security forces in the province.

The revelation follows allegations that the recent murder by the banned Ulster Freedom Fighters (UFF) of a Catholic, Loughlin Maginn, was based on information supplied by the security services. The Royal Ulster Constabulary (RUC) has admitted that documents handed to a BBC reporter by the UFF appear to be genuine. Ulster loyalist sources claim that information comes from all three security forces: the army, the RUC and the Ulster Defence Regiment. The leaks occur out of frustration that, although republican suspects are known, no action can be taken against them.

The Irish government has called for the alleged leaks to be put at the top of the agenda at the next meeting of the Anglo-Irish Council (→14/9).

# Princess Anne and Mark to separate

*Captain Phillips – his bags packed.*

**Aug 31.** Princess Anne and Captain Mark Phillips are to separate, the captain's father, Major Peter Phillips, said last night. The princess is currently visiting Puerto Rico, while her husband has just returned from Canada. Buckingham Palace promised an announcement today.

The royal marriage, which took place in November 1973, has long been seen as less than completely happy. Rumours of a rift intensified after personal letters written to the princess by the Queen's equerry, Cdr Timothy Laurence, were offered to a newspaper earlier this year.

The couple will not divorce but live separately on the Gatcombe Park estate, where Captain Phillips will maintain his duties as estate manager. No reference was made to their two children, 11-year-old Peter and eight-year-old Zara.

# Peter Scott, champion of nature, dies

**Aug 29.** Nature today lost one of its greatest champions with the death of Sir Peter Scott, at the age of 79. The son of the explorer Captain Robert Falcon Scott, who perished in the Antarctic in 1912, Sir Peter devoted his life to the preservation of the world's plants and animals and was associated with dozens of conservation bodies. In 1946 he founded what is now the Wildfowl and Wetland Trust and chaired the World Wildlife Fund from 1961 to 1982. He was the first person to be knighted (1973) for services to conservation and was also a distinguished wildlife artist. The botanist David Bellamy called him simply "the father of conservation".

*Scott at work on his snow geese.*

# Escalating violence in outlying Soviet republics offers big challenge to Moscow

*Moldavian protesters carry a portrait of Gorbachev as well as their flags.*

**Aug 29.** The Soviet president, Mikhail Gorbachev, today faces a major nationalist challenge around the rim of the Soviet Union, at a time when he needs to focus his energy on rescuing his economic reforms from a deepening crisis. In the Baltic republics of Lithuania, Latvia and Estonia there has been a surge of public support for outright independence. And in other parts of the Soviet Union ethnic tensions are mounting.

Georgians and Abkhazians, and Azerbaijanis and Armenians are at each other's throats in the southern Transcaucasus region. There are strikes and demonstrations taking place in Moldavia over the local language and culture. The Central Asian republics are in turmoil after riots which left at least 100 dead and thousands homeless in Uzbekistan. The Ukraine, the second largest Soviet republic after Russia itself, is beginning to stir. The gravity of the situation was underlined today with the official confirmation that Gorbachev was closely involved in the drafting of the ultimatum to Baltic nationalists to halt their campaign for outright secession from the Soviet Union. Gorbachev has signalled that he will not tolerate any further steps towards independence. He sees the ethnic and nationalist unrest as a threat both to the cohesion of the Soviet Union and to his entire *perestroika* reform programme and strategy. It is clear that what applies to the Baltic states applies elsewhere in the country as well.

During the Stalin era, lies, force and terror kept the lid screwed on the bubbling Soviet mixture. Under Gorbachev and *glasnost* the nationalities problem has exploded into the open. Today there is the impression that the crisis is moving inexorably to the point of no return and he must act toughly (→31).

# September
## 1989

| Su | Mo | Tu | We | Th | Fr | Sa |
|----|----|----|----|----|----|----|
|    |    |    |    |    | 1  | 2  |
| 3  | 4  | 5  | 6  | 7  | 8  | 9  |
| 10 | 11 | 12 | 13 | 14 | 15 | 16 |
| 17 | 18 | 19 | 20 | 21 | 22 | 23 |
| 24 | 25 | 26 | 27 | 28 | 29 | 30 |

**1.** S Africa: Bishop Desmond Tutu and 35 others are arrested during a peaceful march in Cape Town (→2).

**1.** US: Bush cuts relations with Panama after Francisco Rodriguez, a Noriega puppet, is sworn in as president.

**1.** UK: The ten England and Wales water authorities become public companies.

**2.** S Africa: Police use tear gas, water cannon, whips and clubs on protesters attempting a march on parliament. →

**3.** Dublin: Neil and Glenys Kinnock survive a car crash in which their chauffeur is killed.

**3.** UK: The 50th anniversary of the outbreak of the Second World War is marked in services of remembrance.

**4.** Colombia: Suspected drug traffickers bomb three banks and a police station in the drug capital of Medellin. →

**4.** Beirut: The Abu Nidal organization says it has executed 15 people as "spies".

**5.** UK: Over 700 are reported to have been killed in an explosion at a secret missile plant in Iraq last month (→7).

**6.** Stockholm: Football fans go wild at a World Cup match between England and Sweden.

**6.** Netherlands: The Christian Democrats win elections (→26/10).

**7.** UK: Graham Gooch is named as England cricket captain for a West Indies tour.

**7.** US: Eduardo Martinez Romera, an alleged accountant of the Medellin cocaine cartel, is extradited from Colombia.

**7.** Iraq: It is acknowledged that an explosion took place at an industrial plant last month; 19 are said to have died.

**8.** UK: GEC and Siemens win control of the electronics group Plessey for £2 billion.

**9.** UK: An opinion poll shows that David Owen is over twice as popular as Paddy Ashdown to lead the political centre.

**DEATH**

**4.** Georges Simenon, Belgian novelist (*13/2/03).→

# Bush commits billions to drugs crusade

*Holding up a bag of crack, Bush tells the nation to wage war on drugs.*

**Sept 6.** In his first address to the nation on prime-time television last night, President George Bush announced a plan costing $7.86 billion to halve drug use in the US by the year 2000.

In what he called a "heart-to-heart" talk, the president urged the American people to pull together to solve the problem. He said: "Drugs are sapping our strength as a nation ... Our most serious problem today is cocaine and, in particular, crack. Let there be no mistake, this stuff is poison."

The government hopes to reduce both supplies and consumption of drugs by ten per cent by 1992 and by 50 per cent by the end of the century. Its plan of campaign, drawn up by William Bennett, the director of drug policy, involves persuading the 50 states to impose harsher penalties, including the loss of driving licences for casual use.

The US will give $200 million – less than predicted – in economic and military aid to drug-exporting countries, including Colombia, Bolivia and Peru. Money will also be spent on more prisons and paying for more police to control what has become a $110 billion industry.

Making the Democrats' official response on television, Senator Joe Biden of Delaware said the president's language was "high on polemic but short on resources" (→7).

# Police criticized at Ward inquest in Kenya

**Sept 4.** An inquest into the death of Julie Ward, a 28-year-old British woman whose charred remains were found last year in a Kenyan game park, heard charges today of poor work by police investigating her death. The solicitor for John Ward, Julie's father, alleged at the hearing in Nairobi that the Suzuki vehicle, in which she was driving alone in the Masai Mara park, was not properly searched and might have been "planted" in the gully where it was found, six miles from her remains. John Ward says his daughter was murdered and has accused the Kenyan authorities – who claimed she was killed by wild animals – of a cover-up (→5/10).

*Julie Ward: a victim of murder?*

# East German police arrest would-be emigrants to West

**Sept 4.** East German security police today broke up a demonstration in Leipzig involving dozens of people seeking free emigration to the West. Several were arrested. The large group of human rights activists and would-be emigrants took part in a service at the Nikolai Church before the demonstration.

During the march through the provincial city's streets protesters chanted "We want out" and "We want a new government". Speakers urged the ruling Communist Party leadership of Erich Honecker to begin introducing both economic and democratic reforms. Thousands of East Germans are now reaching West Germany through Hungary and Austria (→11).

# British athletes win World Cup races

*Linford Christie: victorious again.*

**Sept 9.** Sebastian Coe failed to win what is expected to be his last major race in Europe when he was forced into second place by Abdi Bile, the Olympic champion, in the 1,500 metres race of the World Cup athletics finals in Barcelona today. The 33-year-old Coe found the younger man too strong in the final straight. But victories by Linford Christie and Tom McKean yesterday kept Britain in the running for their best-ever position in the contest (→10).

# De Klerk wins amid "massacre" row

**Sept 7.** South Africa's ruling National Party today celebrated its 11th consecutive election victory since 1948, amid allegations that police last night killed 23 people in townships near Cape Town.

Archbishop Desmond Tutu, the Anglican bishop of Cape Town, and Rev Allan Boesak, the president of the World Alliance of Reformed Churches, claimed at a joint press conference that the police "massacre" followed protests by black and "coloured" (mixed-race) youths against the exclusion of most South Africans from the whites-only poll. Among the dead were one woman aged 69 and a girl aged six, the churchmen said.

The police deny the allegations, saying four people died in gang violence and eight of gunshot wounds in uncertain circumstances. Little credence will be given to this denial by anti-apartheid leaders, who have often been at the sharp end of police clubs, water cannon and whips during several weeks of or-

*Tension between blacks and police has run high throughout the campaign.*

ganized protest against apartheid in the run-up to the white election.

President F W de Klerk won 93 of the 166 seats in parliament. He still has a comfortable majority, therefore, despite losing 13 seats to the anti-apartheid Democratic Party (33 seats) and 17 to the pro-apartheid Conservative Party (39 seats). After a campaign of much fence-sitting to avoid losing more votes to left and right, de Klerk will have to move quickly to prove he is serious about reform (→13).

# Teacher shortage: children sent home

**Sept 5.** Hundreds of children were sent home from school yesterday owing to lack of teachers. London was the worst hit; in one borough 16 per cent have resigned this year. Fifty primary school teachers have been recruited by the Inner London Education Authority from The Netherlands. The authority plans to extend its search and has also advertised in local Asian language newspapers. Increased paperwork, stress and low pay are all factors that have resulted in such poor morale among teachers that one in three want to leave the profession.

**James Spader and Andie MacDowell as the good guys who get the happy ending in Steven Soderbergh's "sex, lies and videotape", a modern fable now opening in London after winning the best film award at Cannes.**

# Charles's vision of Britain under fire

**Sept 8.** Prince Charles has stepped up the debate he is conducting on contemporary architecture by publishing *A Vision of Britain*, which illustrates ten "principles" of good architecture and his choice of good and bad recent buildings. His book has gone straight to the top of the bestseller list, backed by a re-showing of his television film.

The prince says that after 30 years of experiment we ended up with "Frankenstein monsters, alien and largely unloved, except by the professors who have been concocting them in their laboratories". He says there is "profound unease" about architecture which people till recently felt powerless to influence. "What on earth is wrong with desiring surroundings which are traditional, well-tried and beautiful?"

Architects are now hitting back, particularly the president of the RIBA, Maxwell Hutchinson, in a book *The Prince of Wales: Right or Wrong?* "His vision is one in which new buildings must dress in ridiculous, old-fashioned costumes."

# IRA admits murder of soldier's wife

**Sept 8.** The IRA has admitted responsibility for the death of a British soldier's wife in West Germany. They said the killing of 26-year-old Heidi Hazell was a mistake, but gave no apology.

Mrs Hazell was shot 14 times by a single burst of automatic fire as she sat in her car near her home in a Dortmund suburb yesterday. Her husband, Clive, aged 27, was away on exercise at the time.

The prime minister, Margaret Thatcher, immediately condemned the IRA as "evil and cowardly", and the Labour leader, Neil Kinnock, said the killing was the work of a psychopath.

The IRA cell which has killed six people so far is believed to be working from safe houses in northern Germany (→31/10).

# Simenon, creator of Maigret, dies

*Simenon's most popular character.*

**Sept 7.** The prolific Belgian crime writer Georges Simenon gave instructions that his death – aged 86 on September 4 – should remain a secret until after his cremation. Having churned out pulp fiction under 16 aliases, he created Inspector Maigret in 1929 and wrote 84 books about him. He boasted of his productivity, claiming to write a book in seven days. He also claimed to have slept with 10,000 women, an unlikely figure.

# September

## 1989

| Su | Mo | Tu | We | Th | Fr | Sa |
|----|----|----|----|----|----|----|
|    |    |    |    |    | 1  | 2  |
| 3  | 4  | 5  | 6  | 7  | 8  | 9  |
| 10 | 11 | 12 | 13 | 14 | 15 | 16 |
| 17 | 18 | 19 | 20 | 21 | 22 | 23 |
| 24 | 25 | 26 | 27 | 28 | 29 | 30 |

**10.** Danube: Up to 162 people drown in a collision between a pleasure cruiser and a tug.

**10.** Barcelona: British athletes finish third in the World Cup.

**11.** Colombia: Drug traffickers shoot dead Pablo Gonzalez, a former mayor of Medellin (→27).

**11.** USSR: Unprecedented strikes in Azerbaijan in the past week are reported to have cost 132 million roubles.→

**12.** E Germany: Hungary is criticized for allowing East German citizens to cross to the West without visas.

**12.** Namibia: A senior white official of Swapo, Anton Lubowski, is assassinated (→14).

**12.** UK: Simon Hayward, a former Life Guards captain, returns to Britain after two and half years in a Swedish jail for drug smuggling.

**13.** USSR: Delegates from the Russian Federation, the largest republic, set up the United Front of Russian Workers.

**13.** UK: Nineteen thousand ambulance staff start an overtime ban over pay (→23/10).

**14.** Namibia: After nearly 30 years in exile, Sam Nujoma, the president of Swapo, returns home to a rapturous welcome (→14/11).

**14.** S Africa: F W de Klerk is confirmed as president (→20).

**14.** UK: Police Inspector Raymond Codling is shot dead at an M62 service station by a long-time criminal.

**14.** UK: An altered version of the Channel Tunnel rail link is announced.

**15.** US: Exxon halts its clean-up of the Alaskan oil spill.

**16.** Hungary: The Movement for a Democratic Hungary holds its inaugural meeting (→18).

### DEATHS

**15.** Robert Penn Warren, US novelist (*24/4/05).

**16.** Lord (Anthony) Trafford, recently appointed British health minister (*20/7/32).

# Marchers take to streets of Cape Town

*A Cape Town street filled by the biggest anti-apartheid march for 30 years.*

**Sept 13.** Twenty thousand people took to the streets of Cape Town today in South Africa's biggest anti-apartheid march for 30 years.

President F W de Klerk, the acting president, decided to lift the ban on the march, imposed under his government's own state of emergency laws, as long as it remained peaceful and lawful. The march was prompted by the alleged police massacre of 23 people on the day of the whites-only election day last week. The protesters were mainly blacks, but there was a great cross-section of South African society, from trendy young whites to Moslem clerics. The festive air of the march – during which a flag of the banned African National Congress was unfurled for the first time in memory in this city – climaxed outside the town hall, where church and other anti-apartheid leaders made defiant speeches to great cheers from the crowd (→15/10).

## Female bank staff win fight over pay

**Sept 11.** Several thousand female secretaries and typists at Lloyds Bank are set to receive annual pay rises of between £500 and £2,000 following a tribunal decision that they do work of equal value to that of male senior messengers.

After a month-long hearing, the London North tribunal ruled today that the bank's bargaining procedures were "tainted by direct sex discrimination" and that pay inequality sprang from the traditional assumption that "the messenger was a family man and needed to be paid a family wage".

The Equal Opportunities Commission, which backed seven Lloyds staff in bringing the case, said it was delighted with the outcome, claiming that it would have wide implications throughout the banking and finance sector, a large employer of women (→16/10).

# Police admit key documents on IRA have been stolen

**Sept 14.** The deputy chief constable of Cambridgeshire, John Stevens, has been appointed to investigate the disappearance of an intelligence document from a Belfast police station.

He was called in by Royal Ulster Constabulary's chief constable, Hugh Annesley, after the RUC admitted the document had been forcibly removed from a locked cabinet, thought to be inside the RUC station at Dunmurry in south Belfast.

The admission comes after another document went missing from the Ulster Defence Regiment's base at Ballykinler in County Down. Senior officers in the security forces are concerned that the documents have probably been passed to loyalist paramilitary groups for marking potential targets.

It is the first time a police officer from the mainland has been called in to investigate the RUC since John Stalker was brought in to inquire into allegations of a "shoot-to-kill" policy within certain parts of the RUC (→8/10).

# Row follows Thatcher's ban on sex survey

**Sept 10.** The Labour Party and medical researchers have jointly attacked Margaret Thatcher's vetoing of plans to mount the most comprehensive survey of British sexual habits ever. Involving 20,000 people and costing £750,000, it was intended to improve the currently sketchy data available to predict the long-term spread of Aids. The prime minister claimed, however, that it would be a waste of public money and an unjustified invasion of privacy.

**"Installation of Mao Paintings on Mao wallpaper" – one of the works exhibited in "Andy Warhol: a Retrospective" at the Hayward Gallery. This is one of four shows of the eccentric self-publicist's works now in London.**

## Boat people moved from cholera island

**Sept 10.** Hong Kong authorities moved today to combat an outbreak of cholera threatening thousands of Vietnamese boat people held on the island of Tai Ah Chau. About 4,400 detainees were moved in a fleet of ferries to a detention centre on Hei Ling Chau island.

Conditions on Tai Ah Chau have been condemned by local voluntary agencies. The island is without running water or electricity and boat people are forced to use trenches as lavatories. Rations are said to be inadequate – weakening the people and contributing to the outbreak of cholera and numerous cases of malaria, diarrhoea, meningitis and chest infections.

The government have denied reports that disease is "out of control". Mike Hanson, the refugee coordinator, said: "Once we get these people to Hei Ling Chau, they will have much better medical facilities." He admitted that the boat people were on "dry rations" – which might not be suitable for long periods (→25/10).

# Hungary opens refugee floodgates

**Sept 11.** Europe's biggest migration since the end of the Second World War continued apace today when the Hungarians opened their border for East Germans to flee to the West. About 60,000 East Germans are currently in Hungary ostensibly on holiday and many are thought to be poised to make their way to West Germany.

Hungary's decision to open its border for anyone carrying an East German passport followed weeks of negotiations with Bonn and East Berlin, but in the end it was taken unilaterally. When the news was broken to East Germans staying in refugee camps it was greeted with cheers and clapping, followed by feverish packing.

In language reminiscent of the Cold War, the East German news media smeared Budapest with the taint of Judas for accepting "pieces of silver" from Bonn in return for allowing the refugees to leave. At the same time West Germany was bitterly accused of conducting a military-style campaign to lure the refugees to the West (→12).

*A three-year-old East German refugee looks west from her camp in Budapest.*

## Non-communists take over in Poland

*The Polish parliament: the cabinet is first non-communist one for 40 years.*

**Sept 12.** Poland's parliament has voted for a new cabinet, the first not dominated by communists in 40 years. The team put together by the prime minister, Tadeusz Mazowiecki, comprises eleven Solidarity ministers, four communists, four Peasant Party and three Democratic Party ministers. Mazowiecki called on deputies to back a "sovereign, democratic and law-abiding Poland", and he outlined a programme of change. His speech was interrupted when he nearly fainted from exhaustion, having had almost no sleep in recent days.

## SLD sets out to defeat Thatcherism

**Sept 15.** Paddy Ashdown, the leader of the Social and Liberal Democrats, today clearly identified the SLD as left-of-centre, dedicated primarily to end Thatcherism.

He told his party's annual conference in Brighton: "I do not believe that our place is at the comfortable mid-point between the extremes of left and right."

Mr Ashdown's long-term aim – ridiculed by politicians in other parties and seen as unrealistic by many in his own – is still for the Democrats to replace Labour as the main opponent of Toryism.

But with the Democrats at present reduced to around seven per cent support in the opinion polls, he admitted that his immediate target must be a more modest one of having decisive influence in a future hung parliament.

The collapse in public support for the Democrats has been accelerated by the upsurge of the Greens in recent months.

**Sept 16. In defiance of Moscow, thousands of protesters gather in Baku, the capital of Azerbaijan, to call for economic and political "sovereignty" for the Soviet republic and for the resignation of Abdul Rakhman Vezirov, the hated Communist Party chief.**

# September

## 1989

| Su | Mo | Tu | We | Th | Fr | Sa |
|----|----|----|----|----|----|----|
|    |    |    |    |    | 1  | 2  |
| 3  | 4  | 5  | 6  | 7  | 8  | 9  |
| 10 | 11 | 12 | 13 | 14 | 15 | 16 |
| 17 | 18 | 19 | 20 | 21 | 22 | 23 |
| 24 | 25 | 26 | 27 | 28 | 29 | 30 |

**17.** North Sea: Two tankers collide near the Humber estuary, leaking hundreds of tons of crude oil.

**17.** UK: A new newspaper, the *Sunday Correspondent*, makes its debut.

**18.** India: The government agrees to suspend military operations against the Tamil Tigers and remove troops from Sri Lanka by the year end.

**18.** UK: The Serious Fraud Office prepares to launch a formal investigation into Ferranti International Signal.

**18.** Sahara: A French DC-10 crashes with 170 people on board – the suspected victim of a bomb attack (→24).

**19.** US: San Diego is ruled the winner of the 1988 America's Cup, reversing a decision that gave the prize to New Zealand.

**19.** Japan: At the start of a four-day visit, Margaret Thatcher tells the Japanese to cherish free markets.

**20.** USSR: Viktor Chebrikov and Vladimir Shcherbitsky are among five of Mikhail Gorbachev's opponents ousted from the politburo.

**20.** US: The Senate approves a $1.3 billion aid package for Poland and Hungary.

**20.** S Africa: F W de Klerk is sworn in as president.

**20.** Brussels: The European Community announces that it will prosecute Britain over polluted drinking water.

**21.** UK: The government admits that English schools were short of 3,600 teachers at the start of the current term.

**22.** Lebanon: The Christian leader, Michel Aoun, abandons his "war of liberation" against Syria (→23).

**23.** USSR: Margaret Thatcher urges the Soviet people not to lose heart over *perestroika*.

**23.** Lebanon: A nationwide ceasefire, brokered by the Arab League, comes into force (→24).

**DEATH**

**22.** Irving Berlin, US songwriter (*11/5/1888).→

# Ten Royal Marine bandsmen die in IRA bomb blast at music school in Deal

*The Royal Marines' School of Music, where the search for bodies goes on.*

**Sept 22.** Early morning practice at the Royal Marines' School of Music was almost over. It was 8.26am. "I heard music playing and then it went bang and there was glass everywhere," said one witness in the aftermath of the IRA bomb that ripped through the barracks in Deal, Kent, killing ten bandsmen and injuring 22. Of the 12 who are still in hospital, eight are said to be in a serious condition.

Marines, hearing the screams of their injured and dying colleagues, clawed desperately into the rubble searching for survivors before the rescue services arrived. Evidence is mounting over the extent that the barracks was a "soft target" for the IRA. Security was provided by a private firm and has been described as "pathetic". One local man said that "people come and go as they want".

Tom King, the defence secretary, promised a full review of the security arrangements. He gave a message to the "godfathers of Northern Ireland" that the fight against terrorism would go on.

As messages of sympathy pour in, an unrepentant IRA statement claims it still wants peace and the British government to leave "our country". Police believe that more bodies may yet be found (→25).

# Greens fear right or left takeover

**Sept 22.** Astonished by their success in winning 15 per cent of Britain's Euro-election votes, the Greens talked at their annual conference in Wolverhampton today about hiring professional staff to run their growing party.

However, they rejected the concept of having a single party leader and were also suspicious of moves to make their haphazard organization look more conventional. "We are different. That's our attraction," they said. They now have 15,000 members.

Sara Parkin, the Greens' most prominent spokesperson, warned of extremist infiltration by "parasites" from left and right.

*Sara Parkin: leading Green figure.*

# Catholic nuns living in Auschwitz look set to move to new home

**Sept 19.** Cardinal Jozef Glemp, the primate of Poland, who is in Britain to consecrate a Catholic church, revealed that the Carmelite nuns in Auschwitz are likely to move. The 14 nuns, who set up a convent just inside the perimeter of the former concentration camp in 1985, have caused an international row.

Some Jews said the convent defiled the uniquely Jewish experience of the Holocaust. Some Catholics fiercely defended the right of the nuns to commemorate the million non-Jewish victims.

Now, Zygmunt Nissenbaum, a Jewish philanthropist, is talking to the Vatican about the joint funding of a new convent just outside the horror-camp.

*Carmelite nuns tend their garden in Auschwitz: they may now be on the move.*

# Hurricane Hugo hits American coast

**Sept 21.** The weather satellites saw it first, a swirling mass of disturbed air and sea in the Atlantic, moving ominously at a steady 25mph, gaining strength and threatening the Caribbean. The weathermen called it Hugo and began to issue urgent warnings of the most dangerous hurricane in a decade.

Puerto Rico and the Virgin Islands were the first to feel the destructive force of Hugo's 140mph winds that left at least 25 dead, hundreds injured and 100,000 homeless in a matter of hours. Entire homes were swept down flooded rivers, and in St Juan, the capital, sheets of corrugated iron flew down the main street crashing into shop windows.

Hugo moved relentlessly on with the Dominican Republic directly in its path. Newscasters pleaded with people to race to high ground.

The Royal Navy warship *Alacrity* landed basic medical supplies on Montserrat where 12,000 people were left homeless. The Red Cross is flying relief supplies into Puerto Rico where a state of emergency has been declared.

Widespread looting was reported from the Virgin Islands with 1,000 US military police flown in to restore order.

Hugo hit the American mainland last night, lashing the coasts of South Carolina and Georgia. With shops boarded up, schools closed and 100,000 people warned and evacuated, the nation was prepared for Hugo's dying wrath.

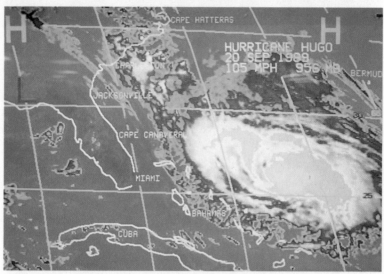
*View from a satellite of Hugo, the most powerful hurricane this decade.*

*Luxury yachts piled up like discarded toys in the wake of the giant hurricane.*

## Thousands of Scots fail to pay poll tax

**Sept 20.** Almost 300,000 people in Strathclyde, Scotland's largest region, have failed to pay the poll tax, according to figures out today. Many live in Glasgow, where one in three adults has defaulted on the tax, introduced in Scotland in April. The Scottish Nationalists and other opponents of payment claim that the high figures reflect the success of their campaign. However, Donald Dewar, Labour's Scottish spokesman, scorned the idea that Strathclyde's defaulters were "a determined army marching in support of a non-payment campaign". He said: "Those involved are victims of circumstance, oppressed by poverty."

## Songwriter Irving Berlin dies at 101

**Sept 22.** Irving Berlin, who died at the age of 101 today, outsold his great song-writing competitors, Gershwin, Kern and Cole Porter, with an output of 900 songs, none of which he could write down. His real name was Israel Baline and his family emigrated from Siberia when he was four. His pseudonym became a household word in 1911 with *Alexander's Ragtime Band*. Hits poured out of him till he was 75, including *Easter Parade*, *Top Hat*, *White Christmas* and *God Bless America*.

## Hungary endorses democratic rule

**Sept 18.** Hungary moved smoothly to free elections today when the ruling Communist Party and the main opposition groups agreed on a legislative package including a modified constitution and a new electoral law. Proposals for the transition to Western-style democracy will now be presented to parliament.

The agreement comes after three months of secret haggling between the communists and a coalition of nine groups. It could lead to free elections before the end of the year, which the communists are unlikely to win (→ 10/10).

# Boeing 737 crashes on takeoff at La Guardia airport: two die

**Sept 21.** A USAir Boeing 737 with 55 passengers on board skidded off the end of the runway late last night when the pilot tried an "accelerate stop" to prevent take-off from La Guardia, New York's oldest airport. The airliner screeched into the East River with its nose-cone propped up by a pier.

Two elderly passengers, both in the buckled centre cabin, died and 45 others were seriously injured. A number scrambled on to the wings for safety. The pier prevented the 737 from sinking and this undoubtedly saved many lives. Experts believe that the crash may have been caused by lax safety standards.

*The wrecked Boeing 737 lies in the East River, its nose resting on the pier.*

# September

## 1989

| Su | Mo | Tu | We | Th | Fr | Sa |
|----|----|----|----|----|----|----|
|    |    |    |    |    | 1  | 2  |
| 3  | 4  | 5  | 6  | 7  | 8  | 9  |
| 10 | 11 | 12 | 13 | 14 | 15 | 16 |
| 17 | 18 | 19 | 20 | 21 | 22 | 23 |
| 24 | 25 | 26 | 27 | 28 | 29 | 30 |

**24.** Beirut: The "Clandestine Chadian Resistance" says it carried out the French DC-10 bombing over the Sahara.

**24.** Beirut: People pour back into the city as the ceasefire organized by the Arab League takes hold.

**24.** Portugal: The British driver Nigel Mansell is fined £30,000 for failing to stop after being disqualified from the Portuguese Grand Prix.

**25.** UK: A review of security at military establishments is announced.

**25.** North Sea: Two people die in a fire aboard the Danish ferry *Tor Scandinivia*.

**26.** UK: A £2 billion trade deficit for August – the third worst ever – is recorded.

**26.** Greece: Paul Bakoyannis, a leading conservative MP, is assassinated by the "17th November" terrorist group.

**27.** US: Britain says it will send a frigate and a small number of soldiers to help the Colombian government in its war against the drug barons.

**27.** Brussels: The European Community publishes new proposals for a Social Charter.

**28.** Yugoslavia: Anti-Slovene marchers in Serbia protest at a new constitution for Slovenia, which guarantees its right to secede from Yugoslavia.

**28.** UK: University vice-chancellors say they are considering charging students full cost for their courses.

**29.** UK: Problems over the future structure of the industry force a six-month delay in electricity privatization (→9/11).

**29.** UK: Ferranti International says it will cancel dividends and take a £185 million write-off against its accounts after the discovery of fraud.

**30.** USSR: In Minsk, the capital of Byelorussia, 15,000 march to demand action to alleviate the consequences of the Chernobyl accident.

**DEATH**

**28.** Ferdinand Marcos, former leader of the Philippines (*11/9/17).→

## Storms of church and state beset Runcie

**Sept 30.** Pope John Paul II and Dr Robert Runcie, the archbishop of Canterbury, attended vespers together at Rome's church of San Gregorio today. It was on this site that Pope Gregory sent out St Augustine to become the first archbishop of Canterbury in 597. But the historic visit of the present archbishop, in the hope of boosting Christian unity, is running into problems. Runcie's offer to recognize the "universal primacy" of the pope has angered many Protestants. Runcie insists he means "spiritual" not political primacy, but this does not satisfy those for whom Rome is also a spiritual enemy.

Even so, Dr Runcie is not going far enough to satisfy the pope, who wants "total fidelity to the faith in Christ" as defined by the apostles. The consecration of the first woman bishop in the US Anglican church has aggravated the differences between them.

*Dr Runcie and Pope John Paul II.*

Dr Runcie is also at the centre of a political row in Britain over an interview he gave to the *Director* magazine, in which he attacks the "Pharisees" of British society who disparage the unsuccessful, the poor and the unemployed.

## Police raid Broadwater Farm for drugs

**Sept 29.** Police marked the fourth anniversary of the riots at Broadwater Farm estate in north London by mounting a large-scale drugs raid involving 400 officers; many wore riot gear while others carried sledgehammers axes and heavy-duty cutting equipment. Five private homes were entered as well as a grocer's, a youth association and a launderette. They found 50 small bags of cannabis, one and a half pounds of cannabis and arrested 30 people. The police issued a long statement justifying their action in such a sensitive area, saying it was necessary to remove the "atmosphere of menace" caused by open cannabis dealing which made the estate impossible to police.

## Europe ties with US to retain Ryder cup

**Sept 24.** Europe retained the Ryder Cup today in a nail-biting contest at the Belfry course near Birmingham. Europe and America finished level, with 14 points each, which means that Europe, as the holders, retain the trophy for another two years. "We did it by the skin of our teeth," said captain Tony Jacklin.

After Paul Azinger unexpectedly beat Spain's Seve Ballesteros it appeared that the Americans might win. Then a series of wild drives into the water at the final hole gave the Europeans their chance – clinched finally by Jose-Maria Canizares of Spain.

*Tony Jacklin with the cherished cup.*

## Hizbollah vows to be revenged against Saudis and Kuwaitis

**Sept 26.** Beneath huge portraits of the late Ayatollah Khomeini in a decaying hotel in west Beirut, four men, all heavily masked, vowed revenge against Saudi Arabia and Kuwait today after the beheading of 16 Shia Moslems. Their public oaths – made at a well-staged press conference with glossy brochures distributed to correspondents – described the public executions as a "terrorist act and an organized crime".

The 16 men were executed for causing bomb explosions in Mecca last July. In videotaped confessions, they said they had been given explosives, timing devices and training in sabotage by the Iranian embassy in Kuwait.

*Under the eyes of the world's press – four masked men take a vow of revenge.*

# Bush offers to ban chemical weapons

**Sept 25.** President George Bush has put forward proposals for the immediate elimination of chemical weapons "from the face of the earth". In his first speech to the United Nations general assembly in New York, Bush said that, if the Soviet Union would sign a treaty banning chemical weapons, the US would destroy 98 per cent of its stockpile within eight years.

Critics point out that Congress has required the Pentagon to destroy old stocks of chemical weapons already. Mr Bush said: "Let's begin today to rid the earth of this scourge."

# Columbia Pictures bought by Sony

**Sept 28.** The Japanese electronics giant Sony has bought Columbia Pictures for $3.4 billion. Sony's interest lies in the film library – one of the largest in the world, with 2,700 titles including such classics as *The Bridge on the River Kwai* – which will ultimately be available on their 8mm video Walkman.

Reactions in America have veered between alarm at the selling of "our patrimony" and a relief that "America's world cultural hegemony is safe" (→31/10).

*The Vietnamese say farewell to Cambodia after ten years of occupation.*

# Last Vietnamese pull out of Cambodia

**Sept 26.** Waving red and yellow national flags with patriotic music blaring from tinny loudspeakers, the last of the Vietnamese army left Cambodia today. There seemed few regrets as the great grins on the faces of soldiers showed. More than 25,000 of their comrades have been killed in Cambodia since 1978, when Vietnam invaded and drove the Khmer Rouge out of the country. Thousands more have been mutilated by the kind of weapons used originally by the Vietcong against the US army. Although United Na-

tions observers appear satisfied that this is a genuine withdrawal, China is claiming that the pull-out is little more than a sham, with thousands of Vietnamese remaining in civilian clothing.

China is backing Prince Norodom Sihanouk against the existing Cambodian government – but the most powerful military force in Cambodia is the Khmer Rouge, whose leaders and policies have not changed. Thousands of fearful civilians are leaving in the wake of the Vietnamese army.

# Social Democrats admit reduced role

**Sept 27.** David Owen, the leader of the Social Democratic Party "rump" which rejected a merger with the Social and Liberal Democrats, admitted today that the SDP is no longer a national force.

He told the SDP conference in Scarborough: "It is not parties but values and ideas which last for ever." Dr Owen's dream is still about a small parliamentary group holding the balance of power some day, and then using new leverage to get Labour to sponsor proportional representation.

# Greek PM on bank swindle charges

**Sept 28.** Andreas Papandreou, the former Greek prime minister, has been committed for trial on charges relating to bank fraud. The multi-million-pound swindle at the Bank of Crete contributed to his defeat in the June elections. Now, accused of accepting bribes from the disgraced banker George Koskotas, Papandreou, and four similarly charged ex-ministers of his socialist (Pasok) government, may face long prison sentences.

# East German refugees pack West German embassy in Prague

**Sept 28. A monument, 24 metres high, of the exiled Philippine leader Ferdinand Marcos, who died today in Honolulu, aged 72. He was finally ousted from power by Corazon Aquino in 1986.**

**Sept 28.** West Germany's embassy in Prague has become the scene of the latest refugee crisis involving thousands of East Germans. More than 2,000 people have got into the building hoping to be given permission to go on to West Germany. Despite difficult conditions with insufficient sleeping places, clusters of East Germans gather around the embassy railings asking journalists and West German tourists to pass on messages home urging relatives and friends to join them in Prague immediately.

Czechoslovakia has been refusing to become directly involved in negotiations and is insisting that the problem is political and one that can only be settled by the two Germanies. East Germany is its closest ally in the Warsaw Pact and West Germany its most important western trading partner (→7/10).

*More East Germans negotiate the West German embassy fence in Prague.*

# October

## 1989

| Su | Mo | Tu | We | Th | Fr | Sa |
|----|----|----|----|----|----|----|
| 1 | 2 | 3 | 4 | 5 | 6 | 7 |
| 8 | 9 | 10 | 11 | 12 | 13 | 14 |
| 15 | 16 | 17 | 18 | 19 | 20 | 21 |
| 22 | 23 | 24 | 25 | 26 | 27 | 28 |
| 29 | 30 | 31 | | | | |

**1. W Germany:** About 7,000 East Germans arrive on special trains from various East European countries (→2).

**1. China:** Protected by stiff security, Chinese leaders celebrate the 40th anniversary of communist rule.

**1. Pakistan:** Pakistan rejoins the Commonwealth after 17 years' absence.

**2. Prague:** About 3,000 more East Germans pour into the West German embassy (→3).

**2. UK:** Hammersmith and Fulham Council admits that its £6 billion worth of money-market deals were illegal.

**3. E Germany:** The border is closed as 6,000 more East Germans are allowed to leave for the West from Prague (→4).

**3. Panama:** A coup attempt by junior officers is foiled by troops loyal to Noriega.→

**4. Prague:** Chartered trains carrying more East German emigrants leave for W Germany.→

**4. UK:** The Bank of England spends up to $1 billion supporting the pound as West German interest rates look likely to rise.→

**4. UK:** Chris Patten, the environment secretary, turns down a plan for a new town at Foxley Wood, Hampshire.

**5. Kenya:** Simon Makalla, the chief warden of the Masai Mara game reserve, is named as the most likely killer of Julie Ward (→27).

**5. US:** Jim Bakker, the disgraced TV evangelist, is found guilty of fleecing his followers of $158 million.

**6. UK:** A group of nuns barricade themselves into hen-houses to prevent the slaughter of chickens said to be infected with the salmonella virus (→13).

**7. USSR:** At least 20,000 people form a human chain across Moscow in an anti-corruption protest.

### DEATHS

**4.** Graham Chapman, British comedian (*8/1/41).→

**6.** Bette Davis, US film actress (*5/4/08).→

# Fury as Lawson ups rate

**Oct 6.** A one-point rise to 15 per cent in base lending rates – the highest for eight years – was signalled by the Bank of England today. There was immediate turmoil in political and financial circles.

Nigel Lawson, the chancellor of the exchequer, had tried desperately and expensively to avoid the increase. It was finally forced on him by the Bundesbank lifting its rates to choke off West German inflation. Without emergency action there would have been a disastrous run on sterling.

Lawson admitted tonight that the situation is "awkward and embarrassing" so close to next week's Tory Party conference and in the middle of this week's Labour conference. In the past few days he has authorized spending of about two billion dollars from the official reserves in what has proved to be a vain effort to defend sterling in the markets. Angry Tory MPs openly

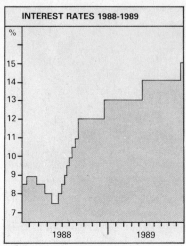

*Rates have doubled since May 1988.*

criticized the chancellor for losing votes to save the pound. They are alarmed over the hostility of home buyers to even higher mortgage payments. Margaret Thatcher is said to be furious. There is obvious tension within the cabinet (→13).

## Failed-coup officer shot dead in Panama

**Oct 6.** The Panamanian leader, General Noriega, is believed to have personally shot dead a ringleader of yesterday's failed *coup,* it was reported in Washington today. The fate of 37 alleged conspirators arrested – including three senior officers – remains unknown. As Noriega's police ring the opposition headquarters – locking up opposition leader, Guillermo Endara, for two hours, evidence is mounting that several units of the Panamanian army were involved in the *coup.* Although Noriega was held prisoner for several hours, his captors refused to hand him over to the United States for trial.

## Death of Graham Chapman mars Monty Python 20-year party

**Oct 4.** *Monty Python's Flying Circus,* BBC TV's smash-hit comedy show of the early seventies, is 20 years old this year, but the celebrations will lack a vital member of the original team.

Graham Chapman died of cancer today. He was 48. Chapman, whose studiously conventional image belied both his successful fight against alcoholism and his determination as a homosexual to advance the cause of gay rights, was the only Python not to capitalize financially on the show's worldwide success.

Fellow-Pythons Michael Palin and John Cleese, his former writing partner, were at his bedside. "He was the most talented actor of us all," said Cleese.

# Nobel peace prize goes to Dalai Lama

**Oct 5.** The award of the Nobel peace prize to the exiled Dalai Lama, the spiritual leader of Tibet, is a slap in the face for the Chinese, who have kept the Tibetan nation in thrall since 1950.

There has been no comment on the award from Beijing. But the Chinese embassy in Oslo has accused the prize committee of meddling in Chinese internal affairs, a stock response to any criticism of their position in Tibet. The Dalai Lama said: "I hope and pray that the decision to give me the Nobel peace prize will encourage all those who pursue the cause of peace."

*The Dalai Lama after the award.*

*Graham Chapman (second from right) with the original Monty Python team.*

# East Germans pour over the border as Gorbachev speaks out for more reforms

# History made in Hungary as Communist Party votes for its own death sentence

*On the way to a new life: East German refugees set out for the west.*

*A red star is taken down in Budapest: political symbols are being removed.*

**Oct 7.** East Germany's communist rulers tackled their most serious political crisis for three decades today as Mikhail Gorbachev, the Soviet leader, told them it was time for fundamental reforms. Visiting East Berlin for celebrations to mark the country's 40th birthday, he told a group of East Germans: "the most important thing is not to panic". But he also warned that countries were in danger if they failed to react to the "impulses" of the times. As head of the Soviet bloc, the Soviet president is the chief guest at the anniversary celebrations, which are being held at a bad time for the ruling East German communists. While Erich Honecker, the East German leader, is hailing his country as a model socialist state, it is suffering a massive human haemorrhage. Tens of thousands are voting with their feet, using Hungary, Poland and Czechoslovakia as exit points for a new life and freedom in West Germany.

For the second time in only a few months Gorbachev has turned up in a country deeply involved in a serious political crisis. In Beijing students invoked his name as a symbol of reforms, and they met with bloody repression. So far Honecker has made it clear he is not going to be dictated to by Moscow about East German reforms (→10).

**Oct 7.** Hungary's communist rulers today turned their back on 40 years of Marxism-Leninism and voted to become social democrats. A death sentence on the party was passed at a Budapest congress with a huge majority. It paves the way for free multi-party elections in Hungary early next year. The new party will be headed by Rezso Nyers, a veteran leader who has been pushing for fundamental reforms. But its policies are likely to be shaped to a large extent by Imre Poszgay and Miklos Nemeth, the prime minister, who fear that Hungary's new opposition groups could sweep the board when the first free elections since 1947 are held (→23).

*Imre Poszgay, who will play a big part in shaping Hungary's future.*

# Costs of Chunnel rise by 50 per cent

**Oct 10.** Costs of the Channel Tunnel have soared by 50 per cent and Eurotunnel, the Anglo-French consortium which will operate the tunnel when it opens in 1993, are seeking £1.6 billion worth of new investments. If costs increase no further, the entire project, of which only one quarter has been built, will require a staggering £7 billion.

Despite Labour objections every penny must come from private investors as the prime minister remains determined that the government shall put no public money in the scheme (→31).

**Oct 7. Bette Davis in "The Scapegoat". The Hollywood star died today in a Paris hotel, aged 81.**

# Labour conference ends on high note

**Oct 5.** "Now we are ready, eager and able to take power." With that confident cry Neil Kinnock this afternoon sent Labour delegates home from the Brighton conference. The party has convinced itself that it has reasons for joy. It has now ditched its vote-losing policies of unilateral nuclear disarmament and large-scale nationalization. Left-wingers are protesting but in disarray. Labour is consistently ahead in the opinion polls. Above all the party leadership reckons the troubled Tory government now has a death wish.

# Staff creche opened by Midland Bank

**Oct 3.** Midland Bank's first creche for staff's children opens today in Sheffield. The bank plans to open 300 more across the country over the next three years. Midland are at the forefront of a national effort to maximise staff potential as the job market tightens. With 56 per cent of their employees being female, provision of nursery care is an obvious way to keep trained staff on the payroll and entice those who have left back to work. Midland already have a five-year career-break scheme as part of their equal opportunities programme.

# October

## 1989

| Su | Mo | Tu | We | Th | Fr | Sa |
|----|----|----|----|----|----|----|
| 1  | 2  | 3  | 4  | 5  | 6  | 7  |
| 8  | 9  | 10 | 11 | 12 | 13 | 14 |
| 15 | 16 | 17 | 18 | 19 | 20 | 21 |
| 22 | 23 | 24 | 25 | 26 | 27 | 28 |
| 29 | 30 | 31 |    |    |    |    |

**8.** W Berlin: The Italian conductor Claudio Abbado is appointed musical director of the Berlin Philharmonic.

**9.** UK: The pound has its steepest one-day fall in more than three years; £6.54 billion is wiped off shares. →

**9.** Stockholm: Michael Bishop and Harold Varmus of the US share the Nobel prize for medicine.

**9.** Philippines: Typhoon Angela kills 50 people and wrecks 5,000 houses.

**10.** E Germany: The flow of refugees to the West continues unabated in spite of curbs. →

**10.** UK: A large quantity of explosives is found dumped on Hampstead Heath.

**11.** UK: The government says it will pay £1 billion before the next election to take the sting out of the poll tax.

**11.** UK: The businessman Michael Knighton pulls out of a deal to buy Manchester United football club.

**11.** Stockholm: Trygve Haavelmo (Norway) wins the Nobel prize for economics.

**12.** Sweden: The conviction of Christer Petersson for the murder of former premier Olof Palme is overturned on appeal.

**12.** Stockholm: Norman Ramsey (US), Hans Dehmelt (US) and Wolfgang Paul (West Germany) share the Nobel prize for physics.

**12.** Stockholm: Sidney Altman and Thomas Cech of the US share the Nobel prize for chemistry.

**12.** Beirut: Michel Aoun denounces draft peace agreement drawn up by Lebanese deputies in Taif, Saudi Arabia.

**12.** Argentina: Leopoldo Galtieri, the former Argentine leader, is freed from jail in an amnesty.

**13.** UK: The IRA says it has proof of British intelligence operations to recruit agents within the Irish community on the continent.

**14.** Colombia: Three alleged drug traffickers are extradited to the US.

## Protests rock cities across East Germany

*Thousands throng the streets of Leipzig in the biggest march since 1953.*

**Oct 10.** The political turmoil which is gripping East Germany shows no sign of abating. There have been huge rallies not only in Leipzig but also in other places such as East Berlin, Potsdam and Halle. There are also violent clashes occurring between police and demonstrators with dozens of arrests and many people being injured.

The trouble in East Berlin broke out during a candle-lit march by several thousand young people near the city's Gethsemane church, a centre for pro-reform groups. As the crowd chanted "No violence" and "We're staying here" the police moved in using their truncheons to beat the youths about the head. But as yet there has been no police violence used against the huge crowds marching in Leipzig and calling for the legalization of the New Forum opposition group.

The demonstrations began within hours of the departure of Mikhail Gorbachev, the Soviet president, after attending celebrations for the country's 40th anniversary. He is believed to have used the visit to urge Erich Honecker, the ageing and inflexible communist leader, to introduce more reforms. Honecker has made it clear there will be no deviation from what he insists is communist orthodoxy. He is the focus of increasing popular discontent, anger and frustration (→15).

## Crash fear follows fall on Wall Street

**Oct 14.** Wall Street shares plunged yesterday in the second biggest dive on record, prompting fears of another global financial crisis. The fall came on Friday the 13th, just a week before the anniversary of the 1987 crash. The Dow Jones index lost more than 190 points, or seven per cent of its value, as 251 million shares changed hands. The collapse was said to have been triggered by recent rises in world interest rates and the failure of British Airways to secure $7.2 billion finance to buy United Airlines. The fate of the markets hinges largely on reaction in Japan when trading begins there early on Monday (→16).

## Remains of Globe theatre discovered

**Oct 12.** The remains of the Globe, Shakespeare's theatre on Bankside in London, have been found close to those of the Rose theatre discovered earlier this year. Two sections of wall, made of chalk and of brick, were unearthed four feet below the surface. Much of the site is covered by a listed building. Shakespeare was one of seven shareholders in the theatre, built in 1599, burnt down and rebuilt in 1613, but demolished after parliament closed the theatres, in 1644.

## Home Office releases Kurdish refugees seeking asylum in UK

**Oct 9.** The Home Office has released 25 Kurds from detention centres in Britain after one man burned himself to death in his cell. The Kurd committed suicide at the Harmondsworth centre near Heathrow after being told he was being recommended for deportation back to Turkey.

Other refugees barricaded themselves in their cells and there were demonstrations outside the Home Office by Kurds who believe they face oppression and torture if they are returned.

The Home Office denied it was bowing to pressure and said the immigrants were only being given temporary admission while their cases were assessed.

*The lucky ones? Kurdish refugees billeted in a hall in Stamford Hill, London.*

# UDR members arrested in leak inquiry

**Oct 8.** Police in Northern Ireland today arrested 28 members of the Ulster Defence Regiment, following investigations into how information on IRA suspects fell into the hands of loyalist paramilitaries. Four of the men have tonight been charged under the Firearms Act.

The investigation, led by John Stevens, the deputy chief constable of Cambridgeshire, began last month after names and addresses of IRA suspects were taken from a

Belfast police station between 11-14 August, and after the outlawed Ulster Freedom Fighters showed documents on IRA suspects to a BBC reporter. Similar documents and stolen ammunition were seized in 30 raids preceding today's arrests. In the past month over 20 documents have come to light, many sent with death threats to alleged IRA suspects. Loyalist paramilitaries claim they have details of hundreds of suspects.

# England qualify for World Cup finals

*Joy for England as the goalless draw with Poland qualifies them for the finals.*

**Oct 11.** Goalkeeping heroics by 40-year-old Peter Shilton today clinched England a place in next year's World Cup finals in Rome. Even when Shilton was beaten, the crossbar came to England's rescue to give England a 0-0 draw against Poland and the single point they

needed. Scotland did not fare so well, losing 3-0 to France in Paris, meaning that they must draw, at least, in the final game against Norway next month. The Republic of Ireland sustained their hopes of the finals by beating Northern Ireland 3-0 in Dublin (→15/11).

# Nuns' chickens pose no risk to health

**Oct 13.** A flock of hens owned by the nuns of Our Lady of the Passion Monastery in Northamptonshire may have been reprieved from slaughter after tests carried out by the Ministry of Agriculture proved that their eggs are not carrying the deadly virus salmonella.

Although the virus has been found in the intestines of five of the chickens, Mr Alan Rawley, QC, appearing in a judicial review of the Ministry's order to slaughter the

flock, stated that the disease could not pass into eggs. The flock, therefore, is not a public health hazard.

The results of the ministry tests had not hitherto been released to the nuns and their Mother Superior accused the ministry of "moving the goalposts".

"We will continue the fight for as long as we can," says 82-year-old Sister Catherine. If the appeal fails the convent will receive compensation of £1.42 per bird (→20).

# Thatcher derides Kinnock "conversion"

**Oct 13.** On her 64th birthday and after ten years of premiership, Margaret Thatcher made a mighty effort today to dispel recent doubts about her leadership style, staying power and grip on events. In her Tory conference speech at Blackpool, she showed much of her old verve in an attack on Labour's leader, Neil Kinnock, and what she called his "policy contortions".

The prime minister said: "Not for us disposable ideas. Not for us throwaway convictions. Not for us rent-a-principle." This was the stuff for which the Tory faithful had braved Blackpool's rigours.

The conference slogan has been "The Right Team for Britain's Future". Party impresarios have struggled to show that Thatcher's recent reshuffle after her sacking of Sir Geoffrey Howe as foreign secretary has produced men keen in new jobs and full of new ideas for improving the quality of life in the nineties.

But on the conference fringes there has been more talk than ever before about the post-Thatcher era. Jockeying for position in the succession stakes is in full swing.

*Tory press joins attack on Lawson.*

Mrs Thatcher wore her ecstatic expression during a speech by the new party chairman, Kenneth Baker. She looked much less happy listening to the chancellor, Nigel Lawson, who has not had an easy week – even the pro-Tory *Daily Mail* has joined his critics (→27).

*A brilliant blue Thatcher flanked by the "Right Team for Britain's Future".*

# Limits put on right to strike in USSR

**Oct 10.** Russia's new parliament has approved a comprehensive law on labour disputes which accepts the workers' right to strike, but will ban stoppages in some key sectors of the economy. The legislation follows a fortnight of strikes in the country's biggest coalfields. The measure is the first major law pas-

sed by the Supreme Soviet, and unprecedented recognition that the strike weapon can be used in the Soviet state. The law bans strikes in transport, in the fuel, energy and defence industries, and in other sectors where a halt in output would have "serious consequences". Also banned are political strikes.

# October

## 1989

| Su | Mo | Tu | We | Th | Fr | Sa |
|----|----|----|----|----|----|----|
| 1 | 2 | 3 | 4 | 5 | 6 | 7 |
| 8 | 9 | 10 | 11 | 12 | 13 | 14 |
| 15 | 16 | 17 | 18 | 19 | 20 | 21 |
| 22 | 23 | 24 | 25 | 26 | 27 | 28 |
| 29 | 30 | 31 | | | | |

**15.** Iraq: Farzad Bazoft, an *Observer* journalist held in Iraq for over a month, is accused of espionage.

**15.** Hungary: Another 4,000 East Germans have left for the West over the weekend (→16).

**16.** World: Fears of a global stock-market crash recede as dealers keep their nerve.

**16.** E Germany: Another protest march, 120,000-strong, is held in Leipzig.→

**17.** UK: Kurt Waldheim, the Austrian leader, is cleared of criminal involvement in the wartime execution of seven British commandoes.

**17.** UK: Corruption proceedings against the police involved in the conviction of the Guildford Four are announced.→

**18.** Hungary: Parliament overwhelmingly approves plans to transform the country into a multi-party democracy.

**19.** Stockholm: Camilo Jose Cela of Spain wins the Nobel prize for literature.

**19.** Madrid: Argentina and Britain formally end hostilities after the 1982 Falklands war.

**19.** UK: The £600,000 damages award to Sonia Sutcliffe against *Private Eye* is overturned on appeal.

**19.** UK: In his Mansion House speech, the chancellor, Nigel Lawson, warns of a economic slowdown (→26).

**19.** Australia: At least 22 people are killed and 20 others seriously hurt in a coach crash.

**20.** UK: Paul Hill is the last of the Guildford Four to be freed.

**20.** UK: The 5,000 chickens belonging to the nuns of Our Lady of the Passion monastery are slaughtered after an appeal fails.

**21.** E Berlin: Several thousand demonstrators form a human chain across the city centre (→30).

**21.** Honduras: A Boeing 727 crashes, killing at least 131.

**DEATH**

**20.** Sir Anthony Quayle, British actor (*7/9/13).

# San Francisco devastated by quake

*A house lists like a sinking boat and ruins smoulder in San Francisco.*

*A collapsed part of the Bay bridge.*

**Oct 19.** At least 273 people are believed to have died and a further 650 been injured today when at 5.04pm local time an earthquake, triggered by the San Andreas fault, struck the San Francisco Bay area. The quake, which measured 6.9 on the Richter scale, wrecked homes and offices, cut off vital services and brought chaos to the cities of San Francisco and neighbouring Oakland. The bulk of the deaths came when a half-mile section of the double-decker Interstate 880 motorway collapsed, crushing those in vehicles travelling on the lower deck. An estimated 253 people were killed, trapped in cars that were reduced in seconds to flattened, twisted wrecks.

California has declared a state of emergency and the cost of the damage, which spreads across some seven counties, may total $1 billion.

Many buildings designed to be "earthquake-proof" withstood the tremor, but older ones collapsed.

San Francisco's last major earthquake came in 1906, when 2,000 died and the entire city was razed by a shock estimated at 8.3 on the scale. Californians have been waiting for the next major tremor ever since. This was not it, but experts are convinced that the "Big One" is only a matter of time (→25).

## South Africa frees eight, including Sisulu

**Oct 15.** There were scenes of great jubilation among South African opposition supporters today following the release at dawn of eight leading black nationalist prisoners.

Among the eight freed by the government of President F W de Klerk is the 77-year-old former secretary general of the African National Congress, Walter Sisulu, who was sentenced to life imprisonment for treason and sabotage with Nelson Mandela in 1963. After Mandela, he has been the most senior ANC figure in captivity.

Between them, the men released today have served nearly two centuries in jail. All are members of the ANC except Jafta Masemola, who belongs to a rival group, the Pan-Africanist Congress. The seven ANC men held a press conference tonight near Sisulu's Soweto home. Sisulu conceded that the government was "beginning to be sensitive to issues that affect the people", but

*Walter Sisulu, freed after 26 years.*

insisted it still had to make "visible efforts" to move towards a negotiated future for the country. On their own release, they said it was only a "half measure" while Nelson Mandela remained a prisoner (→29).

## Doctors monitored under new contract

**Oct 15.** Leaders of Britain's 35,000 family doctors are angry at today's announcement by Kenneth Clarke, the health secretary, that he is to impose new contracts on GPs.

Under the most controversial of their new terms of employment, which are due to begin in April 1990, doctors will be paid less in basic allowances but will receive more for each patient on their list. The government claims that this will encourage practices to compete for patients by offering a wider range of services, but doctors are worried that taking more patients to avoid losing income will mean less time with each patient. It is the imposition of the contract which is "incensing" GPs, according to Dr Michael Wilson of the British Medical Association, whose members voted three to one against the contract in the summer.

## Communists force Honecker to resign

*Honecker before his resignation.*

**Oct 18.** Erich Honecker, the East German Communist Party leader, was ousted today – the scapegoat for the exodus of tens of thousands of East Germans and the slow pace of political reform. His job went to Egon Krenz, at 52 the youngest member of the ruling politburo and who hitherto has also been seen as a hardliner. He has been holding the politburo portfolio for internal security and youth.

During his 18 years as party boss, Honecker personified the hardline approach of East Germany, which sought to maintain the monolithic Stalinist style. He was resisting the pressure for reform to the very end. But the continuing exodus, and the growing protest demonstrations in Leipzig and other cities, have been too much for party reformers, and the Kremlin, to take any longer. Honecker's enforced retirement is expected to open the political floodgates (→21).

*Krenz: new East German leader.*

# Guildford Four go free after 14 years

**Oct 19.** The court of appeal took half an hour today to overturn the murder convictions of four alleged terrorists convicted of pub bombings in 1975. The convictions of the Guildford Four had been based on police lies and the use of fabricated confessions as evidence.

Gerard Conlon, aged 35, Carole Richardson, aged 32, and Patrick Armstrong, aged 39, all walked free, having served 14 years for a crime they did not commit. Paul Hill, aged 35, remains in custody until another case in which he is implicated is resolved.

A judicial inquiry has been ordered into the case. Evidence that senior detectives had tampered with, and even concocted, confessions said to have been made by the accused came to light in May, during inquiries by the Avon and Somerset police, although doubts about alibi and scientific evidence had already been expressed.

Officers from Avon and Somerset found that notes on interviews with Hill and Armstrong had been rewritten, altered and suppressed,

*Gerard Conlon responds to an ecstatic crowd just minutes after his release.*

and that detectives had misled the trial. There are also calls for investigation of the role of the then director of public prosecutions, Sir Norman Skelhorn, now deceased, for his part in the suppression of scientific evidence that conflicted with the falsified confessions. The decision by the court of appeal also has implications for the case of the Maguire family, relations of Conlon whom he is said to have named as bomb manufacturers. The whole family were convicted, despite doubts about the forensic evidence (→20).

## Worldwide ban on ivory trade agreed

**Oct 17.** A global ban on trading in ivory was confirmed today by the Convention on International Trade in Endangered Species (Cites), meeting in Lausanne. The 103-nation conference voted by a large majority for the African elephant to be listed on the Cites Appendix I, which bans all trade. The move comes after a week of wrangling.

The number of elephants in Africa has fallen in the past decade from more than 1.2 million to about 600,000, as poaching has fed a multi-million-pound market in ivory objects to Europe, Japan and the US. However, southern African states such as South Africa, Zimbabwe and Botswana – which have well-stocked herds, used for profitable culling and hunting – objected to being penalized for the failure of countries in central and east Africa to control poaching.

Cites also decided that the 670-ton stockpile of ivory in Hong Kong cannot be sold abroad.

## Pay inequality between sexes worsens

**Oct 16.** Non-manual women workers in Britain earn just 61 per cent of that earned by their male equivalents, a report by the Equal Opportunities Commission out today reveals. This staggering inequality is greater than it has ever been since the Equal Pay Act came into force in 1975. Part-time women workers fare even worse, earning just 49 per cent of their full-time male counterparts. Female manual workers are also underpaid by a significant margin in relation to men.

**The multi-talented Kenneth Branagh makes his debut as film director of "Henry V", seen here as the hero with Emma Thompson as Katherine.**

# October

## 1989

| Su | Mo | Tu | We | Th | Fr | Sa |
|----|----|----|----|----|----|----|
| 1 | 2 | 3 | 4 | 5 | 6 | 7 |
| 8 | 9 | 10 | 11 | 12 | 13 | 14 |
| 15 | 16 | 17 | 18 | 19 | 20 | 21 |
| 22 | 23 | 24 | 25 | 26 | 27 | 28 |
| 29 | 30 | 31 | | | | |

**22. US:** It is revealed that Alan Walters, Mrs Thatcher's personal economic adviser, has published details of the British cabinet split over the European Monetary System (→24).

**22. Japan:** Ayrton Senna is disqualified from the Japanese Grand Prix after a crash; Alain Prost still heads the world drivers' championship.

**22. Saudi Arabia:** At Taif, Lebanese Christian deputies accept a compromise peace plan for Lebanon.

**23. US:** A huge explosion and fire vaporizes a plastics plant in Pasadena, Texas.

**24. UK:** Nigel Lawson, the chancellor, demands on TV that Alan Walters stop making public statements.→

**25. UK:** Plans are revealed forcibly to repatriate Vietnamese refugees from Hong Kong.

**25. US:** The death toll from last week's San Francisco earthquake is now put at 83.

**26. UK:** Kazuo Ishiguro wins the Booker Prize for *The Remains of the Day.*

**26. Netherlands:** Ruud Lubbers's Christian Democrats and the Labour Party agree to form a centre-left coalition.

**27. E Germany:** An amnesty is announced for all those convicted of escaping or trying to escape to the West.→

**28. Costa Rica:** Daniel Ortega, the Nicaraguan leader, threatens not to renew his unilateral ceasefire with the Contras.

**29. Colombia:** A reputed leader of the Medellin drug cartel is extradited to the US.

**30. Algeria:** The death toll from an earthquake rises to 30.

**31. Turkey:** Turgut Ozal is elected president.

**31. New York:** Mitsubishi buys the Rockefeller Center.

### DEATHS

**22.** Ewan McColl, British folk singer and actor (*1915).

**25.** Mary McCarthy, US novelist (*21/6/12).

**28.** Henry Hall, British band leader (*2/5/1898).

## Police take 999 calls in ambulance strike

**Oct 23.** Seven million Londoners face life without a regular ambulance service from today and their emergency calls are being answered by the police, backed by Red Cross and St John Ambulance teams. The stand-in services are struggling to cope, but they are vastly inferior to the regular crews in both equipment and training.

Ambulance crews began a work-to-rule at 7am in support of their current pay claim. Management responded by stopping their pay and declaring the crews "off-duty". The ambulance unions have stated that their members will be available to answer 999 calls without pay.

Both sides are vehement in their condemnation of the situation. Tom Crosby, London's acting chief ambulance officer, described affairs as "a shambles" and claimed that the union action put crews in breach of contract.

The unions reject this argument and accuse management of being intimidated by government. Both sides are demanding talks, before

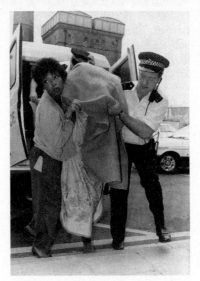

*Police struggling to cope in London.*

the dispute leads to loss of life.

Kenneth Clarke, the secretary of state for health, accused the ambulancemen of "gambling with patients' lives" and walked out of a TV interview, stating: "I am not negotiating with unions who are refusing to negotiate." (→8/11).

## Gonzalez scrapes home in Spanish polls

**Oct 30.** Spanish socialists have secured their third election victory in a row, but with a much reduced majority. A late victory in a Barcelona constituency enabled them to hold on to their absolute majority in the parliament with 176 of the 350 seats. The socialist leader, Felipe Gonzalez, won 39.5 per cent

of the vote, with the conservative Popular Party securing 25.8 per cent. The poll saw a sharp increase in support for the extreme left, with the United Left party taking third place. The rest of the vote was divided among nine regionalist parties, including the political wing of Eta, the Basque separatists.

**Oct 31. The coffins of an RAF corporal, Maheshkumar Islania, and his six-month-old daughter arrive at RAF Northolt, west London. The two were shot dead by the IRA on Thursday at a petrol station in West Germany.**

## Thatcher slammed by Commonwealth

**Oct 23.** Once again, relations with South Africa have dominated a Commonwealth heads of government conference, and once again it was Margaret Thatcher who played the central role. Shortly after the conference had agreed a policy on sanctions, she infuriated the other leaders by issuing a separate statement stressing British reservations.

Australia's Bob Hawke and Canada's Brian Mulroney led the attack on what they regarded as British duplicity, but Mrs Thatcher was unrepentant. Despite being outnumbered by 48 to one, she insisted that she was in step with the people of South Africa. The blacks there did not want sanctions, she argued, because it would cut jobs. "If it is one against 48," she said, "then I am very sorry for the 48."

## Joyful Soweto rally salutes black spirit

**Oct 29.** In the largest such rally ever held in South Africa, 60,000 supporters of the African National Congress (ANC) gathered at the Soweto stadium today. They were celebrating the release from jail of Walter Sisulu and six other veteran ANC leaders. In an upbeat speech, Sisulu said that repression had failed "to dent the spirit of resistance among our people", but that serious talks with the government depended on the release of all 3,000 or so political prisoners still held and the lifting of all political restrictions.

## Rail link postponed

**Oct 31.** British Rail has put off plans to build a high-speed rail link to the Channel tunnel for a least a year. The decision comes in the face of government insistence that the link should be paid for entirely by private money. BR has failed to agree with its private-sector partners on how to finance the project, and it now looks unlikely to be completed before the year 2000. The news is a blow to Eurotunnel, the consortium building the tunnel, which has urged the government to back the link (→3/11).

## Many thousands march in Leipzig

**Oct 30.** Despite leadership changes in East Germany, and promises of major reform, the people of Leipzig have not stopped their huge regular Monday demonstrations. Some half a million took to the streets today in the biggest demonstration of its kind so far in East Germany. The theme of the slogans was that the people are tiring of talk and want action. The Leipzig rallies started six weeks ago as a protest march of a few thousand after a prayer meeting. They have grown into a spontaneous mass event which has proved a major force for change (→4/11).

## Murder verdict in Julie Ward inquest

**Oct 27.** The inquest into the death of Julie Ward, the British woman who died in a Kenyan game reserve last year, decided today that the 28-year-old was the victim of "foul play". She was not, as the Kenyan police maintained, killed by wild animals. The Kenyan chief magistrate said: "Those sharp cuts described by the pathologist were man-made." John Ward, Julie's father, who has spent many thousands of pounds pursuing the case, said he had got the verdict required.

**Oct 23. On the 33rd anniversary of the 1956 uprising, Hungarians gather to proclaim a new republic and Eastern Europe's first post-Stalinist constitution.**

# Lawson resigns in day of high drama

**Oct 26.** Nigel Lawson, the chancellor of the exchequer, resigned tonight. The government is plunged into its greatest agony and turmoil of the Thatcher years.

A day of high drama began with a bitter breakfast-time row between the prime minister and Mr Lawson. He said that his position was untenable. It had been undermined by constant public sniping from Mrs Thatcher's personal economic adviser, Professor Sir Alan Walters. She must promise to sack him by the year-end or Mr Lawson would quit now. The prime minister asked him to reconsider.

In the afternoon she answered teasing Commons questions about Sir Alan's position. She said nothing about the chancellor's resignation threat – and nothing about disowning Sir Alan for having criticized Mr Lawson's backing for British membership of the European Monetary System.

Lawson was livid. He stormed into 10 Downing Street, with his resignation letter in his hand as soon as Mrs Thatcher returned there from the House.

The letter said: "Successful conduct of economic policy is possible only if there is full agreement between the prime mininster and the chancellor of the exchequer." Obviously there was not.

Tonight Mrs Thatcher named

*The ex-chancellor: Nigel Lawson.*

*The other man: Sir Alan Walters.*

*All change: (l. to r.) John Major, once foreign secretary, now chancellor; his replacement, Douglas Hurd; and David Waddington, the new home secretary.*

John Major, her recently appointed foreign secretary, to succeed Mr Lawson and moved Douglas Hurd from being home secretary to foreign secretary. Government whips made frantic "keep calm" appeals.

Anxious Tories asked if the government is falling apart. Can Mrs Thatcher herself last much longer? In the Commons the jubilant Labour MPs sang the *Red Flag* (→31).

## Lawson and Thatcher give their versions

**Oct 31.** In a sensational Commons speech Nigel Lawson tonight denounced Mrs Thatcher's leadership style and repudiated her version of why he resigned as chancellor of the exchequer five days ago.

Mr Lawson startled MPs with a stark account of his final rows with the prime minister. He denied her assertion in a weekend television interview that he had been determined to quit and could not possibly have gone just because of the "small thing" about the position of Sir Alan Walters, her personal economic adviser.

The ex-chancellor also contradicted Mrs Thatcher's claim that she did everything possible to stop him from resigning. Then he continued: "For our system of cabinet

government to work effectively the prime minister must appoint ministers that he or she trusts and then leave them to carry out the policy."

Lawson insisted that Britain must join the exchange rate mechanism of the European Monetary System as soon as practicable instead of putting this off as long as possible – as Mrs Thatcher prefers. This was at the root of their conflict.

John Smith, Labour's shadow chancellor, accused the prime minister of being "less than frank" in her remarks about the cabinet crisis. He said that Lawson was the victim of her "subversion of cabinet government". Speculation continues to rage about where all this will end.

## The man who was Thatcher's guru

**Oct 26.** And who is Sir Alan Walters anyway? Outside government and academic circles in London and the United States this arrogant 65-year-old economist is practically unknown. He is a university professor in Baltimore. For years he has divided his time between teaching there and on both sides of the Atlantic – pouring scorn on the British Treasury. Sir Alan is a political innocent and he has resigned from Mrs Thatcher's staff tonight in a state of shock. Whatever she thinks about Mr Lawson, she is sorry to lose Sir Alan. Her father kept a grocer's shop. His once tried a grocery business – and failed.

# November

## 1989

| Su | Mo | Tu | We | Th | Fr | Sa |
|----|----|----|----|----|----|----|
|    |    |    | 1  | 2  | 3  | 4  |
| 5  | 6  | 7  | 8  | 9  | 10 | 11 |
| 12 | 13 | 14 | 15 | 16 | 17 | 18 |
| 19 | 20 | 21 | 22 | 23 | 24 | 25 |
| 26 | 27 | 28 | 29 | 30 |    |    |

**1.** US: Pan Am subpoenas the CIA and five other government agencies over documents linking a Syrian arms dealer to the Lockerbie bomb.

**1.** Nicaragua: President Ortega ends a 19-month ceasefire with the Contras because of continued US support for them.

**1.** France: SNCF, the national rail service, offers to help BR finance the Channel tunnel rail link (→2).

**1.** UK: Hammersmith and Fulham Council's £6 billion deals on the money markets are ruled unlawful.

**2.** Prague: More East Germans take refuge in the West Germany embassy (→3).

**2.** E Germany: Pro-reformists march in several cities; the mayor of Leipzig quits (→3).

**2.** UK: Cecil Parkinson, the transport secretary, denies involvement in insider share dealing.

**2.** UK: BR imposes large long-distance fare increases, and formally postpones the building of a Channel tunnel rail link (→4).

**3.** E Germany: Egon Krenz, the new leader, purges politburo hardliners and grants refugees in Prague permission to leave for the West.→

**3.** The Hague: The US agrees to repay Iranian assets frozen in the US since the 1979 Tehran embassy siege.

**3.** UK: The water privatization prospectus is issued, showing that the sell-off will cost the taxpayer £1.3 billion.

**3.** UK: BR abandons plans for an 18-mile tunnel from King's Cross to Swanley in Kent; large parts of the Channel tunnel rail link will now run overground through London.

**4.** USSR: Gorbachev appeals for an end to a ten-day strike by coal miners in the Arctic city of Vorkuta.

**4.** Iran: Four men charged with spying for the American CIA are hanged.

**4.** UK: At an Arsenal-Norwich football match, 21 players become involved in a brawl on the pitch (→27).

## A million march for reform in East Berlin

*Demonstrators pack the vast Alexander Platz in the centre of East Berlin.*

**Nov 4.** As East Germans fled west by the thousand today through the newly opened Czechoslovak corridor, an estimated one million marched in East Berlin demanding more reforms. It was the biggest show of opposition in the city since Soviet tanks crushed a revolt by workers in 1953. Police kept a low profile as the huge numbers gathered in the Alexander Platz, half a mile from the Berlin Wall, chanting "Egon, here we come". Speakers called for multi-party elections, freedom of speech and a criminal code to protect individuals.

The changes made so far by the new East German party chief, Egon Krenz, have not satisfied protes-

ters. Yesterday he sacked five members of the politburo and appealed to East Germans not to flee their country – about 167,000 have left for the West this year. The easing of a travel ban, announced early today, has opened a clear path for refugees through Czechoslovakia.

More than 6,000 East Germans, many of whom had been sheltering in the West German embassy, have already left Prague. Others have crossed into Czechoslovakia from East Germany and then headed straight for the West German border. For the first time since the Berlin Wall was built in 1961, East Germans can vote with their feet against communism (→6).

## Three new women in shadow cabinet

**Nov 1.** Three new women tonight joined Jo Richardson, formerly the only female member, in Labour's shadow cabinet. The only surprise election for Neil Kinnock was that of Ann Clwyd, the MP for Cynon Valley, whom he sacked from his front bench last year. The other victors were Margaret Beckett, and Joan Lestor, who came sixth in the overall vote. Gordon Brown, a Treasury spokesman, topped the poll for the second year running; his boss, John Smith, came second.

## Bhutto survives bid to force her out

**Nov 1.** Benazir Bhutto, the prime minister of Pakistan, has narrowly survived a bid by her opponents to force her from office. In a vote of no confidence today in the 237-seat national assembly, Bhutto's Pakistan People's Party (PPP) polled 221 votes against 207 for the Combined Opposition Parties (COP). Unbowed, the COP vowed to continue the campaign to unseat the "corrupt, incompetent and inept" government. A major shake-up of the PPP now seems likely (→13).

## Brooke accused of boosting terrorism

**Nov 3.** Peter Brooke, the new Northern Ireland secretary, stirred up a political wasps' nest today by suggesting that the IRA could not be beaten, and by hinting that the British government might talk to Sinn Fein, the political wing of the IRA, if the terrorists called a ceasefire.

Speaking in interviews to mark his first 100 days in office, Brooke said that normal military means would contain the IRA but not defeat it altogether. He suggested that if the IRA were to renounce violence London should be "flexible and imaginative" in its response.

Ulster Unionists and the Labour Party accused him of encouraging terrorism. His comments angered some Tories, but others insisted that he was only voicing long-held government views.

*Peter Brooke: speaking his mind.*

## Jaguar accepts a £1.6bn Ford escort

**Nov 2.** Jaguar, one of the few remaining British-owned car makers, was swallowed up today by the giant American Ford corporation in a £1.6 billion deal. The purchase became possible after the trade secretary, Nicholas Ridley, removed the government's "golden share", which was designed to prevent just such a takeover. Workers who were given a share in the luxury car company when it was privatized in 1984 stand to make an average of £6,800 each.

# November

## 1989

| Su | Mo | Tu | We | Th | Fr | Sa |
|----|----|----|----|----|----|----|
|    |    |    | 1  | 2  | 3  | 4  |
| 5  | 6  | 7  | 8  | 9  | 10 | 11 |
| 12 | 13 | 14 | 15 | 16 | 17 | 18 |
| 19 | 20 | 21 | 22 | 23 | 24 | 25 |
| 26 | 27 | 28 | 29 | 30 |    |    |

**5.** UK: Margaret Thatcher suggests she may step down as premier after the next election.

**5.** UK: Nigel Lawson, the ex-chancellor, says on TV that Thatcher knew his resignation was caused by Alan Walters, contradicting her version.

**5.** Lebanon: René Moawad, a Maronite Christian moderate, is elected president (→22).

**6.** E Germany: Half a million people march in Leipzig; other cities see their biggest demonstrations yet (→7).

**6.** Greece: Constantine Mitsotakis's New Democracy party fails to win an overall majority in elections.

**6.** UK: *Private Eye* agrees to pay Sonia Sutcliffe £60,000 plus her legal costs in an out-of-court libel settlement.

**7.** E Germany: The entire cabinet resigns (→8).

**7.** USSR: Nationalist protests mar celebrations for the 72nd anniversary of the Revolution.

**8.** E Germany: A new politburo is appointed; Hans Modrow, a liberal reformer, becomes prime minister (→9).

**9.** E Germany: All border points are opened.→

**9.** UK: Police investigate the sale of lead-contaminated cattle feed as fears grow about the number of farms affected.

**9.** China: Deng Xiaoping hands over control of the central military commission to Jiang Zemin.

**10.** UK: Eleven leading City figures are charged with fraud over the County NatWest-Blue Arrow affair.

**11.** Berlin: More than one million East Berliners flood to the West (→16).

**11.** UK: Thatcher rejects US plans to base nuclear-capable B-52 bombers in Britain.

**11.** UK: Neil Kinnock admits on TV that he bungled his Commons attack on Thatcher during the Westland crisis.

**DEATH**

**5.** Vladimir Horowitz, Russian-born pianist (*1/10/04).

# Troops take over ambulance service

*Not quite dressed for the job: Irish Guards walk past a line of ambulances.*

**Nov 8.** Army and RAF ambulances are out on the streets of London tonight in the latest twist to the ambulance workers' dispute.

The government's decision to send in the troops follows the suspension yesterday of the capital's 2,500 ambulance crew members – who are working to rule in a nationwide campaign for better pay and conditions – by their employers, the health service management.

Kenneth Clarke, the health secretary, said yesterday he had reluctantly called in troops because ambulance crews could not guarantee emergency cover. But Roger Poole, the ambulance union negotiator, insisted that his members, who have stayed at their posts despite the suspensions, "are pledged to maintain accident and emergency cover if they are allowed to do so".

Ambulance staff want greater pay parity with the other emergency services. The growing acrimony in the dispute was sharpened last week, when Britain's firefighters won an 8.6 per cent pay rise. Management continues to offer most ambulance workers a rise of 6.5 per cent (→19).

# British Rail blamed for Clapham crash

**Nov 7.** In a report published today, the blame for the Clapham rail crash last December, in which 35 people died and 132 were injured, is laid squarely on the shoulders of the British Rail management. The underlying cause, said Sir Anthony Hidden, the chairman of the inquiry, lay in the "out-dated and damaging" way British Rail ran its business.

While BR professed a commitment to safety, the report continued, there was a distressing lack of organization, which meant that "safety lagged frighteningly behind the idealism of the words".

# Plans for nuclear power sale ditched

**Nov 9.** The British nuclear power industry was dealt a major blow today when John Wakeham, the energy secretary, told the House of Commons that nuclear power stations will not now be sold off to private investors along with the rest of the electricity industry. Plans for the development of pressurized water reactors have also been shelved, in the wake of predictions that nuclear power will cost at least three times as much as fossil-fuel electricity. Lord Marshall, the chairman of National Power, which was due to take over the nuclear stations, is expected to resign.

The announcement marks an U-turn in government policy, and is widely seen as an attempt to save the electricity privatization programme from collapse.

# New York votes for first black mayor

**Nov 6.** David Dinkins, aged 62, will be New York's first-ever black mayor. He was elected with a firm lead over his republican opponent, Rudolph Guiliani – despite a poll trend that suggested strong opposition from white voters. Dinkins has inherited a city with a massive budget deficit, a fast-growing "crack" problem and more than 80,000 homeless people.

**"Fax" art by David Hockney, the man who developed the photo-collage technique. His new work, composed of 144 sheets faxed from Los Angeles, is being mounted in a West Yorkshire gallery as it arrives on the machine.**

# The Berlin Wall becomes a gateway to the West

**Nov 10.** The 28-mile-long scar cutting across central Berlin – ugliest symbol of a divided world – has no meaning any more. Few thought to see it happen in their lifetimes, but last night, at the stroke of midnight, thousands lining both sides of the Berlin Wall gave a great roar and began to pour through checkpoints, as well as climbing up and over the Wall. They danced and trumpeted on the top. They hacked at the loathed monument to repression, loosening chunks of masonry. "I'm no longer in prison!" one young man shouted. They crowded onto the West Berlin streets, spraying champagne and sounding car horns until long past dawn. It all began quietly. With mass protests and the flight of refugees continuing un-abated – and Egon Krenz, the new leader, intent on showing sincerity about reform – Gunter Schabowski, the East Berlin party boss, yesterday held a press conference. He declared that, starting from midnight, East Germans would be free to leave the country, without special permission, at any point along the border, including the crossing points through the Wall in Berlin.

News spread quickly through both parts of the city; at Checkpoint Charlie in West Berlin a crowd formed early, taunting East German border guards with cries of "Open the gate!". As midnight struck, the first East Berliners came through (→11).

*Egon Krenz addresses East German protesters before the opening of the Wall.*

## Wall splits Berlin

The Berlin Wall rose in August 1961 after East Germany sealed off the border between East and West Berlin to stem a growing tide of refugees. In the six weeks before a six-foot-high concrete barrier topped with barbed wire was erected in the Potsdamer Platz, over 45,000 had crossed into West Berlin – adding to the more than two and a half million who had fled since 1949.

In 28 years, at least 75 people have met often violent deaths while trying to escape over the Wall. Its last known victim died in March this year.

*A courageous leap to freedom.*

## Hopes and fears spring from broken Wall

**Nov 10.** Standing at the spot where, in 1963, John F Kennedy declared "*Ich bin ein Berliner*", the mayor of West Berlin, Walter Momper, said: "The Germans are the happiest people in the world today."

Most world leaders also expressed delight. Some, such as George Bush, were "elated". In London, Margaret Thatcher heralded the news as a "great day for freedom" and President Mitterrand talked of "these happy events". The West German chancellor, Helmut Kohl, was clearly concerned that West Germany would be swamped with newcomers. "Our interest must be that the East Germans stay at home," he said. The Soviet Union praised the move as "symbolic" but warned the Bonn government against changing its borders.

The threat to the existing balance of the European Community was in many minds – as was the spectre of a reunified Germany (→11).

## Bulgaria boss goes

**Nov 10.** The Iron Curtain opened a little wider today with the resignation of the Bulgarian leader, Todor Zhivkov. Zhivkov, aged 78 – the longest-serving communist boss in East Europe – was replaced by the foreign minister, Petar Mladenov, after 35 years in power. Although Bulgaria has shown few signs of *perestroika*, a demonstration by 5,000 people demanding reform in the capital last week has clearly alarmed the leadership (→17).

## East Germany is shattered by astonishing pace of change

**Sept 11.** Hungary opens its borders for East Germans to go to the West.
**Sept 30.** Tens of thousands of East Germans are fleeing via Hungary, Poland and Czechoslovakia.
**Oct 7.** Visiting East Berlin, Mikhail Gorbachev urges the government to introduce fundamental reforms.
**Oct 10.** Huge pro-reform marches, sparked by Gorbachev's visit, continue to rock East German cities.
**Oct 18.** Egon Krenz replaces Erich Honecker as East German leader.
**Nov 4.** Spreading dissent across the country culminates in a million-strong protest in East Berlin.
**Nov 4.** The refugee exodus resumes after the lifting of a travel ban.
**Nov 7.** The government resigns.
**Nov 8.** The politburo is replaced; Hans Modrow becomes premier.
**Nov 9.** All border points open.

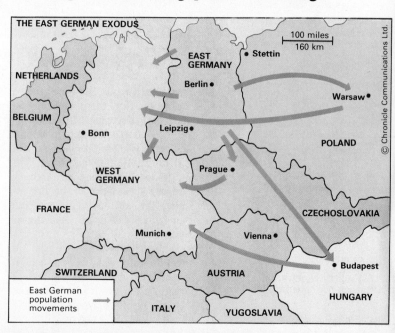

THE EAST GERMAN EXODUS

100 miles
160 km

EAST GERMANY
Stettin
Berlin
NETHERLANDS
Warsaw
BELGIUM
Bonn
Leipzig
POLAND
WEST GERMANY
Prague
FRANCE
CZECHOSLOVAKIA
Munich
Vienna
SWITZERLAND
AUSTRIA
Budapest
East German population movements
ITALY
YUGOSLAVIA
HUNGARY

© Chronicle Communications Ltd.

# November

## East-West traffic swells to a human flood

*The Wall is taken apart at the Potsdamer Platz: soldiers keep the crowd back.*

**Nov 18.** A week after the opening of the Berlin Wall, the streets of West Berlin are again packed with up to two million visitors from East Germany. Some are enjoying tearful reunions with relatives not seen for years; some are shopping or window-shopping; others are simply savouring a taste of the West. A small proportion is here to stay.

The huge traffic between East and West recalls the momentous events of last weekend, which started after bulldozers moved in to make additional crossing points in the Wall. Immense queues formed at all checkpoints from East to West Berlin, and 2.7 million East Germans – a sixth of the popula-

tion – were reported to have been issued with travel visas. Last Saturday saw the largest movement of European people recorded in one day. There were traffic jams up to 30 miles long. Most East German visitors returned home after the weekend, as did West Berliners who had made trips to the East.

As political changes continue apace, the *Volkskammer* [East German parliament] yesterday committed itself to developing a democratic socialist society with a more market-orientated economy. However, the new prime minister, Hans Modrow, attacked the "unrealistic and dangerous" talk in the West of German reunification (→20).

## Paris talks agree aid for East Europe

**Nov 18.** At an emergency Paris summit called by President Mitterrand, European Community heads sat down to dinner tonight to discuss the revolutionary changes in East Europe. They agreed on urgent aid packages for Poland and Hungary, and laid the ground for talks on a full trade and cooperation agreement with East Germany.

Mitterrand said after the dinner: "We should show solidarity with the whole of Europe." But he set the tone for next month's summit in Strasburg – which will focus on economic and monetary union – by stressing the need for the Community to strengthen itself fast.

## Bulgaria sees vast democracy march

**Nov 18.** In the largest political demonstration ever seen in postwar Bulgaria, 100,000 people rallied today in the heart of Sofia. Not satisfied by the reforms introduced by Petar Mladenov – who replaced Todor Zhivkov as party leader a week ago – they were demanding free elections, a new constitution and the sacking of remaining hardliners in the politburo. There were also calls for charges of corruption to be brought against Zhivkov's family.

## Czechoslovak police beat up and detain Prague demonstrators

**Nov 17.** The candles that they carried cast a soft glow on the faces of the Czechoslovak student demonstrators. One of their banners read "Please don't beat students". But candles and banners proved no defence against the truncheons and dogs of the riot police who tonight beat up and detained hundreds of protesters at Prague's biggest anti-government rally for 20 years.

Officially sanctioned to commemorate the death of a student killed by the Nazis in 1939, the event rapidly focused on demands for reform as the marchers chanted "Dinosaurs resign" and "We want free elections". Finally, the police advanced into Wenceslas Square (→19).

*A protester bearing only a candle confronts a line of riot police in Prague.*

# Irish and Scots reach World Cup

**Nov 15.** Sales of the dark liquid reached record levels in Dublin to-night, and distilleries threatened to run dry in Scotland, when Ireland and Scotland won their way to the World Cup finals in Rome next year. Ireland, who have been trying to qualify for 55 years, beat Malta in Valetta by 2-0, with both goals from John Aldridge.

The real drama was at Hampden Park where Scotland, needing only a point, drew 1-1 with Norway. Scotland were in the lead from half-time with a goal by Ally McCoist, but a powerful 40-yard equalizer from Johnsen in the last minute had the 60,000 crowd praying for the final whistle.

*Ireland's McGrath in fine form.*

# Swapo fails to hit Namibia poll target

**Nov 14.** The South West African People's Organization (Swapo) emerged today as the largest party after five days of voting in Namibia's first elections. But it will have to work with its opponents in preparing for independence from South Africa after failing to win the 48 of the 72 seats which it needed to write the country's constitution on its own.

The turnout was around 95 per cent in the poll, in which Swapo won 41 seats; but its main opponents, the conservative Democratic Turnhalle Alliance, came away with 21 seats.

# Death toll mounts in El Salvador war

*Caught in the crossfire: Salvadorean emergency rescue workers hit the ground.*

*A family fleeing from San Salvador.*

**Nov 16.** A death squad entered a university in El Salvador early this morning and dragged six Jesuit priests from their beds. Two were shot in their rooms, four more on the lawns. The killers then shot the priests' cook and her 15-year-old daughter in a room where they were hiding. The deaths of the men – who were in the forefront of the struggle for human rights – add to an estimated toll of over 650 in the worst fighting between left-wing rebels and troops since the El Salvador civil war began ten years ago.

Despite a 24-hour curfew, fighting has continued into a sixth day, with the rebels consolidating their defensive positions in the suburbs around the capital, San Salvador.

"People's governments" have been established in eight provinces, it was claimed.

Shocked by the suddenness and intensity of the guerrilla attacks, the Salvadorean government is using helicopter gunships as its principal weapons. Rocket attacks on shanty-towns around the capital have taken many civilian lives.

# South Africa scraps beach apartheid

**Nov 16.** The tide of change in South Africa took on a literal meaning today when President F W de Klerk announced an end to apartheid on the country's beaches.

De Klerk said in Cape Town that from now on "all members of the public" would be allowed on all beaches. He also gave a pledge that the Separate Amenities Act – a pillar of apartheid under which access to public places such as parks and libraries is restricted according to race – would be abolished next February.

The radical Mass Democratic Movement has recently been targeting segregated beaches as part of a campaign of defiance of apartheid. It gave a cautious welcome to de Klerk's announcements, but said it could not be satisfied before two other key apartheid laws – one classifying people by race and the other deciding where races may live and work – are repealed.

# All passion spent for Spanish heroine

*"La Pasionaria", who became a living symbol of the fight against fascism.*

**Nov 12.** "*La Pasionaria*", the great Republican heroine of the Spanish Civil War, died today at the age of 93. Born Dolores Ibarruri, she became a committed communist at an early age; she once signed an article in the journal *Class Struggle* "*Pasionaria*", and the name stuck. Tall and always dressed in black, she became famous for her rousing, fanatical speeches. Her rallying cry was "*No pasaran*" – "They shall not pass". Equally well-known was her exhortation to Republican troops to die on their feet rather than live on their knees. Exiled to the Soviet Union, she returned to Spain after Franco's death.

# November

### 1989

| Su | Mo | Tu | We | Th | Fr | Sa |
|----|----|----|----|----|----|----|
|    |    |    | 1  | 2  | 3  | 4  |
| 5  | 6  | 7  | 8  | 9  | 10 | 11 |
| 12 | 13 | 14 | 15 | 16 | 17 | 18 |
| 19 | 20 | 21 | 22 | 23 | 24 | 25 |
| 26 | 27 | 28 | 29 | 30 |    |    |

**19.** Prague: Some 20,000 people march on the third day of reformist protests (→20).

**19.** UK: More troops are put on standby in the ambulance dispute (→21).

**19.** UK: Some Sunday postal collections are revived.

**20.** Prague: Up to 200,000 demand the resignation of the communist leaders (→21).

**20.** E Berlin: Hundreds of thousands march in what has become a regular weekly rally for reform (→3/12).

**20.** UK: Wendy Henry is fired as editor of the *People*.

**21.** Czechoslovakia: Ladislas Adamec, the premier, meets the opposition, as marches go on across the country (→23).

**21.** UK: Ambulance crews start a nationwide ban on all but accidents and emergencies.

**22.** El Salvador: Rebels who took at least four US hostages end their siege of the Sheraton hotel in San Salvador (→29).

**22.** India: At least 26 people have died in pre-election clashes amid allegations of widespread ballot fraud (→27).

**22.** UK: The controversial bill to implement sweeping changes to the NHS is published.

**23.** Greece: A new national unity government is sworn in, led by Xenophon Zolotas.

**23.** Czechoslovakia: Alexander Dubcek addresses a rally in Bratislava, as more than 300,000 march in Prague.→

**23.** UK: Haemophiliacs infected with the Aids virus by NHS blood are promised an extra £19 million compensation.→

**24.** S Africa: People win the right to live in residential areas not segregated by race.

**24.** US: Thatcher says on US TV that she has changed her mind about standing down as leader after the next election.

**25.** Lebanon: Elias Hrawi, a Christian who supports Syria's role, is sworn in as president.

**DEATH**

**22.** C C Beck, British cartoonist (*8/6/10).

## Brave backbencher stands against PM

**Nov 23.** Margaret Thatcher is to face her first challenge to the leadership of the Conservative Party since she wrested it away from Edward Heath 14 years ago. The contest will be forced by Sir Anthony Meyer, a backbench MP of resolutely liberal views. He says he would be happy to withdraw in favour of a better-qualified candidate, but so far appears undeterred by either the derision of tabloid newspapers ("Sir Nobody") or pleas for party loyalty.

Only Tory MPs have a vote for party leader. Nobody doubts that Mrs Thatcher will win, but the number of votes against – and abstentions – will be interpreted as a sign of the prime minister's hold on the party (→5/12).

*Sir Anthony and his wife, Barbadee.*

## Massive bomb kills Lebanese president

**Nov 22.** Tortured Lebanon was plunged into chaos today when a bomb made of 550 pounds of TNT killed President Rene Moawad and 23 other people. The dead included Lebanese soldiers, Syrian troops, bodyguards, and more than a dozen civilian bystanders.

Moawad – president for less than three weeks – and other Lebanese leaders were travelling in a motorcade when the bomb, hidden in a shop window, was detonated by remote control. Moawad's Mercedes was blown in the air by the force of the explosion; his body was found among a tangle of limbs in the upturned limousine. As the country's prime minister, Selim el-Hoss, a survivor of the blast, started urgent talks to find a new president, suspicion fell on the Christian leader, Michel Aoun – who had denounced the dead president as a "stooge" only a few hours before the murder. Aoun denied involvement in the killing, which he described as a "loathsome crime".

Moawad's death is considered to be one of the worst disasters in Lebanon's recent bloody history. Whether the country can survive without partition between Moslems and Christians, or a slide into virtual anarchy, remains a matter of grave doubt (→25).

*Lebanese women express their grief for a dead president and a dying country.*

## Television cameras enter the Commons

**Nov 21.** Labour's Bob Cryer made a bit of history today when he opened the debate in the Commons on the Queen's Speech – in front of television cameras. Despite the reluctance of some MPs, who claim it will take the sting out of Commons debate, Britain's voters can now watch their members in action.

MPs are used to donning their best suits and frocks for the Queen's Speech, given earlier in the Lords (which has been on television for years). But today extra care went into tying ties, brushing hair and applying make-up. Although viewers are not allowed to see much more than a speaker's top half, parliament has entered a new era.

*The Labour benches on camera.*

## Controversial test tube bill published

**Nov 23.** The growing debate about research on human embryo cells looks set to become fiercer following the publication today of the government's Human Fertilization and Embryology Bill.

MPs will have a free vote on the bill, which has a choice of clauses either to ban or to permit research on fertilized cells. This would be up to a limit of 14 days, after which embryo cells become distinct.

Supporters of cell research say it is invaluable for treating infertility and genetic disorders. They are opposed by "pro-life" activists who claim life begins with fertilization.

# Prague in ecstasy as leadership quits

**Nov 24.** Czechoslovaks – massed in their tens of thousands to salute the triumphant return to Prague of Alexander Dubcek – erupted in joy tonight at the news that Milos Jakes, the Communist Party leader, and the entire ruling politburo had resigned. Embracing, weeping and cheering, crowds streamed through the Prague streets chanting "Dubcek! Dubcek!" and the name of the playwright Vaclav Havel, the leading opposition figure.

The resignations – accompanied by an admission of failure to bring about democratic reform – were announced after a special meeting of the Communist Party central committee. The hardline Jakes has been replaced by Karol Urbanek, the party leader of the Czech republic, who has no link with the 1968 Soviet-led invasion of the country.

Even before the changes became known, it was clear that support for the government had collapsed. The marches that began just a week ago have mushroomed into a huge popular movement affecting many cities, although centred on the capital. The crowds thronging Wenceslas Square have grown daily, as determination mounted to oust the repressive communist leadership. Addressing a crowd of 200,000 tonight, Dubcek – who has emerged from 20 years' obscurity, which began after the crushing of his 1968 Prague Spring – declared: "We have been too long in darkness. Once already we have been in the light, and we want it again." (→26).

*Crowds in Wenceslas Square hear of the success of their peaceful revolution.*

*Alexander Dubcek and Vaclav Havel join the toast to "a free Czechoslovakia!".*

## Mass tests planned to chart Aids virus

**Nov 24.** Rejecting fears that the government is not fully committed to fighting Aids, the junior health minister, Virginia Bottomley, today announced a new mass anonymous screening programme to measure the spread of HIV, the virus that causes the Aids disease.

Concern about the government's role has been prompted by some recent decisions. Last month Margaret Thatcher was reported to have vetoed a survey of the nation's sexual habits, while earlier this week the Health Education Authority (HEA) disbanded its Aids division. The HEA's chairman puzzlingly declared that this meant Aids would get more attention.

## Boat people riot at deportation threat

**Nov 25.** A report that the Hong Kong government was planning to charter ferries in order to repatriate Vietnamese boat people by force led to rioting and hunger strikes in the colony's detention camps today. A local newspaper claimed that officers were in London looking for ships with open space that could be divided into compartments for 100 people or more. At Sek Kong camp, stones, sharpened tent pegs and metal lances were used as hundreds of Vietnamese fought one other.

# Unbeaten All-Blacks trounce Barbarians

*The All-Blacks rise to the occasion.*

**Nov 25.** The New Zealand All-Blacks took their unbeaten run to 46 matches today when they beat the Barbarians at Twickenham by 21 points to 10. The Baa-Baas were not short of talent, as befits a team drawn from four home nations plus Australia, but their lack of preparation meant they were no match for the powerful and disciplined teamwork of the All-Blacks.

Yet the Barbarians led for a time, after a try was scored by Philip Matthews. Then three tries by the New Zealanders, all forced from short-range scrums, put the result beyond doubt.

# Europe pulls teeth of Social Charter

**Nov 20.** In response to Margaret Thatcher's unrelenting hostility to the European Commission's planned Social Charter, fresh proposals have been drawn up which drop the attempt to fix a minimum wage and accept that linking social security payments across EC nations would be impossible. The Charter, which is a declaration of the rights that all EC workers should have after 1992, is due to be signed at the Strasbourg summit next month. Mrs Thatcher regards it as "back-door socialism" and a threat to jobs (→9/12).

**Helen Sharman and Timothy Mace: the two finalists for the choice of first Briton in space.**

# November

## 1989

| Su | Mo | Tu | We | Th | Fr | Sa |
|----|----|----|----|----|----|----|
|    |    |    | 1  | 2  | 3  | 4  |
| 5  | 6  | 7  | 8  | 9  | 10 | 11 |
| 12 | 13 | 14 | 15 | 16 | 17 | 18 |
| 19 | 20 | 21 | 22 | 23 | 24 | 25 |
| 26 | 27 | 28 | 29 | 30 |    |    |

**26.** Czechoslovakia: The newly formed opposition group Civic Forum publishes a manifesto.→

**26.** USSR: Over 150,000 march for the legalization of the Ukrainian Catholic church.

**26.** S Africa: Calls mount for the prosecution of policemen allegedly implicated in a political assassinations squad.

**27.** Ethiopia: Fears of another disastrous famine are reported.

**27.** Colombia: A Boeing 727 explodes shortly after take-off from Bogota, killing 107.

**27.** Hungary: In the country's first referendum, Hungarians postpone voting for a president until after parliamentary polls.

**27.** Uruguay: In the first free elections since 1971, Luis Lacalle, the head of the Blanco party, is chosen as president.

**27.** UK: Sterling hits a three-year low against the mark.

**27.** UK: A Mori poll puts Labour support at 51 per cent, against 37 per cent for the Tories.

**27.** UK: Arsenal and Norwich are fined for a 21-player brawl at Highbury three weeks ago.

**27.** N Ireland: An IRA bomb destroys a commuter aircraft at Shorts company in Belfast.

**28.** Czechoslovakia: A new government acceptable to Civic Forum is promised (→4/12).

**28.** USSR: Restoration to Azerbaijan of powers over the disputed territory of Nagorny Karabakh angers Armenians.

**28.** UK: A National Audit Office report says the 1988 sale of Rover to British Aerospace shortchanged the taxpayer by up to £100 million.→

**29.** N Ireland: Two men are shot dead in a bar in Ardboe, a republican area.

**29.** El Salvador: Left-wing guerrillas launch an intensive new attack on San Salvador.

**30.** UK: Frank Warren, a boxing promoter, is seriously injured in a shooting attack.

**DEATH**

**30.** Alfred Herrhausen, West German banker (30/1/30).→

## Czechoslovakia halted by general strike

*Traffic in the capital grinds to a standstill during the two-hour strike.*

**Nov 27.** As the people of Czechoslovakia stopped work at noon today, church bells across the country tolled the death knell of communist rule. In Bratislava and Brno, Ostrava and Kosice, workers downed tools and took to the streets in a victory celebration. The two-hour general strike – planned a week ago by the opposition group Civic Forum as a gesture of defiance – had developed into a referendum on the communist power monopoly. There were few reports of people failing to heed the strike call.

In Prague, engulfed by a carnival atmosphere, workers headed for mass meetings in various parts of the city. Waving flags and jangling keys, they rang little bells in a symbolic warning to the communists that their time was up. The sacking this morning of more hardliners, among them Miroslav Stepan – the Prague party boss blamed for police brutality ten days ago – failed to weaken the strength of feeling.

The strike also ended Prague's 11 days of huge protest marches, which have proved such a potent force for change. However, Civic Forum said they would reconvene the demonstrations if their demands for urgent reform, including free elections, were not met. The prime minister, Ladislas Adamec, is due to meet opposition leaders for more talks tomorrow (→28).

## Deceit charges in sale of Rover row

**Nov 30.** In the House of Commons today, in response to Labour accusations of deliberate deception and cries of "rip-off", Margaret Thatcher defended last year's sale of Rover to British Aerospace.

The basis of the attack was a memorandum from the National Audit Office to the Commons public accounts committee – leaked to the *Guardian* – alleging that inducements totalling £38 million had been paid to British Aerospace to conclude the deal and that these had been concealed from the European Commission. The prime minister insisted the government had struck the best deal it could (→7/12).

## DIY chain defies law on Sunday trading

**Nov 26.** It was business as usual today for the B&Q chain of 170 do-it-yourself stores, which last week took its case for Sunday opening of shops to the European court. Five judges in Luxembourg ruled that British restrictions on Sunday opening did not necessarily breach European law. Stores such as B&Q want the Sunday trading laws to be eased; shopworkers' unions and religious groups are equally determined to report any illegal opening to the local authorities.

## Red Army Faction blows up West Germany's leading banker

**Nov 30.** Alfred Herrhausen, the head of West Germany's Deutsche Bank, died instantly today when a bomb blew his armour-plated Mercedes 30 yards along the road in Bad Homburg near Frankfurt. An elaborate detonator was found 150 yards from the car, and beneath it a note bearing the star of the Red Army Faction, the terrorist group founded by Andreas Baader and Ulrike Meinhof in the late 1960s. Police believe the bomb was attached to a bicycle by the roadside.

Herrhausen, aged 59, controlled the most powerful commercial bank in Europe and would have been involved at a high level in West German plans to rebuild the East German economy.

*The crumpled wreck of Herrhausen's armour-plated Mercedes blocks the road.*

# Peer wins £1.5 million for Cossack libel

*Tolstoy: now faces massive payout.*

**Nov 30.** An audible gasp went up in court today when the foreman of the jury announced the amount of damages to be awarded to Lord Aldington in a libel case concerning the repatriation of Cossacks during the Second World War: "One point five million pounds."

Lord Aldington, 75 years old and a former deputy chairman of the Conservative Party, smiled – while the wife of the defendant, Count Nikolai Tolstoy, and his daughter began to cry silently.

The case arose when Tolstoy and his co-defendant, Nigel Watts, a former small businessman, circulated a pamphlet to MPs, peers and Lord Aldington's neighbours, describing him as "a man with the blood of 70,000 men, women and children on his hands" for ordering the repatriation of Yugoslavs and Cossacks after the war, knowing that it would mean their death.

Both defendants, who plan to appeal, face financial ruin as a result of the award, which is three times as high as the previous record. Mr Watts was not in court, having stormed out yesterday, calling the judge a disgrace to British justice.

# Rebel troops attempt coup in Philippines

**Nov 30.** President Corazon Aquino clings to power tonight, after loyal troops apparently fought off the third attempt to overthrow her since she took power in the Philippines in 1986. Rebel army elements attacked Manila's presidential palace at 6.45 this morning, and captured parts of three military bases.

Fighting was also reported near the state broadcasting centre and Manila airport was forced to shut down. Mrs Aquino said the country would not "fall into the hands of tyrants". The leader of the rebels is thought to be the outlawed Colonel Gregorio "Gringo" Honasan, who led an earlier coup attempt (→7/12).

# Bums and knickers convulse Britons

Such unlovable cartoon characters as Fat Slags, Milie Tant and Buster Gonad are set to rival the popularity of old faithfuls from *Beano* and *Dandy* this Christmas when, in its tenth year of publication, the comic *Viz* hits an expected one million sales.

*Viz*, a bi-monthly favouring jokes about farting, vomiting and toilets, is a huge success story. Until 18 months ago the editor, Chris Donald, laid it out in the bedroom of his Newcastle-upon-Tyne home with the help of six others. The first issue cost £60 to produce and sold 150 copies; by 1983 sales had risen to 5,000, reaching 40,000 in 1987.

*"Britain's crappiest magazine."*

# Gandhi gets thumbs-down from voters

*In the shadow of his mother, Rajiv Gandhi addresses a rally in New Delhi.*

**Nov 27.** The foundations of the dynasty which has governed India for most of the 42 years since independence seem decidedly shaky tonight, as Rajiv Gandhi, the prime minister, faces defeat in the general election which ended last Sunday.

Gandhi's Congress Party looks likely to win around 200 of the 545 seats in the *Lok Sabha*, India's lower house, compared with the 415 it won five years ago after the assassination of Rajiv's mother, Indira Gandhi. Although this will still leave Congress as the largest party, it will be about 70 seats short of an absolute majority, and none of the main opposition parties is likely to lift a finger to help Rajiv Gandhi.

He has been heavily criticized for his style of leadership – opponents claim he listens only to a clique of cronies – and for his alleged involvement in the Bofors scandal. This concerned huge "incentives" paid by the Swedish weapons maker Bofors to Indian politicians to further its arms sales to India.

A new minority government could be formed by the National Front, an opposition coalition led by Janata Dal, the party which held power from 1977-80. The Front is expected to win about 150 seats and would need support from Hindu fundamentalists, a shock arrival on the political scene (80 seats), and the communists (50 seats) (→2/12).

# Olympic gymnast Nadia flees Romania

**Nov 29.** The top Romanian gymnast Nadia Comaneci, who won the hearts of millions in 1976, somersaulting from one gold medal to the next at the Montreal Olympics, crossed the border into Hungary last night and asked for political asylum. Unconfirmed reports say that she is now heading for Austria.

By the time she retired in 1984, Comaneci had won 21 gold medals. Her defection is a severe embarrassment to Romania's hardline president, Nicolae Ceausescu, who received her personally after her sporting successes. Comaneci told border officials in Hungary that she had abandoned a flat, a car and financial security in her search for freedom (→1/12).

*Comaneci at the height of her fame.*

# December

## 1989

| Su | Mo | Tu | We | Th | Fr | Sa |
|----|----|----|----|----|----|----|
|    |    |    |    |    | 1  | 2  |
| 3  | 4  | 5  | 6  | 7  | 8  | 9  |
| 10 | 11 | 12 | 13 | 14 | 15 | 16 |
| 17 | 18 | 19 | 20 | 21 | 22 | 23 |
| 24 | 25 | 26 | 27 | 28 | 29 | 30 |
| 31 |    |    |    |    |    |    |

**1.** Rome: Mikhail Gorbachev and Pope John Paul II end 70 years of hostility between the Soviet Union and the Vatican. →

**1.** E Germany: The Communist Party votes to end its monopoly of power (→3).

**1.** US: Nadia Comaneci, the fugitive Romanian gymnast, arrives in New York.

**2.** Malta: Bush invites Gorbachev to a summit meeting in the US next year. →

**3.** E Germany: Egon Krenz is stripped of his powers as Communist Party leader. →

**3.** India: About 800 people are arrested during a protest to mark the fifth anniversary of the Bhopal disaster.

**4.** Prague: Outraged by a limited government reshuffle, tens of thousands again rally to call for further reform. →

**4.** USSR: Moscow officially denounces the 1968 Soviet-led invasion of Czechoslovakia.

**5.** UK: Plans are announced to transfer management of the Atomic Weapons Establishment to private contractors.

**6.** Colombia: At least 40 people are killed by a bomb at Bogota's security police HQ.

**7.** UK: The Courts and Legal Services Bill sets out radical procedural changes, including an end to barristers' monopoly rights in higher courts.

**8.** E Germany: Criminal proceedings start against Erich Honecker and five other members of the old guard.

**8.** UK: Frank Field is de-selected as Labour MP for Birkenhead; trade union votes were decisive in the ballot.

**8.** UK: Government tests find a third of microwave ovens fail to destroy poisonous bacteria.

**9.** USSR: Gorbachev rules out an early move to drop the Communist Party's constitutional "leading role" (→13).

**9.** UK: The water sell-off is 5.7 times subscribed (→12).

### DEATH

**4.** Lord (Frederick) Elwyn-Jones, former British lord chancellor (*24/10/09).

## Britain makes lone stand at Strasbourg

**Dec 9.** On the opening day of the European Community summit in Strasbourg yesterday, Margaret Thatcher made a lone stand on monetary policy and the proposed Social Charter. EC leaders voted by 11-1, with Britain dissenting, for a conference next year to negotiate amendments to the Treaty of Rome for economic and monetary union. By the same margin, they approved the Community Social Charter guaranteeing basic workers' rights.

However, Mrs Thatcher avoided outright confrontation with the other leaders and said today it was "absolute nonsense" to claim Britain was isolated. This followed agreement on a formula for German reunification, proposed by Helmut Kohl, the West German chancellor. The summit endorsed the right of the German people to "regain unity through free self-determination", while respecting existing borders. All 12 leaders approved the setting-up of a Bank of Europe to help Eastern Europe's transition to a market economy.

Adopting a conciliatory tone, Mrs Thatcher insisted that Britain would continue to play a full role in the Community despite differences on a number of issues.

## V P Singh becomes premier of India

**Dec 2.** In what may mark the end of the supremacy in India of the Nehru dynasty – in almost continual power since independence in 1947 – V P Singh today replaced Rajiv Gandhi as prime minister. Although Gandhi's Congress party remains the largest single group in parliament, Singh, the leader of the Janata Dal party, took office with the support of mutually hostile right- and left-wing allies. His rule is threatened by the same fate as Moraji Desai's Janata government in the 1970s – disintegration.

## Rebel soldiers abandon bid to topple Aquino regime

**Dec 7.** Four hundred rebel troops gave up their siege of Manila's business centre today and marched defiantly back to barracks. Shouting "No surrender!", they were greeted by a "Welcome Home" banner and embraces from their colleagues. As far as the capital is concerned, the week-long Philippines revolt is over, although rebels at an airbase in Cebu are still holding out.

This sixth coup attempt against President Corazon Aquino since she came to power in 1986 has cost almost 100 dead and 500 wounded. About 1,200 foreigners were trapped in four central hotels for five days. Although Aquino claimed early on to have contained the revolt, and was later granted US air support, fierce fighting continued for several days.

*Troops loyal to President Aquino fire on rebel positions from a footbridge.*

## Young pop stars give voice to new Ethiopian famine appeal

*New stars sing "Feed the world": the Bros twins embrace Kylie and Jason.*

**Dec 3.** As fears mount of another disastrous famine in Ethiopia, a group of young pop stars gathered today to remake the 1984 Band Aid fund-raising single "Do they know it's Christmas". Bob Geldof, the power behind the original hit record, declined to join in, saying: "It's another generation's thing." The enthusiastic stars who have taken over include Kylie Minogue, Jason Donovan, Bros, Chris Rea, Tears for Fears, Bananarama and Wet Wet Wet. When Kylie, Jason and Bros began an impromptu street performance the police were called to restrain screaming fans.

# Thatcher victorious in leadership fight

**Dec 5.** Despite failing to secure the support of 60 Tory MPs in the ballot for the party leadership – her first contest in 14 years – Margaret Thatcher emerged today with a decisive victory. The prime minister said afterwards she was pleased to have received "this splendid answer". The result was: 314 votes for Thatcher, 33 for the challenger, Sir Anthony Meyer, 24 spoilt papers and three non-votes. Michael Heseltine, the former cabinet minister, was among those reported not to have voted.

# Gunman kills 14 women in Montreal

**Dec 7.** Fourteen women students at the University of Montreal were massacred today by a gunman in his mid-twenties. The man rushed into the university cafeteria and opened fire, yelling: "You're all a bunch of feminists." He continued his rampage through classrooms and hallways before shooting himself dead. He was carrying a three-page denunciation blaming his failures in life on women.

# Rover row worsens

**Dec 7.** Anger over the 1988 sale of Rover to British Aerospace (BAe) grew today when it came out that Lord Young, then trade secretary, asked BAe to choose how to hide from parliament and the European Commission the "sweeteners" of £38 million paid to smooth the sale. Labour called it "calculated deception"; Tories insisted the deal was in the taxpayers' best interests.

# Major TV shake-up

**Dec 7.** A new bill presages the most radical British broadcasting shake-up since ITV came on the air in 1955. It is meant to open the market to smaller companies and boost variety, but there are fears quality may suffer. A regional Channel 3 will replace ITV and franchises sold to the highest bidder. A new Channel 5 will also be put out to tender.

# Superpowers declare end of Cold War

**Dec 3.** At the end of their shipboard summit off Malta – transformed into near-farce by tempestuous weather – Mikhail Gorbachev and George Bush hailed the start of a new era in superpower relations. They envisaged wide new arms cuts and a chance for Moscow to play a full role in the world economy. According to Gennady Gerasimov, the Soviet spokesman, the Cold War finished at 12.45pm today – 11.45am British time. Later Bush gave the thumbs-up sign to a reporter who asked if he agreed.

The US and Soviet leaders detailed plans to sign two arms control pacts in June next year. One would halve strategic nuclear weapons; the other would reduce conventional forces in Europe. There is also hope for accord on chemical weapon destruction. They remained split on naval forces and the Soviet supply of arms to Nicaragua.

Bush promised to end curbs on US-Soviet trade once the Soviet Union opened its borders. He also

*After a stormy but amicable summit, Bush and Gorbachev speak to the press.*

proposed observer status for Moscow in the General Agreement on Tariffs and Trade (Gatt), the body that regulates international trade.

Although the revolution in Eastern Europe pervaded the talks, the two leaders strove to avoid public

comments that could be interpreted as outside interference.

On his way to Malta, Gorbachev visited Pope John Paul II in Rome. It was the first meeting between a communist leader and a pope since the 1917 Bolshevik revolution.

# Communist rule totters in East Germany and Czechoslovakia

## Egon Krenz ousted

**Dec 6.** Amid a rising tide of fury at revelations of gross corruption and abuse of office by the country's former leaders, Egon Krenz was ousted today as East Germany's head of state. The resignation comes just six weeks after Krenz replaced Erich Honecker, and three days after he lost his post as Communist Party chief. Manfred Gerlach, the leader of the Liberal Democratic Party, has taken over as acting head of state.

Krenz – long seen as the heir to Honecker – succeeded his boss after the mass exodus of East Germans from the country and a wave of huge protest marches. He made great efforts to meet demands for reform, opening the Berlin Wall and promising to hold free, multi-party elections. But, as the truth about the previous leaders began to come out, he could not deny his links with financial corruption on a grand scale or take back his public support for the Chinese massacre in Tiananmen Square (→8).

*Krenz: linked with gross corruption.*

*Adamec: accused of lying to public.*

## Adamec bows out

**Dec 7.** The political uncertainty in Czechoslovakia deepened tonight with the resignation of Ladislas Adamec as prime minister and his replacement by another communist, Marian Calfa. A government spokesman said Adamec decided to quit because of "unacceptable demands" from the opposition group Civic Forum. The Forum reacted angrily, accusing Adamec of lying about his negotiations with them.

The writing is on the wall for President Gustav Husak, who was involved in the 1968 Warsaw Pact invasion of the country. Civic Forum said that, if Calfa were to remain in office, the president would have to be a non-communist. The obvious contender is Vaclav Havel, the Forum leader and the most popular man in the country. Havel said he was willing but reluctant to be president: "If, God help us, the situation develops in such a way that the only service I could render my country would be to do this, then of course I would do it." (→10).

# December

## 1989

| Su | Mo | Tu | We | Th | Fr | Sa |
|----|----|----|----|----|----|----|
|    |    |    |    |    | 1  | 2  |
| 3  | 4  | 5  | 6  | 7  | 8  | 9  |
| 10 | 11 | 12 | 13 | 14 | 15 | 16 |
| 17 | 18 | 19 | 20 | 21 | 22 | 23 |
| 24 | 25 | 26 | 27 | 28 | 29 | 30 |
| 31 |    |    |    |    |    |    |

**10.** Bulgaria: Over 50,000 rally in Sofia to demand the abolition of the Communist Party's leading role. →

**10.** E Germany: Gregor Gysi, the new party leader, is challenged by anti-communist rallies in eight cities (→14).

**10.** UK: It is revealed that a burglary took place at the Treasury last weekend.

**11.** UK: A £110 million package is announced to raise by £40 a week the pensions of war widows whose husbands were killed before 1973.

**11.** UK: Manchester airport is halted by a baggage handlers' strike.

**12.** W Germany: The creation of an embryonic European central bank is announced.

**12.** UK: MPs vote for the prosecution of alleged Nazi war criminals living in Britain.

**13.** S Africa: Nelson Mandela meets President F W de Klerk for the first time.

**13.** N Ireland: Two soldiers are killed in an IRA attack at a border checkpoint.

**13.** UK: The game of rugby union abandons its commitment to pure amateurism.

**14.** UK: Plans are announced for 300 miles of no-stopping freeways in Greater London.

**14.** E Germany: It is announced that the secret police are to be disbanded.

**14.** UK: A ban on the film *Visions of Ecstasy* for blasphemy is upheld.

**15.** US: A warning is issued of a new terrorist threat in West Africa or Western Europe.

**15.** Colombia: Police kill Gonzalo Gacha, a leader of the Medellin cocaine cartel.

**15.** Panama: War is declared on the US (→16).

**15.** UK: Inflation rises from 7.3 per cent to 7.7 per cent.

**16.** Panama: A US soldier is shot dead (→20).

**DEATH**

**14.** Andrei Sakharov, Soviet physicist and politician (*21/5/21). →

# Boat people sent home

*Tears of grief and fear from Vietnamese boat people about to be deported.*

**Dec 13.** At dawn on Tuesday a Cathay Pacific Tristar jet carrying 51 Vietnamese boat people touched down at Hanoi airport. The 25 adults and 26 children on board were the first to be returned from the British colony of Hong Kong under a mandatory repatriation scheme for Vietnamese not considered to be genuine refugees.

The Hong Kong government insisted that no force was used, but the clandestine, early morning round-up and deportation of boat people by 150 police in full riot gear has sparked opposition fury in Britain and an international outcry. A US senator compared it to the Allied repatriation of Cossacks to the Soviet Union at the end of the Second World War.

Although the operation has now been temporarily suspended, Hong Kong said it planned eventually to send home all 44,000 Vietnamese deemed not to be refugees. More than 6,000 boat people in three refugee camps today held peaceful

*A symbolic service for the deportees.*

protests against the return of their 51 compatriots to Vietnam. They marched around their camps chanting slogans and carrying banners that said they would rather die in Hong Kong than be sent home.

## Women tube travellers sprayed with acid

**Dec 13.** Six women travellers on the London tube have suffered acute leg burns after being sprayed with acid by a fellow passenger. All the attacks took place at Oxford Circus or Tottenham Court Road stations within the last two days. Transport police have issued a warning to all female passengers, adding that most of the victims were young blondes. The first the women knew of the assault was a burning sensation; all required hospital treatment. Police – who do not even know the sex of the attacker – are in contact with forces in Devon and Cornwall, where similar attacks occurred last weekend.

## Unions reject offer of ambulance truce

**Dec 15.** Further disruption to the ambulance service over Christmas looked certain last night after the breakdown of the latest talks to settle the ambulance workers' three-month-old pay dispute. Duncan Nichol, the chief executive of the NHS, offered to suspend hostilities over the holiday, but Roger Poole, the unions' chief negotiator, said: "We don't want a Christmas truce; we want a settlement." Ambulance crews are seeking an increase on the basic 6.5 per cent pay offer. A petition signed by 4.5 million people in support of the crews was presented to the Commons today.

## Flu epidemic forces hospital red alert

**Dec 11.** As Britain sweats out its worst flu epidemic for 14 years, red alerts – cancelling all routine admissions to hospitals – have been declared by about 20 health authorities. The increasing pressure on hospital beds has been exacerbated by the number of doctors and nurses themselves ill with the virus.

This week the estimate of people infected is up by 24 per cent on last week. Flu vaccine is being flown in from Europe, but is still in such short supply in Britain that only the elderly or those with chest and heart complaints are being advised to have the vaccination.

**Leona Helmsley, New York hotel queen, gets four years in jail and a $7 million fine for tax fraud.**

# Czechoslovaks end communist control

**Dec 10.** More than four decades of communist rule ended in Czechoslovakia today when Gustav Husak swore in the first majority non-communist government since 1948 and at once resigned as president of the country he ruled with an iron fist for 21 years.

Vaclav Havel, the playwright and leader of the main opposition group, Civic Forum, broke the news to an elated crowd of more than 300,000 in Prague's Wenceslas Square. He hailed the achievement of "a peaceful revolution" and read out the names of the new government, whose first task will be to prepare for free elections next year. Civic Forum declared it was backing Havel for president; Alexander Dubcek, who led the 1968 Prague Spring, seems unlikely to run.

# Chile bids farewell to long dictatorship

**Dec 14.** Euphoria swept Santiago, the capital of Chile, today when it became clear that the opposition candidate, Patricio Aylwin, had been elected president with 52.4 per cent of the vote. His election brings to an end the 16-year dictatorship of Augusto Pinochet, who ousted Salvador Allende in a 1973 coup. "We can feel the joy, the happiness of the people. Yet this frightens me," said a Catholic lay worker and local resident. "The day after the election they will think there will be solutions to all our problems."

*President Aylwin: Chile's saviour?*

# Sakharov, symbol of the Soviet soul, dies

*Sakharov: "perestroika started with Sakharov" one Muscovite said today.*

**Dec 14.** Andrei Sakharov, the 68-year-old Soviet nuclear physicist and radical, died tonight at his home in Moscow. When his wife, Elena Bonner, went to wake him from a nap at 10.30pm she found him dead on the floor of his study from a heart attack.

Since 1975, when he won the Nobel peace prize, Sakharov's name has been associated with the fight for human rights by millions around the world. From a top nuclear physicist, who began campaigning for a ban on nuclear test-ing as early as 1955, he had become a dissident with a lowly academic job. In 1980 he was sent into internal exile in Gorky, where he lived until 1986, when a telephone call from Mikhail Gorbachev summoned him back to Moscow.

In 1989 he was elected to the Congress of the People's Deputies, and emerged as unofficial spokesman for the opposition. An ardent believer in a multi-party system, he said to one of his friends shortly before his death: "There'll be a hard fight tomorrow."

# Gorbachev makes shock offer to quit

**Dec 13.** Mikhail Gorbachev threatened to resign during a fierce row at last weekend's plenary meeting of the Communist Party's central committee, it was claimed in Moscow today. Regional party chiefs led the attack, according to an article in today's issue of *Moscow News*. They fear the pace of reforms is too fast and some accuse him of selling out to the West. Yet Gorbachev is this week encountering demands from progressives for an end to one-party communist rule. So far the Soviet president has warded off both attacks, but regional unrest and economic woes still threaten his hold on power.

# Water buyers profit

**Dec 12.** Water shares achieved premiums of up to 68 per cent in hectic first dealings on the Stock Exchange, with more than 15 per cent of shares in the £5.24 billion privatization changing hands. But few small investors were able to benefit from the scramble because they had not yet received their share certificates from last Friday's sale. Despite fears for its success, the offer was subscribed 5.7 times.

# Bulgarians pledge to destroy communist monopoly of power

**Dec 16.** Six weeks after the fall of Todor Zhivkov, the hardline leader, Bulgaria's national assembly has conceded early talks with the opposition and approved reforms to end the Communist Party's political monopoly in the new year. It also agreed to liberalize laws on public gatherings, amend the penal code and grant an amnesty.

Today's moves bring the country into line with other reforming East European states. They come in the wake of mounting popular demonstrations, which culminated yesterday in a siege of the parliament in Sofia by 50,000 marchers. Petar Mladenov, the new Bulgarian leader, made an appeal for calm on the steps of the building, to be greeted with shouts of "Resign!". Shortly after parliament passed today's reform package, demonstrators again packed the streets of Sofia.

*Snowflakes settle on a massive crowd of anti-Stalinist protesters in Sofia.*

# December

## 1989

| Su | Mo | Tu | We | Th | Fr | Sa |
|----|----|----|----|----|----|----|
|    |    |    |    |    | 1  | 2  |
| 3  | 4  | 5  | 6  | 7  | 8  | 9  |
| 10 | 11 | 12 | 13 | 14 | 15 | 16 |
| 17 | 18 | 19 | 20 | 21 | 22 | 23 |
| 24 | 25 | 26 | 27 | 28 | 29 | 30 |
| 31 |    |    |    |    |    |    |

**17. Romania:** Up to 2,000 anti-government protesters are reported massacred in the city of Timisoara (→20).

**17. Prague:** Tens of thousands march in support of Vaclav Havel's presidential candidacy.

**17. UK:** The Labour Party renounces the closed shop as an instrument of trade union power.

**18. Brussels:** The European Community signs a ten-year trade pact with the Soviet Union.

**19. Brazil:** Fernando Collor de Mello is elected president.

**19. UK:** The government pledges £150 million compensation to people who lost money by investment in the Barlow Clowes company.

**20. Romania:** Troops surrender to demonstrators in Timisoara, where up to 4,000 are reported killed; Ceausescu appears on TV to condemn the unrest (→21).

**20. USSR:** The Lithuanian Communist Party votes to break away from the full Soviet Communist Party.

**20. UK:** High street banks pull out of the government's scheme for student loans.

**20. UK:** The Environmental Protection Bill is published.

**21. Romania:** Bloody street fighting rages in Bucharest after a Ceausescu rally erupts into a protest demonstration.→

**22. Panama:** Troops loyal to Noriega bombard the US headquarters in Panama City (→23).

**23. Romania:** The army announces the capture of Ceausescu and his wife; 13,000 lives are believed to have been lost in the past week (→26).

**23. Panama:** Two thousand more US troops arrive to reinforce the 23,000 already in the country.

### DEATHS

**19.** Stella Gibbons, British writer (*5/1/02).

**19.** John Heddle, Conservative MP (*15/9/41).

**22.** Samuel Beckett, Irish writer (*13/4/06) (→26).

# Bush orders US invasion of Panama

In full camouflage: invading American troops on the move in Panama.

America's quarry: Manuel Noriega.

**Dec 21.** American troops have invaded Panama, ousted the dictator president Manuel Noriega, and installed a new government headed by Guillermo Endara. Panama City has become a battleground, with US troops claiming almost complete control of the capital. About 200 civilians, 19 American and 59 Panamanian soldiers are believed killed in the fighting.

Yesterday, President Bush explained that a series of attacks by Noriega's paramilitary "dignity battalions", culminating in the murder of an American soldier, triggered his decision to order the invasion. "General Noriega's reckless threats and attacks ... created an imminent danger to Americans in Panama," he said. So far, Congress, and US public opinion, has backed his decision.

The US army swept through the streets of Panama City today, mopping up pockets of resistance and continuing the search for Noriega. President Bush wants him to stand trial in the US on drug trafficking charges, and has offered a $1 million (£660,000) reward for information leading to his capture.

The failure to net Noriega is proving an embarrassment. It is thought that he is still in Panama City, possibly taking refuge in the Cuban or Nicaraguan embassies. If he is not found soon, the US faces the prospect of a prolonged urban guerrilla war. And with up to a dozen US citizens believed held hostage, the struggle is far from over (→22).

Dec 22. Thousands of East and West Germans gather, despite the rain, to celebrate Christmas and the opening of Berlin's Brandenburg Gate by their leaders, Hans Modrow and Helmut Kohl.

## Tories split over Hong Kong policy

**Dec 22.** Government plans to admit up to 225,000 Hong Kong citizens to Britain were today attacked as "folly" by Norman Tebbit, a former Conservative Party chairman. Mr Tebbit believes as many as 50 Tory MPs will vote against the plan for what he called a "vast wave of immigrants". This could scupper the government's majority as Labour is also opposed to the plan, on the grounds that it is elitist to promise UK passports only to key political and business leaders.

However, although ministers were split over the numbers to be admitted, Douglas Hurd, the foreign secretary, says the move is essential to "anchor" key people in Hong Kong during the years up to 1997, when control of the colony passes to China.

## Huge arms cache uncovered in Wales

**Dec 21.** Two Irishmen were arrested on anti-terrorist charges tonight when they went to check an arms cache in its hiding place on a lonely cliff-top in Dyfed, Wales. The arrest follows round-the-clock police surveillance of the arms dump, discovered some seven weeks ago but left undisturbed in order to trap any claimants.

Police believe that the detonators, firearms and 100 pounds of Semtex plastic explosive were intended to be used by an IRA cell for a bomb attack on the British mainland over the Christmas period. The arrested men will be questioned about recent IRA activities, including the murder of ten Royal Marine bandsmen at Deal in September. Today's operation marks the fourth Semtex find this year.

# Ceausescu overthrown amid Romanian bloodbath

**Dec 22.** Nicolae Ceausescu fled for his life today as civil war ended his 24 years of increasingly tyrannical rule as president of Romania. But there is no end to the blood-letting: secret police (*Securitate*) forces are tonight in combat with the Romanian army, whose support for the protesters was crucial in toppling Ceausescu. Soviet television reported: "As darkness fell, forces loyal to Ceausescu tore into the capital. Violent battles have broken out. Participants in mass meetings were fired on by machine-guns. There are hundreds of dead and injured."

Tanks have also been deployed as the anti-Ceausescu forces defended the television and radio stations. Throughout the day the television station had broadcast live coverage of what has become a revolution. Dissidents, generals and politicians were seen announcing Ceausescu's flight and the formation of a Committee for National Salvation.

For much of the day the mood in the studio and outside on the streets was euphoric. Within a week what had began as a protest by a few hundred people in Timisoara against the threatened arrest of a priest, Laszlo Tokes, had toppled the most feared and dictatorial regime in Eastern Europe.

Only yesterday Ceausescu was speaking from the balcony of the presidential palace, seeking to rally support and blaming "foreign imperialists" for the violence which grew out of the Timisoara protests. It was stage-managed, but a shaken president was greeted by cat-calls and the rally ended with police using tear-gas to disperse the crowd.

Today, 24 hours later, Ceausescu and his wife, Elena, were plucked from the rooftop of their burning palace by helicopter. Tonight their whereabouts is uncertain, but they are believed to be alive.

How many people have died in the last seven days is not known. However, a mass grave containing 4,630 bodies has been discovered in Timisoara and there has been bloodshed in other Romanian cities. Whatever the final figure, it seems certain more people have died here than in any other European conflict since the end of the Second World War. And it is not over yet (→ 23).

*Romanian army tanks in the embattled city of Bucharest come under fire from Securitate forces still loyal to Ceausescu.*

*Ceausescu and his wife, Elena, attempt to rally support in Bucharest yesterday.*

## Romania freed from tyrannical dynasty

The Ceausescu dynasty's rule was more total than that of any other communist regime since Stalin. The official personality cult of Ceausescu and his wife, Elena – seen as the real power in Romania in recent years – embraced their whole family, over 40 members of whom held positions of power. They were kept in place by a propaganda machine which masked the sinister violence of the all-pervasive secret police, the *Securitate*. In a country where food, clothing and energy shortages are the worst in Europe, Ceausescu's most controversial policy involved replacing 7,000 villages with "agro-industrial complexes". He attempted to rebuild Bucharest in his own image, destroying its beauty. His adoption of an independent line from Moscow helped Romania's dealings with the West in earlier years.

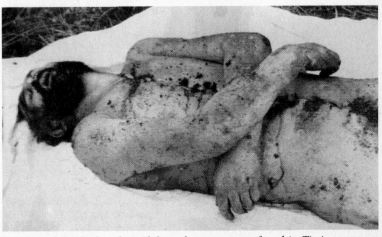

*A bullet-riddled body exhumed from the mass grave found in Timisoara.*

# December

## 1989

| Su | Mo | Tu | We | Th | Fr | Sa |
|----|----|----|----|----|----|----|
|    |    |    |    |    | 1  | 2  |
| 3  | 4  | 5  | 6  | 7  | 8  | 9  |
| 10 | 11 | 12 | 13 | 14 | 15 | 16 |
| 17 | 18 | 19 | 20 | 21 | 22 | 23 |
| 24 | 25 | 26 | 27 | 28 | 29 | 30 |
| 31 |    |    |    |    |    |    |

**24.** Panama: Manuel Noriega, the deposed leader, gives himself up to the papal nuncio in Panama City (→25).

**25.** USSR: Gorbachev attacks Lithuania's decision to break with the full Soviet Communist Party as "illegitimate" (→28).

**25.** Cuba: The government offers sanctuary to Noriega.→

**26.** Romania: A videotape of Ceausescu's trial and bullet-riddled body is shown on TV (→27).

**26.** UK: Desert Orchid wins his third King George VI Chase at Kempton Park.

**27.** Romania: The newly formed National Salvation Front pledges that Romania will abandon communism.→

**27.** Panama: Nine of Noriega's closest associates emerge from the Vatican mission and give themselves up to US troops (→29).

**27.** Egypt: Full diplomatic relations are resumed with Syria after a ten-year break.

**27.** UK: David Owen, the SDP leader, predicts another ten years of Tory rule.

**28.** Czechoslovakia: Alexander Dubcek is elected chairman of the communist-dominated parliament (→29).

**28.** USSR: Latvia votes to abolish the Communist Party's leading role.

**29.** Czechoslovakia: Vaclav Havel is elected president.

**29.** Hong Kong: Thousands of Vietnamese boat people fight with riot police.

**29.** Panama: US troops storm the Nicaraguan ambassador's residence (→30).

**30.** Nicaragua: Twenty US diplomats are expelled.

**31.** Israel: The ruling coalition is in a crisis after Ezer Weizman, a Labour Party minister, is threatened with the sack over PLO contacts.

### DEATHS

**25.** Nicolae Ceausescu, leader of Romania (*26/1/18).→

**26.** Sir Lennox Berkeley, British composer (*12/5/03).

# Ceausescu executed by firing squad

**Dec 31.** Church bells in Romania are tonight ringing out an old year which was scarcely imaginable even two weeks ago.

Out went the dictator Nicolae Ceausescu and his wife Elena: executed on Christmas Day by firing squad after being found guilty by a military tribunal of "crimes against the people" including genocide leading to an alleged 60,000 deaths.

Out went the hated *Securitate* secret police: defeated by the Romanian army after a week of bloody street-fighting although the country's new rulers still live in secret addresses under armed guard for fear of vengeful reprisals.

Out went the Communist Party: formally abolished yesterday as the ruling National Salvation Front laid plans for free elections in April 1990, although it sought to reassure Moscow by announcing that it had no plans to leave the Warsaw Pact.

Mikhail Gorbachev, the Soviet president, responded sympathetically to the birth of the new regime. In a new year message he today pledged Russia's support for Romania – and all East European countries – in their efforts to sustain "socialism with democracy".

Romania's coalition government faces daunting challenges of food shortages and a crippled economy. Yet for all except those who lost loved ones, Romania tonight greets 1990 as a truly happy new year.

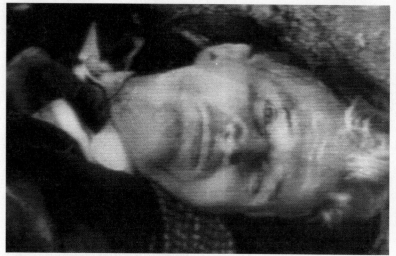

*As seen on Romanian television: Ceausescu after execution by firing squad.*

*A young man waves the Romanian flag, the symbol of communism cut out.*

## Honours list headed by Lockerbie awards

**Dec 30.** The New Year's Honours List salutes the courage of 22 people involved in the traumatic aftermath of the Lockerbie disaster, whose first anniversary was commemorated last week. As well as police officers and several Lockerbie inhabitants, among those honoured are members of the emergency services who coped after Pan Am Flight 103 crashed on to the Scottish town, killing 270 people.

Elsewhere on the list, the former Liberal leader David Steel and the author V S Naipaul are awarded knighthoods, and the actress Maggie Smith becomes a dame. Recipients of sporting honours include the golfer Tony Jacklin and the boxer Frank Bruno.

*Frank Bruno MBE, in the new role of genie, kisses the magic lamp.*

## First fatal quake in Australia kills 11

**Dec 28.** At least 11 people were killed and more than 100 injured in Australia today when an earthquake measuring 5.5 on the Richter scale hit New South Wales, felling many buildings and causing damage worth hundreds of millions of dollars. The quake's epicentre was just west of the coalmining centre of Newcastle, about 100 miles north of Sydney, which took the brunt of the tremors. Most of those who died were in the three-storey Newcastle Workers' Club, which collapsed when the quake struck at about 10.30 am. The deaths were the first recorded fatalities from an earthquake in Australia's history.

# Noriega holes up in Vatican embassy

**Dec 26.** General Manuel Noriega has slipped through the fingers of his American would-be captors and taken refuge in the papal nunciature in Panama City. The Vatican has refused to hand him over, and is believed to be negotiating a haven overseas, possibly in Cuba, for the fugitive dictator.

General Maxwell Thurman – known to his troops as "Mad Max" – has ordered the nunciature compound to be surrounded. President Bush is determined to prise Noriega out. But the rumour is that the CIA (with which Noriega used to have strong connections) is trying to orchestrate his escape in order to prevent it coming under public scrutiny at the general's trial (→27).

# Beckett's wait ends

*Samuel Beckett: creator of Godot.*

**Dec 26.** Samuel Beckett, the Nobel prize-winning Irish writer, died on Friday in Paris, only five months after the death of Suzanne, his companion for 50 years. They were fellow Resistance workers who narrowly escaped the Gestapo. She arranged the first staging of *Waiting For Godot* in Paris in 1953. For many, Beckett was the greatest, most innovative living dramatist. *Godot*, in which two clowns wait with patient fortitude for nothing, moved drama away from imitation of life towards music. It was deeply moving without any "message". After *Endgame* and *Happy Days* his plays grew ever shorter. Beckett was shy, witty and keen on cricket.

# Arts: new life for old ballets and rockers

*Darcey Bussell and Jonathan Cope in "The Prince of the Pagodas".*

A "new" ballet from **Benjamin Britten** and **Kenneth Macmillan** should have been the highlight for the Royal Ballet, but *The Prince of the Pagodas*, composed in 1957 and dropped as unsatisfactory, disappointed critics, despite the brilliance of the young dancers, **Darcey Bussell** and **Tutsuyu Kumaka**. *Hobson's Choice*, a new comedy based on the Harold Brighouse play, is set to give the Sadlers Wells Royal Ballet a more lasting hit.

Opera relied on spectacular effects: Michael Tippett, 85 this year, gave Houston the premiere of his near-rock opera, *New Year*, featuring saxophones, electric guitars and a space ship. *Carmen* filled the vast space of Earl's Court with an arena-sized Spanish fiesta and **Maria Ewing**.

Musically, deaths dominated the year: **von Karajan**, succeeded at the Berlin Philharmonic by **Claudio Abbado**; pianists **John Ogdon** and **Vladimir Horowitz**, who lived long enough to return to his native Russia; and, in Britain, composer **Sir Lennox Berkeley**. Middle-aged rockers such as **The Who** went on tour, but **Kylie Minogue** and **Jason Donovan** ruled the charts.

In a year of hyped films, the ubiquitous **Kenneth Branagh** stood up to comparison with Laurence Olivier as a Shakespeare film-maker by directing and playing a *Henry V* completely rethought for its contemporary relevance. **Peter Brook** filmed the sprawling Hindu religious epic *The Mahabharata*, for cinema and television, but a bigger TV audience followed **Michael Palin** in *Around the World in 80 Days* for the BBC and later bought the book.

Musicals remained the chief moneyspinners on stage, with *Miss Saigon* and *Aspects of Love*. There were notable classical performances, too: **Ian McKellen's** studiously evil Iago, **John Wood's** ravaged Prospero and Solness, **Judi Dench's** volatile Madame Ranevskaya, even **Dustin Hoffman's** offbeat, if lightweight, Shylock. Death claimed **Anthony Quayle**, a King Lear of actor-managers, as well as **Lord Olivier**, whose death along with many other arts events was covered earlier in this book.

*Michael Palin boards the train for his epic and hugely popular voyage.*

# Things they said in the year 1989 ...

*The Communist Party has no God-given right to rule.* **M Gorbachev.**

*Frankly I wish I had written a more critical book.* **Salman Rushdie.**

*Only little people pay taxes.* **Leona Helmsley, New York hotel queen.**

*If this is justice, I am a banana.* **Ian Hislop, editor of Private Eye, after the Sonia Sutcliffe libel award.**

*Nigel [Lawson] had determined that he was going to put in his resignation. I did everything possible to stop him.* **Margaret Thatcher.**

*At last I understand why [Thatcher] has taken to calling herself "We". It is less lonely that way.* **N Kinnock.**

*I am not Lord Longford in drag.* **The Princess Royal on her jail visits.**

*My goal, if the hour of history allows it, is the unity of the nation.* **H Kohl.**

*If this party had a leader, it would no longer be the Green Party.* **David Icke.**

*Sometimes I wish I was a check-out girl.* **Kylie Minogue.**

*Well, it's not been a wholly dull year.* **John Major.**

# The hits of the year

**TOP FILMS**
Indiana Jones and the Last Crusade; Batman; Rainman.

**TOP SINGLES**
Ride on Time (Black Box); Swing the Mood (Jive Bunny); Too Many Broken Hearts (Jason Donovan).

**TOP PAPERBACKS**
Complete Hip and Thigh Diet (Rosemary Conley); Rivals (Jilly Cooper); A Twist in the Tale (Jeffrey Archer).

**TOP HARDBACKS**
Guinness Book of Records; Chronicle of the 20th Century; A Brief History of Time (S Hawking).
*(Sources: Screen International, Today, Bookwatch/Bookseller.)*

# The World's Nations

*This section gives brief updated facts on each nation's geographical location, population, area, language, religion, political status, and membership in international organizations. The head of state and head of government are also named. Figures provided for Gross National Product (GNP) and population are the latest available. Currency values are based on Sept. 30, 1989, indicative rates. The texts provide a short summary of the main events of 1989 up to early December. A list of abbreviations used is provided on page 123.*

## Afghanistan

Central Asia
251,773 sq. mi
Pop: 10-12m.
UN

*Capital:* Kabul (Pop: 2m.)
*Official languages:* Pushtu, Dari (Persian)
*Religion:* Moslem (Shia, Sunni)
*Political status:* People's republic
*Head of state:* Najibullah (since 1987)
*GNP per capita:* $250 (1985)
*Currency:* afghani (£1 = 99.25)

Despite the withdrawal of the last Soviet troops on February 15, under the terms of the April 1988 US and Soviet-guaranteed Geneva peace accords, war-torn Afghanistan continued to be rocked by major clashes between government forces and rebel fighters. Much of the bloodshed occurred around the strategic eastern city of Jalalabad, where Afghan rebels repeatedly tried to break the Soviet-equipped army's hold on the town. Mujahedin guerrillas also repeatedly launched rocket attacks on the capital, often causing heavy civilian casualties. In February, President Najibullah declared a state of emergency, appointing a 20-man Supreme Military Council to replace Prime Minister Hasan Sharq. The Council took over full control of economic, political and military policy. In July, US freelance photographer Tony O'Brien was released after having been held for six weeks by the security forces.

## Albania

Southeastern
Europe
11,101 sq. mi
Pop: 3.08m.
UN

*Capital:* Tirana (Pop: 206,000)
*Official language:* Albanian
*Religion:* Officially atheist
*Political status:* Socialist people's republic
*Head of state:* Ramiz Alia (since 1982)
*Head of government:* Adil Carçani (since 1982)
*GNP per capita:* $930 (1986)
*Currency:* lek (£1 = 10.24)

Tensions with Belgrade over the presence of some 1.7 million ethnic Albanians in Yugoslavia's Kosovo province remained high in 1989. In June, Albania welcomed China's crackdown on student demonstrators.

## Algeria

North Africa
919,595 sq. mi
Pop: 23.85m.
UN, AL, OAU, OPEC

*Capital:* Algiers (Pop: 1,721,607)
*Official language:* Arabic
*Religion:* Sunni Moslem
*Political status:* Socialist republic
*Head of state:* Chadli Bendjedid (since 1979)
*Head of government:* Mouloud Hamrouche (since 1989)
*GNP per capita:* $2,570 (1986)
*Currency:* Algerian dinar (£1 = 12.84)

The adoption in February of a new constitution paved the way for a multi-party system after some 25 years of rule by the socialist FLN Party. By year's end, Algeria was however faced with a severe economic crisis.

## Andorra

Southern
Europe
180 sq. mi
Pop: 51,400

*Capital:* Andorre la Vieille (Pop: 15,639)
*Official language:* Catalan
*Religion:* Roman Catholic
*Political status:* Principality
*Heads of state:* The Spanish Bishop of Urgel, Mgr Joan Marti y Alanis, and French President François Mitterrand
*Head of government:* Josef Pintat Solans (since 1986)
*GNP per capita:* $9,000
*Currencies:* Franc and peseta

Andorra's 6,500 voters were in late December voting to elect the 28 members of the ruling body, the General Council, and nationalist candidates seemed well-placed to win.

## Angola

Southwestern
Africa
481,351 sq. mi
Pop: 9.39m.
UN, OAU

*Capital:* Luanda (Pop: 1.2m.)
*Official language:* Portuguese
*Religions:* Roman Catholic 55%, Protestant 9%, animist 34%
*Political status:* Socialist people's republic
*Head of state:* José Eduardo dos Santos (since 1979)
*GNP per capita:* $500 (1985)
*Currency:* kwanza (£1 = 48.59)

After 14 years of civil war, a ceasefire came into force in June following the historic reconciliation between President dos Santos and Jonas Savimbi, leader of the South African-backed, pro-Western Unita rebel forces. More than 70,000 civilians died in the conflict, while some 400,000 Angolans were forced to flee abroad. The ceasefire came after the start of the phased pull-out of an estimated 50,000 Cuban troops sent in to support Luanda's Marxist regime. The withdrawal is due to be completed by July 1991. However, the ceasefire accord was repeatedly violated by both sides. In October, President Mobutu of Zaire tried to bring the two sides back to the negotiating table, while UN envoys sought to foster a settlement to the conflict that has devastated the country.

## Antigua and Barbuda

Caribbean
171 sq. mi
Pop: 81,500
UN, OAS, Caricom, CW

*Capital:* St John's (Pop: 30,000)
*Official language:* English
*Religion:* Christian (mostly Anglican)
*Political status:* Constitutional monarchy
*Head of state:* Queen Elizabeth II
*Head of government:* Vere C. Bird (since 1981)
*GNP per capita:* $2,380 (1986)
*Currency:* Eastern Caribbean dollar (£1 = 4.28)

## Argentina

South America
1,073,358 sq. mi
Pop: 31.06m.
UN, LAIA, OAS

*Capital:* Buenos Aires (Pop: 9,927,404)
*Official language:* Spanish
*Religion:* Roman Catholic 92%
*Political status:* Federal republic
*Head of state:* Carlos Menem (since 1989)
*GNP per capita:* $2,350 (1986)
*Currency:* austral (£1 = 1,031.25)

From the time he took office as President on July 8, Peronist leader Menem battled against the country's worst economic crisis ever. A policy of wage freezes succeeded in cutting inflation to nine per cent in September, from 200 per cent in July. Relations with Britain, broken off after the 1982 Falklands war, improved considerably.

The Conservative Party won 15 of the 17 parliamentary seats in a March poll despite gains by centrist candidates. In September, the country was badly hit by Hurricane Hugo.

## Australia

South Pacific
2,966,200 sq. mi
Pop: 16.25m.
UN, ANZUS, CW, OECD

*Capital:* Canberra (Pop: 285,800)
*Official language:* English
*Religions:* Anglican 36%, other Protestant 25%, Roman Catholic 33%
*Political status:* Federal constitutional monarchy
*Head of state:* Queen Elizabeth II
*Head of government:* Robert Hawke (since 1983)
*GNP per capita:* $11,910 (1986)
*Currency:* Australian dollar (£1 = 2.09)

The country's Labor government, in serious electoral trouble since the middle of the year, suffered a stinging rebuff in crucial November state elections in South Australia. The vote marked a five per cent swing away from the Labor Party. The result was seen as a sign of trouble for the government of Prime Minister Bob Hawke and of growing discontent with high interest rates resulting from the Canberra's efforts to slow down an overheated economy. This setback came as Mr Hawke mapped out his strategy for general elections, due by the middle of 1990. Mr Hawke, who turned 60 in December, will be seeking a record fourth term. In May, the country's foreign debt crossed the psychological threshold of 100 billion Australian dollars. In August, a pay dispute led to the resignation of 1,645 airline pilots, plunging air travel into chaos. Military planes were used to ferry stranded passengers. By year's end the dispute was close to a final settlement.

# Austria

Western Europe
32,376 sq. mi
Pop: 7.58m.
UN, EFTA,
OECD

*Capital:* Vienna (Pop: 1,479,841)
*Official language:* German
*Religions:* Roman Catholic 84.3%, Protestant 5.6%
*Political status:* Federal parliamentary republic
*Head of state:* Kurt Waldheim (since 1986)
*Head of government:* Franz Vranitzky (since 1986)
*GNP per capita:* $12,297 (1986)
*Currency:* schilling (£1 = 20.69)

In July, Austria asked to join the EC, but by year's end the issue seemed unlikely to be decided until 1993. Thousands of East German refugees poured into Austria from Hungary in September and October.

# Bahamas

Caribbean
5,353 sq. mi
Pop: 236,171
UN, OAS, CW,
Caricom

*Capital:* Nassau (Pop: 135,437)
*Official language:* English
*Religions:* Baptist 29%, Anglican 23%, Roman Catholic 22%
*Political status:* Constitutional monarchy
*Head of state:* Queen Elizabeth II
*Head of government:* Sir Lynden O. Pindling (since 1967)
*GNP per capita:* $7,190 (1986)
*Currency:* Bahamian dollar (£1 = 1.58)

The year was marked by a huge surge in tourist revenue as nearly four million people visited the country. An MP was indicted in the US in March on charges of conspiring to launder illegal drug money.

# Bahrain

Middle East
265.5 sq. mi
Pop: 421,040
UN, AL, GCC

*Capital:* Manama (Pop: 151,500)
*Official language:* Arabic
*Religions:* Moslem 85%, Christian 7.3%
*Political status:* Emirate
*Head of state:* Isa bin Sulman Al-Khalifa (since 1961)
*Head of government:* Khalifa bin Sulman Al-Khalifa (since 1973)
*GNP per capita:* $8,530 (1986)
*Currency:* Bahrain dinar (£1 = 0.59)

The end of the Iran-Iraq conflict gave rise to hopes that Bahrain would quickly reclaim its position as the Gulf's main banking centre. The drop in oil revenue affected the economy.

# Bangladesh

Southern Asia
55,598 sq. mi
Pop: 104.1m.
UN, CW

*Capital:* Dhaka (Pop: 3,440,147)
*Official language:* Bangla
*Religions:* Moslem 80%, Hindu, Buddhist, Christian
*Political status:* Presidential republic
*Head of state:* Hossain Mohammad Ershad (since 1983)
*Head of government:* Moudud Ahmed (since 1988)
*GNP per capita:* $140 (1986)
*Currency:* Taka (£1 = 49.20)

The disastrous floods that killed more than 2,000 people in late 1988 led the government to take steps such as reforestation and improved inland water drainage aimed at preventing future disasters. However, malnutrition and disease remained a problem. In November, a dysentery epidemic left 350 people dead.

# Barbados

Caribbean
166 sq. mi
Pop: 253,881
UN, CW, OAS,
Caricom

*Capital:* Bridgetown (Pop: 7,466)
*Official language:* English
*Religions:* Anglican 70%, Methodist, Moravian, Roman Catholic
*Political status:* Constitutional monarchy
*Head of state:* Queen Elizabeth II
*Head of government:* Erskine Sandiford (since 1987)
*GNP per capita:* $4,668 (1987)
*Currency:* Barbados dollar (£1 = 3.19)

In February, former Finance Minister Richard Haynes set up the National Democratic Party and became opposition leader. Despite a poor sugar-cane harvest, the economy remained healthy owing to a tourist boom.

# Belgium

Western Europe
11,778 sq. mi
Pop: 9.88m.
UN, EEC,
NATO, OECD

*Capital:* Brussels (Pop: 970,346)
*Official languages:* French, Dutch, German
*Religion:* Mostly Roman Catholic
*Political status:* Constitutional monarchy
*Head of state:* King Baudouin I (since 1951)
*Head of government:* Wilfried Martens (since 1981)
*GNP per capita:* $9,230 (1986)
*Currency:* Belgian franc (£1 = 61.70)

Plans to liberalize an 1867 law on abortion sparked an uproar which nearly toppled the government. Abortion foes failed to block debate in parliament of the issue, which remained unresolved at year's end. In October, a leader of Belgium's Jewish community was murdered, six months after the killing in Brussels of a high ranking Moslem dignitary.

# Belize

Central America
8,866 sq. mi
Pop: 176,000
UN, Caricom,
CW

*Capital:* Belmopan (Pop: 3,500)
*Official language:* English
*Religions:* Roman Catholic 62%, Protestant 28%
*Political status:* Constitutional monarchy
*Head of state:* Queen Elizabeth II
*Head of government:* George Price (since 1989)
*GNP per capita:* $1,170 (1986)
*Currency:* Belize dollar (£1 = 3.17)

Centre-left candidate George Price beat incumbent democrat Manuel Esquivel in September elections seen as crucial for the consolidation of democracy in the former British colony.

# Benin

West Africa
43,483 sq. mi
Pop: 4.44m.
UN, OAU

*Capital:* Porto Novo (Pop: 208,258)
*Official language:* French
*Religions:* Mainly animist, Christian, Moslem
*Political status:* Socialist people's republic
*Head of state:* Ahmed Kerekou (since 1972)
*GNP per capita:* $270 (1986)
*Currency:* franc CFA (£1 = 499.13)

President Kerekou's hard-line government in December officially renounced the Marxist-Leninist ideology that has dominated the country's politics and economics since 1974.

# Bhutan

South Asia
18,000 sq. mi
Pop: 1.4m.
UN

*Capital:* Thimphu (Pop: 15,000)
*Official languages:* Dzongkha, Lhotsam (Nepali), English
*Religions:* Buddhist 75%, Hindu 25%
*Political status:* Monarchy
*Head of state:* Jigme Singye Wangchuk (since 1972)
*Head of government:* Council of ministers
*GNP per capita:* $160 (1987)
*Currency:* Ngultrum (£1 = 26.30)

In April, a royal decree made the wearing of Bhutan's colourful national dress compulsory for all citizens as part of a plan to "preserve and promote" the tiny Himalayan kingdom's national identity.

# Bolivia

South America
424,165 sq. mi
Pop: 7m.
UN, LAIA,
OAS

*Capital:* Sucre (legal), La Paz (de facto; pop: 992,592)
*Official languages:* Spanish, Quechua, Aymara
*Religion:* Roman Catholic 95%
*Political status:* Presidential republic
*Head of state:* Jaime Paz Zamora (since 1989)
*GNP per capita:* $540 (1986)
*Currency:* boliviano (£1 = 4.55)

Barely three months after his inauguration, President Paz Zamora was forced to declare a nationwide state of emergency in mid-November as social unrest and labour disputes threatened to plunge the country into a crisis. This move came nearly a month after the World Bank agreed in principle to provide Bolivia with a 2.175-billion-dollar loan over three years, on condition that the country remained stable and its government acted to cut down public spending. The president rejected huge wage claims by teachers, some 2,000 of whom responded by going on hunger strike.

## Botswana

Southern Africa
220,000 sq. mi
Pop: 1.21m.
UN, CW, OAU

*Capital:* Gaborone (Pop: 110,973)
*Official languages:* English, Setswana
*Religions:* Bahai, Moslem, Hindu, Christian
*Political status:* Presidential republic
*Head of state:* Quett Ketumile Joni Masire (since 1980)
*GNP per capita:* $840 (1986)
*Currency:* pula (£1 = 3.11)

In October, President Masire's ruling Botswana Democratic Party won fraud-free general elections, capturing 31 of the 34 National Assembly seats. The opposition Botswana National Front lost two of its five seats.

## Brazil

South America
3,286,487 sq. mi
Pop: 144.3m.
UN, LAIA, OAS

*Capital:* Brasilia (Pop: 410,999)
*Official language:* Portuguese
*Religions:* Roman Catholic 89%, Protestant 6.6%, Spiritualist
*Political status:* Federal republic
*Head of state:* José Sarney (since 1985)
*GNP per capita:* $1,740 (1986)
*Currency:* cruzado (£1 = 6.74)

Mired in its worst-ever economic crisis and facing triple-digit inflation and a crushing foreign debt, the country sought desperately in 1989 to find lasting solutions to the problem. Wage freezes and public spending cutbacks sparked a wave of strikes that culminated in a two-day general strike in March. In a November poll, Workers Party candidate Luis Ignacio da Silva won the right to run for the presidency in a mid-December election against centre-right candidate Fernando Collor de Mello. Mr da Silva promised to trim government bureaucracy, remove barriers to foreign investment, promote free-market policies and tax the rich to help the poor. He also vowed to reduce payments on the 110-billion-dollar foreign debt.

## Brunei

Southeast Asia
2,226 sq. mi
Pop: 226,300
UN, CW, ASEAN

*Capital:* Bandar Seri Begawan (Pop: 63,868)
*Official languages:* Malay, Chinese
*Religions:* Moslem 63%, Buddhist 14%, Christian 10%
*Political status:* Sultanate
*Head of state:* Sultan Muda Hassanal Bolkiah Mu'izzadin Waddaulah (since 1967)
*Head of government:* Sultan Muda Hassanal Bolkiah Mu'izzadin Waddaulah
*GNP per capita:* $15,400 (1986)
*Currency:* Brunei dollar (£1 = 3.09)

With a fortune estimated at more than £16 billion, Brunei's ruler in 1989 remained by far the world's wealthiest individual, thanks largely to the small Asian kingdom's enormous oil and natural gas reserves.

## Bulgaria

Southeastern Europe
42,823 sq. mi
Pop: 8.97m.
UN, CMEA, Warsaw Pact

*Capital:* Sofia (Pop: 1,128,859)
*Official language:* Bulgarian
*Religions:* Mostly Orthodox, Moslem 7%
*Political status:* Socialist people's republic
*Head of state:* Petar Mladenov (s. 1989)
*Head of government:* Georgi Atanasov (since 1986)
*GNP per capita:* $6,460
*Currency:* lev (£1 = 1.33)

In May, Sofia strongly denied Western charges that it was heavily involved in the international drugs traffic, while in August the US recalled its ambassador to Sofia as a protest against repeated human rights violations. Tensions with neighbouring Turkey remained high as Ankara accused Bulgaria of forcing its ethnic Turkish inhabitants to "Bulgarize" their names. In a mid-November shake-up, hard-line leader Todor Zhivkov was ousted and replaced by the pro-Gorbachev Petar Mladenov.

## Burkina Faso

Western Africa
105,839 sq. mi
Pop: 8.53m.
UN, OAU

*Capital:* Ouagadougou (Pop: 442,223)
*Official language:* French
*Religions:* Animist 45%, Moslem 43%, Christian 12%
*Political status:* Presidential republic
*Head of state:* Blaise Compaoré (since 1987)
*Head of government:* Blaise Compaoré
*GNP per capita:* $150 (1986)
*Currency:* franc CFA (£1 = 499.13)

Strongman Blaise Compaoré further consolidated his hold on power in September when he ordered the execution of two senior military officers who had tried to oust him.

## Burma

Southeast Asia
261,228 sq. mi
Pop: 39.84m.
UN

*Capital:* Rangoon (Pop: 2,458,712)
*Official language:* Burmese
*Religion:* Buddhist
*Political status:* Socialist people's republic
*Head of state:* Saw Mung (since 1988)
*Head of government:* Saw Mung (since 1988)
*GNP per capita:* $200 (1986)
*Currency:* kyat (£1 = 10.78)

In August, a government-decreed amnesty led to the release of nearly 19,000 prisoners, many of whom had been jailed for taking part in banned political activities. In November, martial law was lifted in several northern provinces and the year-old military regime announced that the country's first general elections since 1960 would be held in May 1990.

## Burundi

Central Africa
10,759 sq. mi
Pop: 5.13m.
UN, OAU

*Capital:* Bujumbura (Pop: 272,600)
*Official languages:* Kirundi, French
*Religions:* Roman Catholic 60%, traditional tribal beliefs 32%
*Political status:* Presidential republic
*Head of state:* Pierre Buyoya (since 1987)
*Head of government:* Adrien Sibomana (since 1988)
*GNP per capita:* $240 (1988)
*Currency:* Burundi franc (£1 = 253.24)

Burundi in September celebrated the second anniversary of the founding of the country's third republic and the government appealed to citizens to help get the hard-hit, agriculture-based economy back on its feet.

## Cambodia

Southeast Asia
69,898 sq. mi
Pop: 6.23m.
UN

*Capital:* Phnom Penh (Pop: 500,000)
*Official language:* Khmer
*Religions:* Theravada Buddhism, Roman Catholic and Moslem minorities
*Political status:* People's republic
*Head of state:* Heng Samrin (since 1979)
*Head of government:* Hun Sen (since 1985)
*GNP per capita:* No accurate estimate available
*Currency:* riel (£1 = 236.25)

The last Vietnamese soldiers withdrew from Cambodia in late September, ten years and nine months after they were sent in to topple the bloodthirsty Khmer Rouge regime held responsible for the massacre of hundreds of thousands of Cambodians between 1975 and 1978. Vietnam's troops, which suffered casualties estimated at well over 50,000 dead, pulled out after failing to defeat the well-armed, Chinese-backed, anti-communist guerrillas, of which Khmer Rouge forces remained the chief component. Attempts to reach a lasting peace settlement failed due to disagreements within the anti-communist alliance. Following the Vietnamese pull-out, government troops appeared ill-prepared to cope with the guerrilla forces and there were fears among the population and in the West that the Khmer Rouge, which in November scored major military victories in the south and south-west, would succeed in making a political comeback.

## Cameroon

Western Central Africa
179,558 sq. mi
Pop: 11m.
UN, OAU

*Capital:* Yaoundé (Pop: 435,892)
*Official languages:* French, English
*Religions:* Animist 39%, Roman Catholic 21%, Moslem 22%, Protestant 18%
*Political status:* Presidential republic
*Head of state:* Paul Biya (since 1982)
*GNP per capita:* $910 (1986)
*Currency:* franc CFA (£1 = 499.13)

Cameroon in 1989 reported a bumper cotton crop and sought to convince Canadian and West European businessmen to invest in the country. Despite an anti-Aids programme, the disease claimed 100 lives in 1989.

## Canada

North America
3,553,357 sq. mi
Pop: 25.6m.
UN, NATO, CW, OECD, OAS

*Capital:* Ottawa (Pop: 819,263)
*Official languages:* English, French
*Religions:* Roman Catholic, Protestant
*Political status:* Parliamentary monarchy
*Head of state:* Queen Elizabeth II
*Head of government:* Martin Brian Mulroney (since 1984)
*GNP per capita:* $14,100 (1986)
*Currency:* Canadian dollar (£1 = 1.87)

In April elections, Newfoundland's Liberal Party put an end to 17 years of conservative rule in the province. The same month saw the printing of Canada's last one-dollar bill. These are to be replaced by coins. Montreal police in April seized half a ton of Colombian cocaine in Canada's biggest-ever drug bust. Also in April, budgetary constraints led to the cancellation of plans to spend an estimated eight billion Canadian dollars on French- or British-built nuclear submarines. July was marked by the visit of the Queen Mother, 50 years after her first trip abroad with King George VI. Shortly after, the Duke and Duchess of York celebrated their third wedding anniversary among Stanley Mission's Cree Indians. Relations with the US improved after President Bush agreed in February to open talks on the controversial acid rain issue. Canada's huge foreign debt remained a major problem, forcing Ottawa to cut military spending and raise taxes. At the July summit meeting of leaders of the world's seven richest countries, Mr Mulroney expressed satisfaction over plans to fight threats to the Earth's ecology. Also in July, devastating forest fires spread through Manitoba, Saskatchewan and Ontario. In September, Quebec's Premier Robert Bourassa was re-elected for a fourth term, despite gains by the pro-independence candidate. In October, Canada joined the OAS, paving the way for closer ties with Latin America. Mr Mulroney in November made a successful visit to Moscow.

# Cape Verde

Atlantic
1,557 sq. mi
Pop: 359,000
UN, OAU

*Capital:* Praia (Pop: 37,676)
*Official language:* Portuguese
*Religion:* Roman Catholic 98%
*Political status:* Republic
*Head of state:* Aristides Maria Pereira (since 1975)
*Head of government:* Pedro Verona Rodrigues Pires (since 1975)
*GNP per capita:* $460 (1986)
*Currency:* escudo Caboverdiano (£1 = 130.30)

Faced with ever-increasing demographic problems, the country in 1989 continued to rely heavily on international aid. The government also sought to provide incentives for foreign investment programmes.

# Central African Republic

Central Africa
240,324 sq. mi
Pop: 2.86m.
UN, OAU

*Capital:* Bangui (Pop: 596,776)
*Official language:* French
*Religions:* Animist beliefs 57%, Roman Catholic 20%, Protestant 15%, Moslem 8%
*Political status:* Presidential republic
*Head of state:* André Kolingba (since 1981)
*GNP per capita:* $290 (1986)
*Currency:* franc CFA (£1 = 499.13)

The rescheduling under favourable conditions of the country's foreign debt burden considerably eased economic hardships, although General Kolingba in 1989 stressed the need for further budgetary efforts.

# Chad

Central Africa
495,752 sq. mi
Pop: 5.4m.
UN, OAU

*Capital:* N'Djaména (Pop: 511,700)
*Official languages:* French, Arabic
*Religions:* Moslem 44%, animist 38%, Christian 17%
*Political status:* Presidential republic
*Head of state:* Hissène Habré (since 1982)
*GNP per capita:* $88 (1984)
*Currency:* franc CFA (£1 = 499.13)

After talks between Chad's leader and Libya's Colonel Gadaffi, the two nations in August signed a peace accord aimed at ending fighting over a strip of desert that has been the focus of 16 years of bloodshed.

# Chile

South America
284,520 sq. mi
Pop: 12.68m.
UN, LAIA, OAS

*Capital:* Santiago (Pop: 4,858,342)
*Official language:* Spanish
*Religions:* Roman Catholic, Protestant, Jewish
*Political status:* Presidential republic under a military regime
*Head of state:* Augusto Pinochet Ugarte (since 1974)
*GNP per capita:* $1,320 (1986)
*Currency:* Chilean peso (£1 = 503.65)

In mid-December, Chileans were poised to vote in historic presidential and legislative elections. In the run-up to the ballot, General Pinochet and senior military officers vowed that the ballot would be free and promised to abide by the result. In October, the president disbanded the political police force, CNI, but warned that he would not stand idly by if a new civilian government were to take action against the military establishment. Christian Democrat opposition leader Patricio Aylwin was widely tipped to win the presidential election.

# China

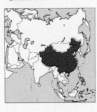

East Asia
3,682,131 sq. mi
Pop: 1,072.2m.
UN

*Capital:* Beijing (Peking; pop: 5.86m.)
*Official language:* Chinese
*Religions:* Officially atheist; Confucianism, Buddhism, Taoism
*Political status:* People's republic
*Head of state:* Yang Shangkun (since 1989)
*Head of government:* Li Peng (since 1987)
*GNP per capita:* $250 (1986)
*Currency:* Renminbi yuan (£1 = 5.88)

The brutal crushing in June of the pro-democracy movement, which sent shock waves around the world, cast a shadow over the historic reconciliation between China and the Soviet Union, sealed during a May visit to Beijing by Soviet leader Mikhail Gorbachev. The visit was aimed an ending a 30-year rift between the two communist states. The June events, which left hundreds if not thousands of people dead, led to an unprecedented wave of repression and dozens of executions. The Communist Party's reformist leader Zhao Ziyang was dismissed and replaced by hardliner Jiang Zemin. Tensions with the US increased after a leading Chinese dissident and his wife were granted refuge inside the US Embassy in Beijing. International condemnation of the regime's actions was nearly unanimous, with only Albania and East Germany expressing approval. Britain, the US and other Western governments froze their diplomatic relations with China and applied economic and other sanctions, thus deepening the country's economic woes. In October, China said it was considering borrowing fresh foreign funds to meet some of the 40-billion-dollar external debt it must repay in the 1990s. The repression in China sparked grave fears among the people of Hong Kong, due to pass from British to Chinese control in 1997. In November, paramount leader Deng Xiaoping resigned from his last post within the Communist Party leadership and was replaced by Mr Jiang.

# Colombia

South America
440,829 sq. mi
Pop: 27.9m.
UN, LAIA, OAS

*Capital:* Bogota (Pop: 3,982,941)
*Official language:* Spanish
*Religion:* Roman Catholic
*Political status:* Democratic presidential republic
*Head of state:* Virgilio Barco Vargas (since 1986)
*GNP per capita:* $1,129 (1986)
*Currency:* peso (£1 = 646.90)

The drug crisis worsened dramatically in 1989, as the regime launched an all-out offensive against traffickers, who responded by assassinating judges, forcing Justice Minister Monica de Grieff out of office and, in August, gunning down Senator Luis Galan, a leading presidential candidate. US aid and equipment to fight the drug lords was sharply increased.

# Comoros

Indian Ocean
719 sq. mi
Pop: 422,500
UN

*Capital:* Moroni (Pop: 20,112)
*Official languages:* French, Arabic
*Religions:* Moslem (Sunni) 99%, Christian
*Political status:* Federal Islamic republic
*Head of state:* Vacant
*GNP per capita:* $280 (1986)
*Currency:* Comorian franc (£1 = 499.13)

President Abderemane, in power since he set up an Islamic republic in 1978, was killed in November shortly after winning a referendum that would have allowed him to stay in office until the mid-1990s.

# Congo

Central Africa
132,046 sq. mi
Pop: 2.27m.
UN, OAU

*Capital:* Brazzaville (Pop: 585,812)
*Official language:* French
*Religions:* Roman Catholic 54%, Protestant 24%, animist 19%, Moslem 3%
*Political status:* People's republic
*Head of state:* Denis Sassou-Nguesso (since 1979)
*Head of government:* Ange-Edouard Poungui (since 1984)
*GNP per capita:* $1,040 (1986)
*Currency:* franc CFA (£1 = 499.13)

The country in February marked ten years of Colonel Sassou-Nguesso's rule amid continued economic problems. In September, the Labour Party won parliamentary elections with more than 99 per cent of the vote.

# Costa Rica

Central America
19,730 sq. mi
Pop: 2.81m.
UN, OAS

*Capital:* San José (Pop: 241,464)
*Official language:* Spanish
*Religion:* Roman Catholic
*Political status:* Democratic republic
*Head of state:* Oscar Arias Sanchez (since 1986)
*Head of government:* Rodrigo Arias Sanchez
*GNP per capita:* $1,420 (1986)
*Currency:* colone (£1 = 130.92)

The worsening economic situation, repeated charges of widespread government corruption and his failure to push forward his regional peace plan in 1989 eroded President Arias's already sagging popularity.

## Cuba

Caribbean
44,206 sq. mi
Pop: 10.24m.
UN, CMEA

*Capital:* Havana (Pop: 2,014,800)
*Official language:* Spanish
*Religions:* Roman Catholic, Methodist, Baptist
*Political status:* Socialist republic
*Head of state:* Fidel Castro Ruz
*GNP per capita:* $2,696 (1981)
*Currency:* peso (£1 = 1.21)

Marking the 30th anniversary of the Cuban revolution, Fidel Castro in January lashed out against the Soviet government's reform policies and vowed to stand firm against any attempts to spread *perestroika* or *glasnost* to his country. Relations between Havana and Moscow remained chilly despite an April visit by Mr Gorbachev. In February, the UN criticized Cuba for continued human rights violations. The year also saw the start of the withdrawal of Cuban troops from Angola, where some 5,000 Cubans were reported to have died.

## Cyprus

Southern Europe
3,572 sq. mi
Pop: 680,400
UN, CW

*Capital:* Nicosia (Pop: 164,500)
*Official languages:* Greek, Turkish
*Religions:* Greek Orthodox 80%, Moslem 19%
*Political status:* Republic
*Head of state:* George Vassiliou (since 1988)
*GNP per capita:* $6,831 (1987)
*Currency:* Cyprus pound (£1 = 0.78)

Despite efforts spearheaded by the UN, tensions between the island's Greek and Turkish communities remained strong and little progress was made towards a pull-out of Turkish troops. In November, seven British soldiers died in a road accident.

## Czechoslovakia

Central Europe
49,383 sq. mi
Pop: 15.5m.
UN, CMEA,
Warsaw Pact

*Capital:* Prague (Pop: 1,194,000)
*Official languages:* Czech, Slovak
*Religion:* Roman Catholic 24%
*Political status:* Federal socialist republic
*Head of state:* Gustav Husak (since 1975)
*Head of government:* Marian Calfa (since 1989)
*GNP per capita:* $8,700 (1985)
*Currency:* Czech koruna (£1 = 15.6)

The wind of change that roared through Eastern Europe in late 1989 did not spare Czechoslovakia. As millions of people took to the streets in November to protest against Communist Party domination and demand free elections, President Husak and Prime Minister Ladislav Adamec suffered humiliating setbacks when they were ousted from the Politburo. Party leader Milos Jakes stepped down and was replaced by Karel Urbanek. After 20 years of political oblivion, Alexander Dubcek, leader of the failed 1968 "Prague Spring" movement, made a triumphant return to the capital in late November. In early December, Mr Adamec was replaced by Marian Calfa, a 43-year-old lawyer.

## Denmark

Northern Europe
16,631 sq. mi
Pop: 5.13m.
UN, EEC,
NATO, OECD

*Capital:* Copenhagen (Pop: 619,985)
*Official language:* Danish
*Religion:* Lutheran 90%
*Political status:* Constitutional monarchy
*Head of state:* Queen Margrethe II (since 1972)
*Head of government:* Poul Schlueter (since 1982)
*GNP per capita:* $12,640 (1986)
*Currency:* krone (£1 = 11.42)

Denmark was a major donor of Third World aid in 1989. November local elections saw gains by the far-right. Denmark in October became the first state to grant full rights to homosexuals, including the right to wed.

## Djibouti

Northeastern Africa
8,960 sq. mi
Pop: 484,000
UN, AL, OAU

*Capital:* Djibouti (Pop: 290,000)
*Official languages:* French, Arabic
*Religion:* Mostly Moslem
*Political status:* Presidential republic
*Head of state:* Hassan Gouled Aptidon (since 1977)
*Head of government:* Barkat Gourad Hamadou (since 1978)
*GNP per capita:* $760 (1984)
*Currency:* Djibouti franc (£1 = 279)

The closure of Ethiopia's border with Djibouti in May did little to slow the flood of refugees from that famine-stricken country. This added a new burden to Djibouti's economy.

## Dominica

Caribbean
290 sq. mi
Pop: 94,191
UN, CW, OAS,
Caricom

*Capital:* Roseau (Pop: 20,000)
*Official language:* English
*Religion:* Roman Catholic 80%
*Political status:* Republic
*Head of state:* C.A. Seignoret (since 1983)
*Head of government:* Mary Eugenia Charles (since 1980)
*GNP per capita:* $1,210 (1986)
*Currencies:* French franc, £ sterling and East Caribbean dollar (£1 = EC$4.28)

Hurricane Hugo in mid-September caused severe damage to the country, wiping out 80 per cent of the banana crop and wrecking fishing boats.

## Dominican Republic

Caribbean
18,700 sq. mi
Pop: 6.7m.
UN, OAS

*Capital:* Santo Domingo (Pop: 1,313,172)
*Official language:* Spanish
*Religion:* Roman Catholic
*Political status:* Presidential republic
*Head of state:* Joaquin Balaguer (since 1986)
*GNP per capita:* $710 (1986)
*Currency:* peso oro (£1 = 10.63)

Tensions with neighbouring Haiti grew despite attempts to settle a dispute over compensation for the accidental death in January of 50 Haitians.

## Ecuador

South America
104,505 sq. mi
Pop: 9.64m.
UN, LAIA,
OAS, OPEC

*Capital:* Quito (Pop: 1,110,248)
*Official languages:* Spanish, Quechua
*Religion:* Roman Catholic
*Political status:* Presidential republic
*Head of state:* Rodrigo Borja Cevallos (since 1988)
*GNP per capita:* $1,160 (1986)
*Currency:* sucre (£1 = 910.00)

Marking his first year in office, President Borja vowed in August to press ahead with democratic reforms. In September, he declared a state of emergency after widespread strikes threatened the ailing economy.

## Egypt

North Africa
386,900 sq. mi
Pop: 49.28m.
UN, AL, OAU

*Capital:* Cairo (Pop: 6,325,000)
*Official language:* Arabic
*Religions:* Sunni Moslem 90%, Coptic Christian 7%
*Political status:* Presidential republic
*Head of state:* Hosni Mubarak (since 1981)
*Head of government:* Atef Mohamed Naguib Sidki (since 1986)
*GNP per capita:* $760 (1986)
*Currency:* Egyptian pound (£1 = 4.10)

Israel in March handed back the Taba enclave to Egypt after a lengthy dispute. The visit to Cairo of Foreign Minister Eduard Shevardnadze led to closer Soviet-Egyptian ties. In 1989, Egypt restored relations with many Arab nations who had broken off links after the Camp David accords. In August, Egypt expressed concern over the activities of its fundamentalist groups.

## El Salvador

Central America
8,236 sq. mi
Pop: 5.48m.
UN, OAS

*Capital:* San Salvador
*Official language:* Spanish
*Religion:* Roman Catholic
*Political status:* Presidential republic
*Head of state:* Alfredo Cristiani (since 1989)
*GNP per capita:* $820 (1986)
*Currency:* colon (£1 = 7.86)

Mr Cristiani, leader of the right-wing Arena Party won February elections with 53.8 per cent of the vote and took office on June 1. His efforts to restore stability suffered a setback in late October when leftist, Soviet and Nicaraguan-armed rebels launched a large-scale offensive which left many hundreds dead. Press freedom was suspended during the crisis and government troops raided church groups and humanitarian organizations. The November murder of six Jesuit priests was blamed by the Roman Catholic Church on far-right death squads. However, the rebels failed to spark a national insurrection. US economic and military aid remained high, at around 500 million dollars.

# Equatorial Guinea

West Africa
10,831 sq. mi
Pop: 336,000
UN, OAU

*Capital:* Malabo (Pop: 10,000)
*Official language:* Spanish
*Religions:* mostly Roman Catholic, Protestant
*Political status:* Presidential republic
*Head of state:* Teodoro Obiang Nguema Mbasogo (since 1979)
*GNP per capita:* $420 (1983)
*Currency:* franc CFA (£1 = 499.13)

President Nguema, who ran unopposed in June presidential elections, won a new seven-year term with 99.96 per cent of the vote. Only 69 voters cast their ballots against him.

# Ethiopia

Northeastern
Africa
471,800 sq. mi
Pop: 46m.
UN, OAU

*Capital:* Addis Abada (Pop: 1,412,575)
*Official languages:* Amharic, Galla
*Religions:* Moslem 45%, Ethiopian Orthodox 40%
*Political status:* People's democratic republic
*Head of state:* Mengistu Haile Mariam (since 1977)
*GNP per capita:* $120 (1986)
*Currency:* birr (£1 = 3.25)

The regime survived a May coup attempt. In September and November, former US President Jimmy Carter chaired talks between the government and the rebel Eritrean People's Liberation Front aimed at ending the 28-year conflict in northern Ethiopia, Africa's longest war. Threats of a famine were reported in November.

# Fiji

South Pacific
7,076 sq. mi
Pop: 715,375
UN

*Capital:* Suva (Pop: 71,608)
*Official language:* English
*Religions:* Christian 42%, Hindu 33%, Moslem 6%
*Political status:* Republic
*Head of state:* Ratu Sir Penaia Ganilau (since 1987)
*Head of government:* Ratu Sir Kamisese Mara (since 1987)
*GNP per capita:* $1,810 (1986)
*Currency:* Fiji dollar (£1 = 2.40)

The country's 68-year-old premier said in April that he planned to retire from politics in late December, at the end of his current term. Fiji's Finance Minister Josevata Kamikamica was set to succeed him.

# Finland

Northern
Europe
117,615 sq. mi
Pop: 4.94m.
UN, NC,
OECD, EFTA

*Capital:* Helsinki (Pop: 490,034)
*Official languages:* Finnish, Swedish, Lappish
*Religions:* Lutheran 89.2%, Greek Orthodox 1.1%
*Political status:* Democratic parliamentary republic
*Head of state:* Mauno Koivisto (since 1982)
*Head of government:* Harri Holkeri (since 1987)
*GNP per capita:* $18,118 (1987)
*Currency:* Finnmark (£1 = 6.73)

In May, Finland became the 23rd member state of the 40-year-old Council of Europe. During an October visit to Helsinki, Soviet leader Gorbachev vowed to withdraw his nation's nuclear-armed Golf-class submarines from the Baltic Sea.

# France

Western Europe
211,968 sq. mi
Pop: 55.84m.
UN, EEC,
OECD, NATO

*Capital:* Paris (Pop: 2,188,918)
*Official language:* French
*Religion:* Roman Catholic 76%, Moslem 4.5%, Protestant 1.4%
*Political status:* Parliamentary republic
*Head of state:* François Mitterrand (since 1981)
*Head of government:* Michel Rocard (since 1988)
*GNP per capita:* $10,740 (1986)
*Currency:* French franc (£1 = 9.98)

It was above all the year of the bicentennial of the French Revolution of 1789, which was celebrated spectacularly on July 14. The event, attended by Mrs Thatcher and dozens of other leaders, was followed by an estimated 800 million television viewers worldwide. The festivities brought an unprecedented tourist boom, as millions came to attend the Bastille Day parade and the 100th anniversary of the Eiffel Tower. The year was also marked in March by local elections which brought gains for conservative candidates, for the extreme-right National Front, and a major setback for the once-powerful Communist Party. In a June ballot for the European Parliament, the newly formed pro-ecology Green Party made a good showing. The socialist government's attempts to bring lasting peace to the French South Pacific territory of New Caledonia suffered a setback in May when a moderate local leader was killed. In September, a terrorist bomb ripped apart a French DC-10 airliner over Africa, killing all 171 people on board. By year's end, owing to exceptional weather conditions, France was revelling in what was said to be the best wine vintage in a century.

# Gabon

Central Africa
103,346 sq. mi
Pop: 1.22m.
UN, OAU,
OPEC

*Capital:* Libreville (Pop: 350,000)
*Official language:* French
*Religions:* Christian 84% (mostly Roman Catholic), animist
*Political status:* Presidential republic
*Head of state:* Omar Bongo (since 1967)
*Head of government:* Léon Mébiame (since 1975)
*GNP per capita:* $3,020 (1986)
*Currency:* franc CFA (£1 = 499.13)

President Bongo in August reshuffled his cabinet, cutting the number of ministers from 46 to 42. In early October, authorities said they had foiled a plot to assassinate the president and seize the premier.

# Gambia

West Africa
4,127 sq. mi
Pop: 788,163
UN, OAU, CW

*Capital:* Banjul (Pop: 44,188)
*Official language:* English
*Religions:* Moslem 70%, Christian, animist
*Political status:* Republic
*Head of state:* Dawda Kairaba Jawara (since 1970)
*GNP per capita:* $230 (1986)
*Currency:* dalasi (£1 = 12.14)

The country in February celebrated the 24th anniversary of its independence. In March, former Finance Minister Sherif Sisay, who resigned in February for health reasons, died in a London hospital.

# Germany (East)

Central Europe
41,827 sq. mi
Pop: 16.6m.
UN, CMEA,
Warsaw Pact

*Capital:* East Berlin (Pop: 1,223,309)
*Official language:* German
*Religions:* Protestant 80.5%, Roman Catholic 11%
*Political status:* Socialist republic
*Head of state:* Egon Krenz (since 1989)
*Head of government:* Hans Modrow (since 1989)
*GNP per capita:* $10,400 (1985)
*Currency:* GDR mark (£1 = 2.94)

For East Germany, 1989 was the most momentous year since the country's birth, as its citizens watched one of the most powerful symbols of the post-war division of Europe crumble before their eyes. Already jolted by the ousting in October of hard-line leader Erich Honecker, replaced by the younger Egon Krenz, East Germans reacted with an unprecedented outpouring of joy to the start of the dismantling of the Berlin Wall, on November 9. This historic event, which allowed hundreds of thousands of exultant East Germans to flood into West Berlin, was almost universally welcomed in the West, although many of Western Europe's leaders warned about the possible effect of the rapid changes in East Germany on the post-war European order. Mr Honecker's downfall and the opening of the Berlin Wall came after the country had been rocked by repeated and massive pro-democracy demonstrations, and by an unprecedented wave of emigration to the West. The exodus of tens of thousands of East German refugees began during the summer months. It became a flood after Hungary opened its border with Austria on September 10 to allow an estimated 60,000 East German refugees to reach the West. East Germany's new leader and his reformist Prime Minister, Hans Modrow, acted quickly in November to defuse growing tensions, marked by persistent calls for reform and even for the Krenz government's resignation. Mr Krenz was in particular criticized for having praised the Chinese leadership after the June crushing of the pro-democracy student movement in central Beijing. Mr Krenz responded by promising free elections and steps aimed at putting the country's ailing economy back on its feet. Mr Modrow vowed to introduce a radical decentralization of the economy by abolishing more than half of the state-decreed plans for industry. The government however stressed that it had no intention of restoring capitalism in East Germany, adding it would act quickly to curb black market currency trading, a problem that had contributed to East Germany's decision to build the Berlin Wall. A special Communist Party congress was scheduled for mid-December, amid intense speculation over whether Mr Krenz would succeed in staying in power.

# Germany (West)

Central Europe
96,025 sq. mi
Pop: 61m.
UN, EEC,
NATO, OECD

*Capital:* Bonn (Pop: 291,400)
*Official language:* German
*Religions:* Protestant 49%, Roman
Catholic 44.6%
*Political status:* Federal republic
*Head of state:* Richard von Weizsäcker
(since 1984)
*Head of government:* Helmut Kohl (since
1982)
*GNP per capita:* $12,080 (1986)
*Currency:* deutschemark (£1 = 2.94)

The historic events in Eastern Europe, particularly in neighbouring East Germany, profoundly affected West Germans, who were faced in September and October with the problems caused by the sudden influx of tens of thousands of East German refugees. These difficulties became more acute after the breaching in November of the Berlin Wall, which had divided the city since August 13, 1961. The urgent need to find housing and employment for the refugees soon became the top priority for West Germany's government. By year's end, Turkish and other immigrant workers were complaining that East German job-seekers were being given preferential treatment. In West Berlin itself, the authorities, already faced with 100,000 unemployed, attempted to cope with thousands of new arrivals from the East. Chancellor Kohl meanwhile sought to reassure his country's neighbours, several of whom had expressed concern over the possibility of German reunification. He reaffirmed his government's commitment to both the EC and Nato after several EC leaders had voiced fears that West Germany would gradually turn towards the Eastern Bloc and away from the its western allies.

# Ghana

West Africa
92,010 sq. mi
Pop: 13.8m.
UN, CW, OAU,
ECOWAS

*Capital:* Accra (Pop: 867,459)
*Official language:* English
*Religions:* Christian 52%, Moslem 13%,
traditional beliefs
*Political status:* Republic
*Head of state:* Jerry John Rawlings (since
1981)
*GNP per capita:* $390 (1986)
*Currency:* cedi (£1 = 449.26)

The number of Aids victims in Ghana rose by nearly 35 per cent in 1989 despite a government anti-Aids programme. In March, the country signed an agreement aimed at increasing British investment there.

# Greece

Southeastern
Europe
50,949 sq. mi
Pop: 9.99m.
UN, EEC,
NATO, OECD

*Capital:* Athens (Pop: 3,027,331)
*Official language:* Greek
*Religion:* Greek Orthodox 98%
*Political status:* Democratic parliamentary
republic
*Head of state:* Christos Sartzetakis (since
1985)
*Head of government:* Xenophon Zolotas
*GNP per capita:* $4,710 (1987)
*Currency:* drachma (£1 = 259.78)

A political crisis stemming from two inconclusive elections, in June and early November, was resolved when the three main parties agreed in late November to an all-party government that would rule until new elections could be held in April 1990. A former governor of the Bank of Greece, 85-year-old Xenophon Zolotas, was appointed to head the six-month interim coalition government.

# Grenada

Caribbean
120 sq. mi
Pop: 88,000
UN, CW, OAS,
Caricom

*Capital:* St George's (Pop: 4,788)
*Official language:* English
*Religions:* Roman Catholic, Anglican,
Methodist
*Political status:* Constitutional monarchy
*Head of state:* Queen Elizabeth II
*Head of government:* Herbert Blaize (since
1985)
*GNP per capita:* $1,240 (1986)
*Currency:* Eastern Caribbean dollar
(£1 = 4.28)

Despite continued US development assistance and attempts to modernize the island's cocoa industry, Grenada was in 1989 forced to turn to the IMF and Western Europe for aid.

# Guatemala

Central America
42,042 sq. mi
Pop: 8.99m.
UN, OAS,
Caricom

*Capital:* Guatemala City (Pop: 1.5m.)
*Official language:* Spanish
*Religion:* Roman Catholic
*Political status:* Presidential republic
*Head of state:* Vinicio Cerezo Arevalo
(since 1986)
*GNP per capita:* $930 (1988)
*Currency:* quetzal (£1 = 4.48)

Mr Cerezo survived a military coup attempt in May. A UN report said in February that 50 people had been killed by death squads in 1988, compared to 64 the previous year.

# Guinea

West Africa
94,926 sq. mi
Pop: 6.53m.
UN, OAU

*Capital:* Conakry (Pop: 705,280)
*Official language:* French
*Religions:* Moslem 69%, tribal beliefs 30%,
Christian 1%
*Political status:* Presidential republic
*Head of state:* Lansana Conté (since 1984)
*GNP per capita:* $320 (1985)
*Currency:* Guinea franc (£1 = 475.5)

Mr Conté in April marked the fifth anniversary of his inauguration. He did not rule out a return to a civilian regime in the country.

# Guinea-Bissau

West Africa
13,948 sq. mi
Pop: 932,000
UN, OAU

*Capital:* Bissau (Pop: 109,214)
*Official languages:* Portuguese, Crioulo
*Religions:* Moslem 30%, Christian 5%
*Political status:* Republic
*Head of state:* Joao Bernardo Vieira (since
1980)
*GNP per capita:* $170 (1988)
*Currency:* peso (£1 = 1,030.25)

The tiny West African nation, one of the world's poorest, continued to rely heavily on Western and Soviet economic assistance in 1989.

# Guyana

South America
83,000 sq. mi
Pop: 812,000
UN, Caricom,
CW

*Capital:* Georgetown (Pop: 188,000)
*Official language:* English
*Religions:* Christian 52%, Hindu 34%,
Moslem 9%
*Political status:* Presidential republic
*Head of state:* Hugh Desmond Hoyte
(since 1985)
*Head of government:* Hamilton Green
(since 1985)
*GNP per capita:* $500 (1986)
*Currency:* Guyana dollar (£1 = 47.30)

# Haiti

The former British colony in July signed four agreements under which Britain will provide approximately £20 million in financial as well as technical assistance.

Caribbean
10,700 sq. mi
Pop: 5.3m.
UN, OAS

*Capital:* Port-au-Prince (Pop: 449,831)
*Official language:* French
*Religions:* Roman Catholic, voodoo
*Political status:* Presidential republic
*Head of state:* Prosper Avril (since 1988)
*GNP per capita:* $330 (1986)
*Currency:* gourde (£1 = 7.93)

Marking the end of his first year in power, General Avril, who crushed a coup attempt in April, said in September that he remained committed to restoring full democracy.

# Honduras

Central America
43,277 sq. mi
Pop: 4.3m.
UN, OAS

*Capital:* Tegucigalpa (Pop: 604,600)
*Official language:* Spanish
*Religion:* Roman Catholic
*Political status:* Presidential republic
*Head of state:* José Azcona Hoyo (since
1986)
*GNP per capita:* $740 (1986)
*Currency:* lempira (£1 = 3.14)

During a three-day visit to Honduras in September, the Princess Royal toured a centre in the capital for sick children and a hospital for children suffering from cancer.

# Hungary

Central Europe
35,911 sq. mi
Pop: 10.6m.
UN, CMEA,
Warsaw Pact

*Capital:* Budapest (Pop: 2.1m.)
*Official language:* Hungarian
*Religions:* Roman Catholic 49%, Protestant 23.5%
*Political status:* Republic
*Head of state:* Mathias Szuros (since 1989)
*Head of government:* Miklos Nemeth
(since 1988)
*GNP per capita:* $2,010 (1986)
*Currency:* forint (£1 = 94.05)

In September the government took the unprecedented decision to open the country's borders with Austria to allow the passage of tens of thousands of East Germans fleeing to the West. Hungary in October took the historic step of ending 41 years of Communist Party rule. The country declared itself a republic and rejected basic principles of communism such as the dictatorship of the proletariat. In late November, the US Congress approved an emergency 81-million-dollar aid package, as the EC stepped up its economic assistance. In the country's first democratic nationwide vote since the communist takeover in 1948, four of the newly formed opposition parties won a narrow victory in a late November referendum that forced the government to postpone presidential elections scheduled for January 1990. A new parliament, due to be elected by June 1990, would instead choose a president of the republic. The country's economic outlook remained bleak. The government stopped subsidizing most staple goods and the cost of food, public transport and heating soared.

# Iceland

North Atlantic
39,758 sq. mi
Pop: 247,357
UN, OECD,
NATO, EFTA,
NC

*Capital:* Reykjavik (Pop: 93,245)
*Official language:* Icelandic
*Religion:* Evangelical Lutheran
*Political status:* Parliamentary republic
*Head of state:* Vigdis Finnbogadottir (since 1980)
*Head of government:* Steingrimur Hermannsson (since 1988)
*GNP per capita:* $15,252 (1986)
*Currency:* krona (£1 = 97.50)

Iceland's premier in September reshuffled her government to include members of the moderate-right Bourgeois Party, in a bid to have the working majority to push through badly needed economic reforms.

# India

Southern Asia
1,222,713 sq. mi
Pop: 748m.
UN, CW

*Capital:* New Delhi (Pop: 5,714,000)
*Official languages:* Hindi, English
*Religions:* Hindu 82.7%, Moslem 11.2%, Christian 2.6%, Sikh 1.9%, Buddhist, Jain
*Political status:* Federal parliamentary republic
*Head of state:* R. Venkataraman (since 1987)
*Head of government:* Vishwanath Pratap Singh (since 1989)
*GNP per capita:* $270 (1986)
*Currency:* rupee (£1 = 26.30)

Rajiv Gandhi resigned in late November after suffering a major defeat in general elections. In early December, Mr Pratap Singh, head of the centrist National Front opposition party was appointed the country's seventh prime minister. For the first time in India's history, the incoming premier headed a minority government.

# Indonesia

Southeast Asia
741,098 sq. mi
Pop: 172m.
UN, ASEAN,
OPEC

*Capital:* Jakarta (Pop: 6,503,449)
*Official language:* Bahasa Indonesian
*Religions:* Moslem 78%, Christian 11%, Buddhist, Hinduist
*Political status:* Presidential republic
*Head of state:* Gen Raden Suharto (since 1968)
*GNP per capita:* $510 (1986)
*Currency:* rupiah (£1 = 2,867)

General Suharto, who has been in power for 21 years, indicated in 1989 that his current term, due to end in 1993, may be his last, sparking intense jockeying among opposition and government politicians.

# Iran

Middle East
634,724 sq. mi
Pop: 53.92m.
UN, OPEC

*Capital:* Tehran (Pop: 6,042,584)
*Official language:* Farsi (Persian)
*Religion:* Moslem (Shi'a 96%, Sunni 3%)
*Political status:* Islamic republic
*Head of state:* Ali Akbar Rafsanjani (since 1989)
*Head of government:* Ali Akbar Rafsanjani (since 1989)
*GNP per capita:* $1,690 (1986)
*Currency:* rial (£1 = 116.90)

The death of Ayatollah Khomeini in June did little to improve relations between Tehran and the West. In August, the country's leaders ruled out the possibility of negotiations with the "hated" US government, accusing the Bush administration of supporting Israel's July abduction of a leading pro-Iranian sheikh in Lebanon. President Rafsanjani said in August he would help free Western hostages in Lebanon only when the West proves it is no longer hostile to Iran. In early November, thousands of club-wielding Iranians demonstrated in Tehran to mark the tenth anniversary of the takeover of the US Embassy there. The same month, the US released 567 million dollars in frozen Iranian assets, but this move did little to reduce tensions between the two nations.

# Iraq

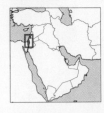

Middle East
167,925 sq. mi
Pop: 17.06m.
UN, AL, OPEC

*Capital:* Baghdad (Pop: 4,648,609)
*Official language:* Arabic
*Religions:* Moslem 64%, Christian 2%
*Political status:* Socialist presidential republic
*Head of state:* Saddam Hussein at-Takriti (since 1979)
*Head of government:* Saddam Hussein at-Takriti
*GNP per capita:* $2,140 (1984)
*Currency:* Iraqi dinar (£1 = 0.49)

The ending in August 1988 of the war against Iran allowed Iraq's regime to play a far more active role in regional affairs in 1989 and to begin to rebuild its ravaged economy. There was practically no progress in 1989 in negotiations for a lasting settlement of the Gulf War. The arrest in September of a British nurse and an Iranian-born British journalist, who was accused of espionage, caused a major dispute between the two nations.

# Ireland

Western Europe
26,600 sq. mi
Pop: 3.54m.
UN, EEC,
OECD

*Capital:* Dublin (Pop: 920,956)
*Official languages:* Irish (Gaelic), English
*Religions:* Mostly Roman Catholic, Church of Ireland, Presbyterian, Methodist
*Political status:* Parliamentary republic
*Head of state:* Patrick Hillery (since 1976)
*Head of government:* Charles Haughey (since 1987)
*GNP per capita:* $5,080 (1986)
*Currency:* Irish pound (£1 = 1.11)

Basing his decision on a series of highly favourable opinion polls, Ireland's premier called early parliamentary elections in mid-June, hoping to gain a majority of seats. The gamble did not pay off. Mr Haughey's Fianna Fail party lost three seats and he was forced to form a coalition government. Despite a slight upturn in the economy in 1989, the government remained faced with a 17 per cent unemployment rate, one of the highest in Western Europe, a continued emigration problem and some social unrest. In September, a dispute broke out between Dublin and London over allegations of collusion between police and Protestant extremists in Northern Ireland. In early October, the EC strongly criticized Ireland for allowing excessive urban pollution. However, the year ended on an upbeat note when, for the first time, Ireland qualified for the soccer World Cup in November by beating Malta.

# Israel

Near East
8,017 sq. mi
Pop: 4.44m.
UN

*Capital:* Jerusalem (Pop: 482,700)
*Official languages:* Hebrew, Arabic
*Religions:* Jewish 82%, Moslem 13%
*Political status:* Parliamentary republic
*Head of state:* Chaim Herzog (since 1983)
*Head of government:* Yitzhak Shamir (since 1986)
*GNP per capita:* $6,350 (1986)
*Currency:* new shekel (£1 = 3.18)

After nearly two years and more than 600 Palestinian deaths, the "intifada", or uprising, showed no sign of abating by year's end. The violent Palestinian protest against Israel's occupation of the West Bank and Gaza weighed heavily on the country's economy and its internal politics. Much-publicized reports of actions undertaken by Israeli security forces to quell the protests drew international criticism. The opening of a dialogue between the US and the PLO, as well as PLO chief Yasser Arafat's official visit to France in May, where he was greeted as Palestine's president, caused considerable bitterness in Israel. In July, Israel came under fire for the kidnapping in Lebanon of a pro-Iranian dignitary. The year was however marked by a warming of relations between Jerusalem and East Bloc nations, most of which had broken ties with Israel after the 1967 Arab-Israeli War. A November visit to the White House by Mr Shamir saw no real progress on implementation of a US peace plan, which Israel refused to accept without further guarantees.

# Italy

Southern Europe
116,319 sq. mi
Pop: 57.4m.
UN, EEC,
NATO, OECD

*Capital:* Rome (Pop: 2,817,227)
*Official language:* Italian
*Religion:* Roman Catholic
*Political status:* Parliamentary republic
*Head of state:* Francesco Cossiga (since 1985)
*Head of government:* Giulio Andreotti (since 1989)
*GNP per capita:* $8,570 (1986)
*Currency:* lira (£1 = 2,162)

Faced with a budget deficit of nearly 50 billion dollars, the coalition government repeatedly attempted to cut down public spending, notably in the health and education sectors. These moves were greeted by strikes and social unrest. In a November visit to Rome, Soviet leader Mikhail Gorbachev held an historic meeting at the Vatican with Pope John Paul II.

# Ivory Coast

West Africa
124,503 sq. mi
Pop: 11.63m.
UN, OAU

*Capital:* Abidjan (Pop: 1.85m.)
*Official language:* French
*Religions:* Animist 44%, Christian 32%,
Moslem 24%
*Political status:* Presidential republic
*Head of state:* Félix Houphouët-Boigny
(since 1960)
*GNP per capita:* $740 (1986)
*Currency:* franc CFA (£1 = 499.13)

The country's ageing president in 1989 continued his policy of dialogue with South Africa, much criticized by other African leaders. His costly project to build Christianity's biggest cathedral also came under fire.

# Jamaica

Caribbean
4,411 sq. mi
Pop: 2.3m.
UN, OAS, CW,
Caricom

*Capital:* Kingston (Pop: 524,638)
*Official language:* English
*Religion:* Mostly Protestant
*Political status:* Constitutional monarchy
*Head of state:* Queen Elizabeth II
*Head of government:* Michael Manley
(since 1989)
*GNP per capita:* $1,068 (1987)
*Currency:* Jamaican dollar (£1 = 9.11)

Jamaica's premier travelled widely in 1989, seeking support for his country's ailing economy, burdened by a constantly rising foreign debt, and for his government's plans to set up an armed, international anti-drug force.

# Japan

Northwestern
Pacific Ocean
145,874 sq. mi
Pop: 122.26m.
UN, OECD

*Capital:* Tokyo (Pop: 8,209,000)
*Official language:* Japanese
*Religions:* Buddhist, Shintoist
*Political status:* Parliamentary monarchy
*Head of state:* Emperor Akihito (since 1989)
*Head of government:* Toshiki Kaifu (since 1989)
*GNP per capita:* $14,039 (1986)
*Currency:* yen (£1 = 223.5)

Political scandals rocked Japan in 1989 nearly as often as earth tremors did. Although expected, after a long illness, Emperor Hirohito's death in January had a profound effect on the people of Japan. The end of the emperor's long reign was soon followed by the so-called "Recruitgate" scandal, in which leading politicians admitted having received huge payoffs from the Recruit firm. This led to the April resignation of premier Noboru Takeshita, who was replaced in the following month by Sousuke Uno of the Liberal Democratic Party. In July, Mr Uno became involved in a sex scandal and was forced to resign after his party suffered a crushing defeat in upper house elections, where the LDP lost its majority for the first time since 1955. In August, with the LDP in disarray, Toshiki Kaifu, a former education minister, was appointed prime minister. However, this constant political turmoil did not harm the country's buoyant economy, which in October marked 46 consecutive months of growth. On the international front, Japan and the Soviet Union were by year's end working on plans to hold a summit meeting in 1991. During a visit to Toyko in September, Mrs Thatcher called on Japan to import more goods from the United Kingdom.

# Kiribati

Pacific
276.9 sq. mi
Pop: 66,250
CW

*Capital:* Tarawa (Pop: 24,598)
*Official language:* English
*Religions:* Protestant, Roman Catholic
*Political status:* Presidential republic
*Head of state:* Ieremia Tabai (since 1979)
*GNP per capita:* $390 (1985)
*Currency:* Australian dollar (£1 = 2.09)

The tiny island nation, whose economy relies heavily on fishing, in January accused South Korea of illegally fishing in its waters.

# Jordan

Middle East
34,443 sq. mi
Pop: 2.97m.
UN, AL

*Capital:* Amman (Pop: 777,500)
*Official language:* Arabic
*Religion:* Sunni Moslem 80%
*Political status:* Constitutional monarchy
*Head of state:* King Hussein II (since 1952)
*Head of government:* Zeid bin Shaker
(since 1989)
*GNP per capita:* $1,540 (1986)
*Currency:* dinar (£1 = 1.05)

The kingdom's first general elections in 22 years saw a major victory for Moslem fundamentalists, who captured more than 30 seats in the 80-member parliament. The victory was a setback for King Hussein.

# Korea (North)

Northeastern
Asia
46,540 sq. mi
Pop: 21.89m.

*Capital:* Pyongyang (Pop: 2.64m.)
*Official language:* Korean
*Religions:* Buddhist, Chondoist, Christian
*Political status:* Democratic people's
republic
*Head of state:* Kim Il Sung (since 1972)
*Head of government:* Yon Hyong Muk
(since 1989)
*GNP per capita:* $1,180 (1985)
*Currency:* won (£1 = 1.54)

At year's end, North and South Korea were set for the second exchange of separated families since the end of the Korean War, but tensions remained high between the two nations.

# Kenya

Eastern Africa
224,960 sq. mi
Pop: 22.8m.
UN, CW, OAU

*Capital:* Nairobi (Pop: 827,775)
*Official language:* Kiswahili
*Religions:* Protestant 19%, Roman Catholic 27%, other Christian 27%, Moslem 6%,
tribal beliefs 19%
*Political status:* Presidential republic
*Head of state:* Daniel arap Moi (since 1978)
*GNP per capita:* $300 (1986)
*Currency:* Kenya shilling (£1 = 34.00)

# Korea (South)

Northeastern
Asia
38,232 sq. mi
Pop: 42m.

*Capital:* Seoul (Pop: 9,645,824)
*Official language:* Korean
*Religions:* Animist, Buddhist, Confucianist, Christian
*Political status:* Presidential republic
*Head of state:* Roh Tae-Woo (since 1988)
*Head of government:* Kang Young-Hoon
(since 1988)
*GNP per capita:* $3,450 (1988)
*Currency:* won (£1 = 1,072.40)

The government in September said it would forbid marriage for women before the age of 18, as part of a plan to cut down the birth rate, one of the world's highest.

In February, Prime Minister Kang Young-Hoon, in office since December 1988, promised to hold a national referendum before the end of the year. However, plans to hold the ballot were shelved indefinitely in March after the premier met Kim Dae-Jung, leader of the opposition Peace and Democracy Party. Mr Kim had earlier supported calls for a full inquiry into the 1980 massacre of demonstrating students and workers at Kwangju. The political climate worsened in April after a leading opposition figure travelled to North Korea for talks with President Kim Il Sung. The government responded by ordering the arrest of scores of people, sparking a wave of often-violent anti-government demonstrations in several cities. On the economic front, the situation remained bright throughout 1989, despite a slight downturn in the growth rate. In November, President Roh vowed to pursue his policy of working for improved relations with communist North Korea, adding that this process should ultimately lead to the peaceful reunification of the two nations.

# Kuwait

Middle East
6,880 sq. mi
Pop: 1.96m.
UN, AL, OPEC,
GCC

*Capital:* Kuwait (Pop: 44,335)
*Official language:* Arabic
*Religions:* Sunni Moslem 78%, Shia Moslem 14%, Christian 6%
*Political status:* Emirate
*Head of state:* Shaikh Jabir al-Ahmad al-Jabir al-Sabah (since 1977)
*Head of government:* Shaikh Saad al-Abdullah as Salim as Sabah (since 1978)
*GNP per capita:* $13,890 (1986)
*Currency:* dinar (£1 = 0.47)

The ending of the Iran-Iraq war was hailed with considerable relief in Kuwait, which had feared that the fighting would spill over its borders. In July, Kuwait signed a major trade pact with the Soviet Union.

# Laos

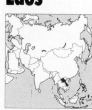

Southeast Asia
91,400 sq. mi
Pop: 3.83m.
UN

*Capital:* Vientiane (Pop: 377,409)
*Official language:* Lao
*Religions:* Mostly Buddhist, tribal 34%
*Political status:* Democratic people's
republic
*Head of state:* Phoumi Vongvichit
*Head of government:* Kaysone Phomvihane (since 1975)
*GNP per capita:* $220 (1984)
*Currency:* new kip (£1 = 924.05)

Soviet-backed Laos in 1989 improved its relations with China, while at the same time stepping up its ties with its non-communist neighbour, Thailand. The regime also launched a more liberal economic policy.

# Lebanon

Near East
4,036 sq. mi
Pop: 3.5m.
UN, AL

*Capital:* Beirut (Pop: 702,000)
*Official language:* Arabic
*Religions:* Moslem (Sunni, Shiite, Druze), Christian (mostly Maronite and Greek Orthodox)
*Political status:* Parliamentary republic
*Head of state:* Elias Hrawi (since 1989)
*Heads of governments:* Dr Selim Hoss (Moslem); Michel Aoun (Christian)
*GNP per capita:* no reliable figures available
*Currency:* Lebanese pound (£1 = 724.33)

The year began in a state of political vacuum, due to the existence of two rival governments, a Christian one and a Moslem one. In March, Christian General Michel Aoun launched a "war of liberation" against occupying Syrian forces, who responded by blockading and bombing Christian sectors, killing more than 1,000 civilians over a six-month period. In May, Arab leaders asked representatives of Morocco, Saudi Arabia and Algeria to seek a lasting solution to the Lebanese crisis. The last remaining US diplomats were evacuated from Beirut in September after General Aoun accused Washington of having sold out Lebanon to Syria. In November, as a political settlement seemed near, newly appointed President René Moawad was assassinated in Beirut. He was quickly replaced by a Syrian-backed Maronite Christian, Elias Hrawi. Meanwhile, Mr Hoss formed a government of national union composed of 14 ministers, drawn equally from the Christian and Moslem communities.

# Lesotho

Southern Africa
11,720 sq. mi
Pop: 1.67m.
UN, CW, OAU

*Capital:* Maseru (Pop: 109,382)
*Official languages:* Sesotho, English
*Religions:* Protestant 49%, Roman Catholic 44%
*Political status:* Constitutional monarchy
*Head of state:* King Moshoeshoe II (since 1966)
*Head of government:* Gen Justin Lekhanya (since 1986)
*GNP per capita:* $410 (1986)
*Currency:* loti (£1 = 4.20)

General Lekhanya was in October acquitted of the murder of a student. In early May, the Roman Catholic Archbishop of Maseru, Alphonsus Morapeli, died of a heart attack.

# Liberia

West Africa
42,989 sq. mi
Pop: 2.44m.
UN, ECOWAS, OAU

*Capital:* Monrovia (Pop: 425,000)
*Official language:* English
*Religions:* Moslem 26%, Christian, traditional beliefs
*Political status:* Presidential republic
*Head of state:* Samuel Kanyon Doe (since 1980)
*GNP per capita:* $450 (1986)
*Currency:* Liberian dollar (£1 = 1.58)

Faced with a major economic crisis, President Doe in November announced an immediate 54 per cent increase in the price of rice, the staple food of Liberians, and taxes of up to 100 per cent on luxury goods.

# Libya

North Africa
679,358 sq. mi
Pop: 3.96m.
UN, AL, OAU, OPEC

*Capital:* Tripoli (Pop: 990,697)
*Official language:* Arabic
*Religion:* Sunni Moslem 97%
*Political status:* Socialist people's state
*Head of state:* Muammar Gadaffi (since 1969)
*Head of government:* Abdessalam Jalloud
*GNP per capita:* $7,180 (1985)
*Currency:* dinar (£1 = 0.48)

In mid-September, Colonel Gadaffi celebrated the 20th anniversary of his revolution amid persistent reports that he had ordered the closure of the offices in Tripoli of more than 70 self-styled "liberation movements". The Libyan leader in 1989 considerably toned down his criticism of the US and British governments, signalling what some saw as a new era of pragmatism. Libya's economy was in 1989 badly hit by plummeting oil revenues.

# Liechtenstein

Western Europe
61.8 sq. mi
Pop: 27,700
EFTA

*Capital:* Vaduz (Pop: 4,606)
*Official language:* German
*Religions:* Roman Catholic 87%, Protestant 8.6%
*Political status:* Constitutional monarchy
*Head of state:* Prince Hans Adam II (since 1989)
*Head of government:* Hans Brunhart (since 1978)
*GNP per capita:* $15,000 (1984)
*Currency:* Swiss franc (£1 = 2.58)

In November, Prince Hans Adam II became the ruler of the tiny but wealthy principality following the death of his father, Prince Francis Joseph II, who died at the age of 83 after 51 years on the throne. Prince Hans Adam had in fact been running the government since 1984.

# Luxembourg

Western Europe
998 sq. mi
Pop: 372,100
UN, EEC, NATO, OECD

*Capital:* Luxembourg (Pop: 76,640)
*Official languages:* Luxemburgish, French, German
*Religion:* Roman Catholic 95%
*Political status:* Constitutional monarchy
*Head of state:* Grand Duke Jean (since 1964)
*Head of government:* Jacques Santer (since 1984)
*GNP per capita:* $15,680 (1986)
*Currency:* Luxembourg franc (£1 = 61.65)

In general elections held in mid-June, the ruling coalition lost six parliamentary seats. However, an agreement hammered out the following month between the socialist and Christian democrat parties allowed Mr Santer to remain prime minister. He was also appointed minister of the treasury and minister of culture.

# Madagascar

Indian Ocean
226,658 sq. mi
Pop: 10.92m.
UN, OAU

*Capital:* Antananarivo (Pop: 703,000)
*Official languages:* Malagasy, French
*Religions:* Christian 50%, Moslem 3%, animist 47%
*Political status:* Republic
*Head of state:* Didier Ratsiraka (since 1975)
*Head of government:* Victor Ramahatra
*GNP per capita:* $230 (1987)
*Currency:* Malagasy franc (£1 = 2,273)

President Ratsiraka was re-elected in March with 62.7 per cent of the vote, although this was 18 per cent less than his score in the 1982 presidential elections. Opposition candidates won surprise victories in several major cities, including the capital.

# Malawi

Southern Africa
36,325 sq. mi
Pop: 7.1m.
UN, CW, OAU

*Capital:* Lilongwe (Pop: 186,800)
*Official languages:* Chichewa, English
*Religions:* Mostly Christian, Moslem 7%
*Political status:* Presidential republic
*Head of state:* H. Kamuzu Banda (since 1966)
*GNP per capita:* $160 (1986)
*Currency:* kwacha (£1 = 4.40)

Drought, a poor maize crop, the spread of Aids and the continued arrival of refugees from the conflict in Mozambique were added burdens on the country's ailing economy.

# Malaysia

Southeast Asia
127,317 sq. mi
Pop: 17m.
UN, ASEAN, CW

*Capital:* Kuala Lumpur (Pop: 937,875)
*Official language:* Malay
*Religions:* mostly Moslem, Buddhist, Hindu, Christian
*Political status:* Federal constitutional monarchy
*Head of state:* Sultan Azlan Shah (since 1989)
*Head of government:* Mahathir Mohamad (since 1981)
*GNP per capita:* $1,850 (1986)
*Currency:* ringgit (£1 = 4.27)

Azlan Shah, a British-educated jurist, became Malaysia's ninth king in September, as the government was set to sign an accord to end a decades-long communist insurgency.

# Maldives

Indian Ocean
115 sq. mi
Pop: 200,000
UN, CW

*Capital:* Malé (Pop: 46,334)
*Official language:* Divehi
*Religion:* Moslem
*Political status:* Presidential republic
*Head of state:* Maumoon Abdul Gayoom (since 1978)
*GNP per capita:* $310 (1986)
*Currency:* rufiyaa (£1 = 14.28)

The last of the 1,200 Indian troops sent in following a bloody 1988 coup attempt left the Indian Ocean island nation in early November.

# Mali

West Africa
478,832 sq. mi
Pop: 7.78m.
UN, OAU

*Capital:* Bamako (Pop: 404,022)
*Official language:* French
*Religions:* Sunni Moslem 90%, animist 9%, Christian 1%
*Political status:* Presidential republic
*Head of state:* Moussa Traoré (since 1969)
*GNP per capita:* $170 (1986)
*Currency:* franc CFA (£1 = 499.13)

A relatively good 1989 cotton crop and government austerity measures contributed to a slight upturn in the country's economy, which however continued to rely heavily on foreign, notably US, assistance.

# Malta

Southern Europe
121.9 sq. mi
Pop: 345,636
UN, CW

*Capital:* Valletta (Pop: 9,239)
*Official languages:* Maltese, English
*Religion:* Roman Catholic
*Political status:* Democratic parliamentary republic
*Head of state:* Vincent Tabone (since 1989)
*Head of government:* Eddie Fenech Adami (since 1987)
*GNP per capita:* $3,470 (1987)
*Currency:* Lira Maltija (£1 = 0.56)

Malta in September celebrated its 25th anniversary. Its government in 1989 succeeded in improving relations with the West after years of militant socialism and non-alignment.

# Mauritania

West Africa
398,000 sq. mi
Pop: 1.89m.
UN, AL, OAU

*Capital:* Nouakchott (Pop: 500,000)
*Official languages:* Arabic, French
*Religion:* Sunni Moslem 99%
*Political status:* Republic
*Head of state:* Maaouia Ould Sidi Mohamed Taya (since 1984)
*GNP per capita:* $440 (1986)
*Currency:* ouguiya (£1 = 135.57)

Some 200 people died in May when a border dispute with Senegal erupted into riots. About 100,000 Mauritanians in Senegal and 85,000 Senegalese in Mauritania had to be repatriated.

# Mauritius

Indian Ocean
787 sq. mi
Pop: 1.057m.
UN, CW, OAU

*Capital:* Port Louis (Pop: 138,038)
*Official language:* English
*Religions:* Hindu 53%, Christian 30%, Moslem 13%
*Political status:* Constitutional monarchy
*Head of state:* Queen Elizabeth II
*Head of government:* Anerood Jugnauth (since 1982)
*GNP per capita:* $1,720 (1987)
*Currency:* rupee (£1 = 24.65)

Sir Anerood in September asked other Indian Ocean states to help him turn the region into a "zone of peace". The government in October said that the serious hard drugs problem had been brought under control.

# Mexico

North America
756,198 sq. mi
Pop: 82.7m.
UN, OAS, LAIA

*Capital:* Mexico City (Pop: 12,932,116)
*Official language:* Spanish
*Religion:* Roman Catholic 92.6%
*Political status:* Federal republic
*Head of state:* Carlos Salinas de Gortari (since 1988)
*GNP per capita:* $1,850 (1986)
*Currency:* peso (£1 = 4,084)

Since Mr Salinas was elected president in late 1988, there has been a marked improvement in the often-tense relations between Mexico and the US. In early 1989, the Salinas government launched a major anti-drug effort that won immediate praise from Washington. By September, Mexican police had seized 22 tons of cocaine, the equivalent of all the cocaine seized during the six-year rule of Mr Salinas's predecessor. Mexico's leader also clamped down on the thousands of emigrants crossing the US-Mexican border and opened up the country to US and West European investors. An anti-pollution project was launched in 1989 in Mexico City, by far the world's most polluted capital.

# Monaco

Southern Europe
481 acres
Pop: 27,063

*Capital:* Monaco
*Official language:* French
*Religion:* Roman Catholic
*Political status:* Constitutional principality
*Head of state:* Prince Rainier III (since 1949)
*Head of government:* Jean Ausseil (since 1985)
*GNP per capita:* $10,000
*Currency:* French franc (£1 = 9.98)

Prince Rainier in June celebrated his 40 years on the throne as the tiny principality's economy continued its unprecedented boom, resulting largely from tourism, banking and, to a lesser degree, gambling.

# Mongolia

Eastern Asia
605,022 sq. mi
Pop: 2m.
UN, CMEA

*Capital:* Ulan Bator (Pop: 500,000)
*Official language:* Mongolian
*Religion:* Tibetan Buddhist Lamaism
*Political status:* People's republic
*Head of state:* Jambyn Batmunkh (since 1984)
*Head of government:* Dumaagiyn Sodnom (since 1984)
*GNP per capita:* $940 (1978)
*Currency:* tugrik (£1 = 5.32)

Soviet-style reform made its debut in 1989 in Mongolia. Past errors were denounced and schools began teaching a new version of Mongolian history from which the negative Soviet view of Mongol conqueror Genghis Khan had been removed. The regime said it planned to strengthen economic ties with Japan and Europe.

# Morocco

North Africa
177,116 sq. mi
Pop: 23m.
UN, AL

*Capital:* Rabat (Pop: 518,616)
*Official language:* Arabic
*Religions:* Sunni Moslem 98%, Christian 2%
*Political status:* Constitutional monarchy
*Head of state:* Hassan II (since 1961)
*Head of government:* Azzeddine Laraki (since 1986)
*GNP per capita:* $590 (1986)
*Currency:* dirham (£1 = 13.31)

To mark his 60th birthday, King Hassan in July released some 300 prisoners. In August, the King made his first trip to Libya since Colonel Gadaffi came to power in 1969. This came as relations between the two states were gradually improving after years of tension. In November, the government launched economic reforms, notably the privatization of some of the 700 state-run firms.

# Mozambique

Southern Africa
308,642 sq. mi
Pop: 14.9m.
UN, OAU

*Capital:* Maputo (Pop: 882,814)
*Official language:* Portuguese
*Religions:* Animist 60%, Christian 18%, Moslem 16%
*Political status:* People's republic
*Head of state:* Joaquim Alberto Chissano (since 1986)
*Head of government:* Mario da Graça Machungo
*GNP per capita:* $90 (1986)
*Currency:* metical (£1 = 1,280)

For Mozambique, it was a year of continuous struggle to put a war-ravaged economy back on its feet. The regime followed often-painful IMF guidelines, including big cuts in social spending. The destruction of schools during the conflict left more that 500,000 children with no access to education, while poor health care and malnutrition continued to claim lives.

# Namibia

Southern Africa
318,261 sq. mi
Pop: 1.29m.

*Capital:* Windhoek (Pop: 114,500)
*Official languages:* Afrikaans, English
*Religions:* Protestant, traditional beliefs
*Political status:* South African-controlled territory
*Head of state:* Louis Pienaar (since 1985)
*GNP per capita:* $1,020 (1986)
*Currency:* South African rand (£1 = 4.20)

The last South African soldiers left Namibia in late November, thus ending a 23-year conflict against Marxist Swapo fighters and Cuban-backed Angolan troops. The South Africans left behind an enemy who lost virtually every battle but won the war. No official figures have been released by South Africa detailing the cost in manpower and money of its low-tech border war in Namibia. Also in November, mineral-rich Namibia, which has lived under South African administration since 1915 and is Africa's last remaining colony, made a giant step towards independence with the holding of UN-sponsored elections. The once-outlawed South West Africa People's Organization, led by Sam Nujoma, won 57.3 per cent of the popular vote. The elections were by far the most danger-fraught phase of the implementation of the UN plan for the territory's independence. The new Constituent Assembly in December began the drawn-out process of drafting and approving the future nation's first-ever constitution.

# Nauru

Pacific
8,108 sq. mi
Pop: 8,042
CW

*Capital:* Yaren (Pop: 4,000)
*Official languages:* Nauruan, English
*Religions:* Roman Catholic, Protestant
*Political status:* Republic
*Head of state:* Kenas Aroi (since 1989)
*GNP per capita:* $9,091 (1985)
*Currency:* Australian dollar
(£1 = 2.09)

After 21 years as head of the world's smallest republic, President Hammer DeRoburt was ousted in August by his long-time political ally Kenas Aroi. Mr DeRoburt however remained in charge of trade policy.

# Nepal

South Asia
56,827 sq. mi
Pop: 16.63m.
UN

*Capital:* Kathmandu (Pop: 235,160)
*Official language:* Nepali
*Religions:* Hindu 90%, Buddhist 5%, Moslem 3%
*Political status:* Constitutional monarchy
*Head of state:* Birendra Bir Bikram Shah Dev (since 1972)
*Head of government:* Marich Man Singh Shrestha (since 1986)
*GNP per capita:* $160 (1986)
*Currency:* Nepalese rupee (£1 = 38.04)

A trade dispute with India, which threatened to choke Nepal's economy, erupted in March, as India refused to renew bilateral transit and trade agreements. India shut down most of its 15 border posts with Nepal.

# Netherlands

Northwestern
Europe
16,163 sq. mi
Pop: 14.71m.
UN, EEC,
NATO, OECD

*Capital:* Amsterdam (Pop: 691,738)
*Official language:* Dutch
*Religions:* Roman Catholic 36%, Dutch Reformed 19%
*Political status:* Constitutional monarchy
*Head of state:* Queen Beatrix (since 1980)
*Head of government:* Ruud Lubbers (since 1982)
*GNP per capita:* $8,500 (1984)
*Currency:* guilder (£1 = 3.32)

Like many of its EC neighbours, the Netherlands spent 1989 gearing up for Europe's single market, scheduled for the end of 1992. European integration and the environment were the chief issues of September general elections which returned Christian-Democrat leader Ruud Lubbers to power at the head of a centre-left coalition government.

# New Zealand

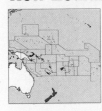

South Pacific
103,736 sq. mi
Pop: 3.3m.
UN, CW,
OECD

*Capital:* Wellington (Pop: 325,200)
*Official language:* English
*Religions:* Anglican, Presbyterian, Roman Catholic, Methodist
*Political status:* Constitutional monarchy
*Head of state:* Queen Elizabeth II
*Head of government:* Geoffrey Palmer
*GNP per capita:* $7,110 (1988)
*Currency:* New Zealand dollar (£1 = 2.71)

The country's vice-premier Geoffrey Palmer was elected prime minister in August following the resignation of David Lange for health reasons. Mr Palmer vowed to pursue his predecessor's anti-nuclear policies. These have long been a major source of disagreement between Wellington and Washington and caused New Zealand's withdrawal from the 1951 Anzus military pact linking Australia, New Zealand and the US The Palmer government was in 1989 outspoken in defence of the environment, calling for international action to protect the Antarctic. Relations with France, at an all-time low since the 1985 sinking of the Greenpeace ecological movement's ship *Rainbow Warrior* by French secret agents, warmed considerably in 1989. In November, the murder of an English tourist, the third killing of a foreign visitor since January, prompted strong opposition criticism of police efficiency.

# Nicaragua

Central America
49,363 sq. mi
Pop: 3.5m.
UN, OAS

*Capital:* Managua (Pop: 682,111)
*Official language:* Spanish
*Religion:* Roman Catholic 91%
*Political status:* Republic
*Head of state:* Daniel Ortega Saavedra (since 1984)
*GNP per capita:* $790 (1986)
*Currency:* new cordoba (£1 = 33,451)

Nicaragua's leader Daniel Ortega in April travelled to several West European capitals in a bid to raise the £160 million the country urgently needed to stave off economic collapse. By mid-1989, its foreign debt stood at seven billion dollars, most of it owed to the Soviet Union and other East Bloc states. On the political front, Nicaragua's Sandinista government and several opposition parties in August signed an accord aimed at guaranteeing that anti-Sandinista candidates would be able to participate in elections set for February 1990.

# Niger

West Africa
458,075 sq. mi
Pop: 7.19m.
UN, OAU

*Capital:* Niamey (Pop: 399,100)
*Official language:* French
*Religions:* Moslem 97%, animist
*Political status:* Republic
*Head of state:* Ali Seybou (since 1987)
*Head of government:* Mamane Oumarou (since 1988)
*GNP per capita:* $260 (1986)
*Currency:* franc CFA (£1 = 499.13)

In a September referendum, a massive 99.3 per cent of voters approved a new constitution. At year's end, voters were going back to the polls for presidential elections in which President Seybou stood unopposed.

# Nigeria

West Africa
356,667 sq. mi
Pop: 105m.
UN, ECOWAS,
CW, OAU,
OPEC

*Capital:* Lagos (Pop: 1,097,000)
*Official language:* English
*Religions:* Moslem 48%, Christian 34%
*Political status:* Federal republic
*Head of state:* Ibrahim Babangida (since 1985)
*GNP per capita:* $730 (1986)
*Currency:* Naira (£1 = 11.62)

The government in early 1989 was forced to increase fuel prices by 44 per cent. On the political front, preparations were underway for a return to civilian rule in 1992.

# Norway

North Europe
125,049 sq. mi
Pop: 4.2m.
UN, EFTA,
NATO, NC,
OECD

*Capital:* Oslo (Pop: 453,730)
*Official language:* Norwegian
*Religions:* Mostly Evangelical Lutheran, Roman Catholic
*Political status:* Constitutional monarchy
*Head of state:* King Olav V
*Head of government:* Gro Harlem Brundtland (since 1986)
*GNP per capita:* $16,400 (1986)
*Currency:* krone (£1 = 10.94)

The country's prime minister in May marked her third year in office at the head of a minority labour government. Mrs Brundtland was still faced in 1989 with a difficult economic situation and a high foreign debt.

# Oman

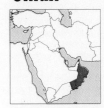

Middle East
105,000 sq. mi
Pop: 1.2m.
UN, AL, GCC

*Capital:* Muscat (Pop: 250,000)
*Official language:* Arabic
*Religions:* Ibadhi Moslem 75%, Sunni Moslem
*Political status:* Sultanate
*Head of state:* Qaboos bin Said (since 1970)
*Head of government:* Qaboos bin Said
*GNP per capita:* $4,990 (1986)
*Currency:* Rial Omani (£1 = 0.61)

For the first time in Omani history, a woman was in June elected to the national Chamber of Commerce. In November, Britain's Defence Secretary Tom King discussed military cooperation with Sultan Qaboos.

# Pakistan

South Asia
307,293 sq. mi
Pop: 102.2m.
UN

*Capital:* Islamabad (Pop: 201,000)
*Official languages:* Urdu, English
*Religions:* Moslem 97%, Christian, Hindu
*Political status:* Federal Islamic republic
*Head of state:* Ghulam Ishag Khan (since 1988)
*Head of government:* Benazir Bhutto (since 1988)
*GNP per capita:* $350 (1986)
*Currency:* rupee (£1 = 33)

A year after she became the first woman to govern a Moslem country, Miss Bhutto was in December still grappling with the three main problems that face Pakistan: poverty, corruption and violence. In November, she narrowly escaped being ousted as her political opponents failed by 12 votes to push through a no-confidence vote at the National Assembly. At year's end, the premier was said to be set for a government reshuffle after coming under fire for not fulfilling her electoral promises.

# Panama

Central America
29,768 sq. mi
Pop: 2.32m.
UN, OAS

*Capital:* Panama City (Pop: 386,393)
*Official language:* Spanish
*Religions:* Roman Catholic 85%, Protestant 5%, Moslem 4.5%
*Political status:* Presidential republic
*Head of state:* Francisco Rodriguez (since 1989)
*GNP per capita:* $2,330 (1986)
*Currency:* balboa (£1 = 1.58)

The political crisis that had been rocking the country since the cancellation, amid widespread violence, of May presidential elections came to a head in October, when a group of military officers tried to overthrow Panama's strongman, General Manuel Antonio Noriega, the nation's de facto leader. The coup bid failed and General Noriega cracked down on his opponents. A few days after the election was declared null, President Bush called on Panamanians to oust General Noriega and sent in 2,000 troops to reinforce the 10,000 already stationed in the Canal Zone. The wave of political violence led to international condemnation, the recall of the US ambassador and a December evacuation of US citizens.

# Papua New Guinea

Pacific
170,702 sq. mi
Pop: 3.48m.
UN, CW

*Capital:* Port Moresby (Pop: 152,100)
*Official language:* English
*Religions:* Protestant 63%, Roman Catholic 31%, local religions
*Political status:* Constitutional monarchy
*Head of state:* Queen Elizabeth II
*Head of government:* Rabbie Namaliu (since 1988)
*GNP per capita:* $690 (1986)
*Currency:* kina (£1 = 1.37)

Premier Namaliu in May moved to reassure foreign investors that his country was overcoming its problems, including months of violence that closed the Bougainville copper mine.

# Paraguay

South America
157,042 sq. mi
Pop: 4.01m.
UN, LAIA, OAS, LAES

*Capital:* Asuncion (Pop: 729,307)
*Official languages:* Spanish, Guarani
*Religion:* Roman Catholic 97%
*Political status:* Presidential republic
*Head of state:* Gen Andres Rodriguez (since 1989)
*GNP per capita:* $880 (1986)
*Currency:* guarani (£1 = 1,977.89)

The February overthrow of General Stroessner, in power since 1954, marked the end of Latin America's longest military dictatorship. His successor became president in May.

# Peru

South America
496,222 sq. mi
Pop: 21.3m.
UN, LAIA, OAS

*Capital:* Lima (Pop: 5,258,600)
*Official languages:* Spanish, Quechua
*Religion:* Roman Catholic over 90%
*Political status:* Republic
*Head of state:* Alan Garcia Perez (since 1985)
*Head of government:* Luis Alberto Sanchez (since 1989)
*GNP per capita:* $970 (1985)
*Currency:* inti (£1 = 8,515)

1989 was a particularly difficult year for President Garcia, who was faced with inflation running at around 2,000 per cent annually, a huge foreign debt, growing labour unrest and an active extreme-left guerrilla movement. He vowed in July to spend his final year in office looking for solutions to the country's economic woes. The Shining Path Maoist guerrilla movement failed to impose a boycott of a November municipal ballot held as a run-up to the April 1990 general elections. The ballot was marked by a clear swing to the right.

# Philippines

Southeast Asia
115,830 sq. mi
Pop: 58.72m.
UN, ASEAN

*Capital:* Manila (Pop: 1,630,485)
*Languages:* Filipino, English, Tagalog
*Religions:* Roman Catholic 83%, Protestant 9%, Moslem 5%
*Political status:* Republic
*Head of state:* Corazon C. Aquino (since 1986)
*GNP per capita:* $614 (1986)
*Currency:* peso (£1 = 33.40)

The September death in exile in Hawaii of former dictator Ferdinand Marcos was followed in early December by yet another military coup attempt aimed at toppling Mrs Aquino's government. Her regime survived the bloody revolt, believed to have been led by backers of the late

president, but the fighting left scores dead. President Bush ordered US Air Force Phantom fighters based near Manila to intervene in support of Mrs Aquino, although they did not open fire on the rebel-held positions.

# Poland

Eastern Europe
120,628 sq. mi
Pop: 37.8m.
UN, CMEA, Warsaw Pact

*Capital:* Warsaw (Pop: 2,432,000)
*Official language:* Polish
*Religion:* Roman Catholic 93%
*Political status:* Socialist republic
*Head of state:* Wojciech Jaruzelski (since 1985)
*Head of government:* Tadeusz Mazowiecki (since 1989)
*GNP per capita:* $2,070 (1986)
*Currency:* zloty (£1 = 3,295)

Poland in 1989 underwent some of the most profound changes in its recent history. In June, Poland held its first semi-democratic elections. In July, the country restored diplomatic relations with the Vatican. These had been broken in 1945 after the Communist Party came to power. The appointment in August of 62-year-old Tadeusz Mazowiecki as premier, after months of political and social turmoil, marked the end of 40 years of Communist Party domination in Poland. Mr Mazowiecki, a Roman Catholic and close associate of Solidarity leader Lech Walesa, thus became the first non-communist to head an East Bloc government. This historic event however brought little immediate relief to the country's economic crisis. Inflation was expected to hit 900 per cent by year's end. During a July visit to Warsaw, President Bush announced a major economic aid plan for Poland, while the EC rushed in food assistance in the form of beef and grain. During a· November visit to the West, Mr Walesa called for massive Western investment in Poland. In December, Mr Walesa made his first visit to London, as Britain increased its aid to Poland.

# Portugal

Southwestern Europe
35,516 sq. mi
Pop: 10.29m.
UN, NATO, OECD, EEC

*Capital:* Lisbon (Pop: 807,937)
*Official language:* Portuguese
*Religion:* Roman Catholic 94.5%
*Political status:* Parliamentary republic
*Head of state:* Mario Soares (since 1986)
*Head of government:* Anibal Cavaco Silva (since 1985)
*GNP per capita:* $2,230 (1986)
*Currency:* escudo (£1 = 251.10)

Portugal's premier said in November, after four years in power, that the 13 per cent inflation rate, one of the highest in the EC, was the country's most pressing problem.

# Qatar

Middle East
4,415 sq. mi
Pop: 371,863
UN, AL, OPEC, GCC

*Capital:* Doha (Pop: 217,294)
*Official language:* Arabic
*Religion:* Moslem 95%
*Political status:* Emirate
*Head of state:* Khalifa bin Hamad Al-Thani (since 1972)
*GNP per capita:* $22,940 (1984)
*Currency:* riyal (£1 = 5.74)

The arid Gulf peninsula, which relies heavily on oil revenues, faced some belt-tightening in 1989, but great hopes were pinned on a huge, newly discovered natural gas well.

# Romania

Southeastern Europe
91,699 sq. mi
Pop: 22.8m.
UN, CMEA, Warsaw Pact

*Capital:* Bucharest (Pop: 2,272,526)
*Official language:* Romanian
*Religions:* Orthodox 80%, Roman Catholic 6%
*Political status:* Socialist republic
*Head of state:* Nicolae Ceausescu (since 1967)
*Head of government:* Constantin Dascalescu (since 1982)
*GNP per capita:* $2,540 (1981)
*Currency:* leu (£1 = 14.22)

Virtually alone among East Bloc nations, Romania in 1989 steadfastly rejected any attempts at Soviet-style economic and political reforms. Any political dissent was ruthlessly crushed, while the government pressed ahead with its widely criticized centralization programme which involves the levelling of an estimated 10,000 small rural villages. Mr Ceausescu, who was unanimously re-elected in November for his sixth term as Communist Party chief and head of state, lashed out against any deviation from his brand of "scientific socialism" and pledged to strengthen the army to "defend revolutionary achievements". Such barbs aimed at Soviet reform policies led to tension between Bucharest and Moscow. Romanians were faced with chronic shortages of food, energy and nearly all consumer goods. The November defection of former star gymnast Nadia Comaneci was a serious blow to the regime's prestige.

# Rwanda

Central Africa
10,169 sq. mi
Pop: 6.71m.
UN, OAU

*Capital:* Kigali (Pop: 156,650)
*Official languages:* French, Kinyarwanda, Kiswhahili
*Religions:* Christian 68%, traditional 23%, Moslem 9%
*Political status:* Republic
*Head of state:* Juvenal Habyarimana (since 1975)
*GNP per capita:* $290 (1986)
*Currency:* Rwanda franc (£1 = 127.13)

The presence of more than 60,000 refugees from 1988 massacres in Burundi placed a heavy strain on the economy, also hit by early 1989 flooding. Overpopulation remained a major concern during 1989.

# St Christopher and Nevis

Caribbean
103 sq. mi
Pop: 43,700
UN, CW, OAS, Caricom

*Capital:* Basseterre (Pop: 14,283)
*Official language:* English
*Religions:* Protestant 76.4%, Roman Catholic 10.7%
*Political status:* Constitutional monarchy
*Head of state:* Queen Elizabeth II
*Head of government:* Kennedy A. Simmonds (since 1983)
*GNP per capita:* $1,700 (1986)
*Currency:* East Caribbean dollar (£1 = 4.28)

The government, which came to power in 1983 after nearly 30 years of socialist rule, won a third consecutive victory in March elections. The drop in world sugar prices was a blow to the country's economy.

# St Lucia

Caribbean
238 sq. mi
Pop: 146,600
UN, CW, OAS, Caricom

*Capital:* Castries (Pop: 52,868)
*Official language:* English
*Religion:* Roman Catholic 86%
*Political status:* Constitutional monarchy
*Head of state:* Queen Elizabeth II
*Head of government:* John Compton (since 1982)
*GNP per capita:* $1,320 (1986)
*Currency:* East Caribbean dollar (£1 = 4.28)

The island nation, which in February marked the tenth anniversary of its independence, was boosted by a record banana crop in 1989.

# St Vincent and the Grenadines

Caribbean
150 sq. mi
Pop: 112,614
UN, CW, OAS, Caricom

*Capital:* Kingstown (Pop: 28,942)
*Official language:* English
*Religions:* Anglican 47%, Methodist 28%, Roman Catholic 13%
*Political status:* Constitutional monarchy
*Head of state:* Queen Elizabeth II
*Head of government:* James Mitchell (since 1984)
*GNP per capita:* $960 (1986)
*Currency:* East Caribbean dollar (£1 = 4.28)

The ruling left-wing New Democratic Party won all 15 seats in the House of Assembly in a May vote, the third since independence in 1979.

# San Marino

Southern Europe
24.1 sq. mi
Pop: 22,746

*Capital:* San Marino (Pop: 4,363)
*Official language:* Italian
*Religion:* Roman Catholic 95%
*Political status:* Republic
*Heads of state:* Two co-regents appointed every 6 months
*Currency:* Italian lira (£1 = 2,162)

The tiny republic, founded in 1686, continued to rely on funds sent by its citizens living abroad.

# Sao Tome and Principe

Atlantic Ocean
387 sq. mi
Pop: 115,600
UN, OAU

*Capital:* Sao Tome (Pop: 34,997)
*Official language:* Portuguese
*Religion:* Roman Catholic 80%
*Political status:* Republic
*Head of state:* Manuel Pinto da Costa (since 1975)
*GNP per capita:* $340 (1986)
*Currency:* dobra (£1 = 169.37)

The year was marked by further democratization of the regime and the economy as the government prepared for general elections in 1990.

# Saudi Arabia

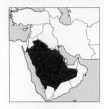

Middle East
849,400 sq. mi
Pop: 11.52m.
UN, AL, GCC, OPEC

*Capital:* Riyadh (Pop: 666,840)
*Official language:* Arabic
*Religions:* Sunni Moslem 85%, Shiite 15%
*Political status:* Kingdom
*Head of state:* King Fahd ibn Abdul Aziz (since 1982)
*Head of government:* King Fahd ibn Abdul Aziz
*GNP per capita:* $6,930 (1986)
*Currency:* rial (£1 = 5.91)

Saudi Arabia in 1989 strictly enforced Islamic law, often applying the death penalty to violators. More than 70 people, 16 of whom were Kuwaiti fundamentalists accused of terrorism, were publicly executed.

# Senegal

West Africa
75,750 sq. mi
Pop: 6.98m.
UN, OAU

*Capital:* Dakar (Pop: 978,553)
*Official language:* French
*Religions:* Moslem 91%, Christian 6%, animist 3%
*Political status:* Republic
*Head of state:* Abdou Diouf (since 1981)
*GNP per capita:* $420 (1986)
*Currency:* franc CFA (£1 = 499.13)

Senegal's government and its neighbour in Gambia in late September decided to dissolve the confederation created by the two nations in 1981 which was known as Senegambia.

# Seychelles

Indian Ocean
175 sq. mi
Pop: 67,000
UN, CW, OAU

*Capital:* Victoria (Pop: 23,000)
*Official languages:* Creole, English, French
*Religion:* Roman Catholic 96%
*Political status:* Republic
*Head of state:* France Albert René (since 1977)
*GNP per capita:* $3,590 (1988)
*Currency:* Seychelles rupee (£1 = 9.00)

President Albert René was elected for a third term in June with 96.1 per cent of the vote after running unopposed in general elections. The country improved its relations with western nations during 1989.

# Sierra Leone

West Africa
27,925 sq. mi
Pop: 3.88m.
UN, ECOWAS, CW, OAU

*Capital:* Freetown (Pop: 469,776)
*Official language:* English
*Religions:* tribal 52%, Moslem 39%, Christian 8%
*Political status:* Republic
*Head of state:* Joseph Saidu Momoh (since 1988)
*GNP per capita:* $310 (1986)
*Currency:* leone (£1 = 99.10)

Tension with neighbouring Liberia over the late 1988 expulsion of more than 70 of its citizens from that country decreased in 1989 following mediation efforts by Togolese and Nigerian representatives.

# Singapore

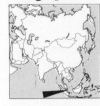

Southeast Asia
238.7 sq. mi
Pop: 2.61m.
UN, ASEAN, CW

*Capital:* Singapore (Pop: 2,612,800)
*Official languages:* Chinese, Malay, Tamil, English
*Religions:* Buddhist, Taoist, Moslem, Hinduist, Christian
*Political status:* Parliamentary republic
*Head of state:* Wee Kim Wee (since 1985)
*Head of government:* Lee Kuan Yew (since 1959)
*GNP per capita:* $7,464 (1987)
*Currency:* Singapore dollar (£1 = 3.09)

After 30 years in power, Singapore's premier said in September, on the occasion of his 66th birthday, that he would retire within one year on condition however that Deputy Prime Minister Goh Chok Tong was prepared to replace him. Mr Lee added however that he planned to remain a member of Singapore's cabinet.

# Solomon Islands

Pacific
10,640 sq. mi
Pop: 285,796
UN, CW

*Capital:* Honiara (Pop: 26,000)
*Official language:* English
*Religions:* Protestant 76%, Roman Catholic 19%
*Political status:* Constitutional monarchy
*Head of state:* Queen Elizabeth II
*Head of government:* Solomon Mamaloni (since 1989)
*GNP per capita:* $530 (1986)
*Currency:* Solomon Island dollar (£1 = 3.79)

In March, Mr Mamaloni, who was premier from 1981 to 1984, was returned to power. In July, the government said it could not afford to fund a UN embassy in New York.

# Somalia

Northeastern Africa
246,201 sq. mi
Pop: 6.26m.
UN, AL, OAU

*Capital:* Mogadishu (Pop: 250,000)
*Official languages:* Somali, Arabic
*Religion:* Sunni Moslem 99%
*Political status:* Republic
*Head of state:* Mohammed Siyad Barre (since 1969)
*Head of government:* Mohammed Ali Samater
*GNP per capita:* $280 (1986)
*Currency:* Somali shilling (£1 = 649.85)

President Barre in October marked his 20 years in office as head of a country still ravaged by civil war, ethnic strife and a seemingly endless famine. In July, an estimated 1,500 people died in anti-government rioting and the regime came under heavy fire for repeated human rights violations.

# South Africa

Southern Africa
433,678 sq. mi
Pop: 29.6m.
UN

*Capital:* Pretoria (Pop: 528,407)
*Official languages:* Afrikaans, English
*Religion:* Mainly Christian
*Political status:* Republic
*Head of state:* Frederik Willem de Klerk (since 1989)
*GNP per capita:* $1,800 (1986)
*Currency:* rand (£1 = 5.16)

Whites-only elections in September were marred by the bloodiest explosion of anti-government violence in three years which left up to 23 blacks dead and more than 100 injured. On election day, an estimated three million black workers staged a strike in the country's major cities. Despite this, Mr de Klerk claimed voters had given him a "mandate for reform". The ballot was far from a whole-hearted endorsement for Mr de Klerk's policies. For the first time since 1953, his

ruling National Party failed to win the majority of white votes, although it retained control of the government. In the 166-member House of Assembly, the Nationalists lost a quarter of their seats to rivals on both right and left, dropping from 123 seats to a bare 93. In November, Mr de Klerk promised to put an end to so-called "petty apartheid" as soon as possible. This is the practice of banning black citizens from such public places as beaches.

# Spain

Southwestern Europe
194,884 sq. mi
Pop: 39m.
UN, NATO, EEC, OECD

*Capital:* Madrid (Pop: 3,123,713)
*Official language:* Spanish
*Religion:* Roman Catholic
*Political status:* Constitutional monarchy
*Head of state:* King Juan Carlos I
*Head of government:* Felipe Gonzalez Marquez (since 1982)
*GNP per capita:* $5,198 (1986)
*Currency:* peseta (£1 = 187)

In January, the Basque separatist group Eta declared a truce in its fight for an independent homeland and talks aimed at reaching a lasting solution got underway with the government. These soon broke down as Eta terrorist attacks spread. Relations with Britain continued to improve despite the long-running dispute over Gibraltar's sovereignty. In October general elections, the ruling Socialist Party lost its overall majority.

# Sri Lanka

South Asia
25,332 sq. mi
Pop: 16.6m.
UN, CW

*Capital:* Colombo (Pop: 587,647)
*Official language:* Sinhala
*Religions:* Buddhist 69%, Hindu 15%, Christian 7%, Moslem 7%
*Political status:* Republic
*Head of state:* Ranasinghe Premadasa (since 1989)
*Head of government:* D.B. Wijeratne (since 1989)
*GNP per capita:* $400 (1986)
*Currency:* Sri Lankan rupee (£1 = 63.00)

The year was marked by continued bloodshed in the vicious conflict between separatist Tamil guerrillas and the Sinhalese-dominated government. The fighting left an estimated 10,000 dead since the start of the year. During 1989, Indian peace-keeping troops deployed in the north and east of the country since 1987 continued their phased withdrawal, scheduled to be over by year's end.

# Sudan

North Africa
967,500 sq. mi
Pop: 25.56m.
UN, AL, OAU

*Capital:* Khartoum (Pop: 476,218)
*Official language:* Arabic
*Religions:* Moslem 73%, animist 18%, Christian 9%
*Political status:* Republic
*Head of state:* Omar Hassan Ahmed el Beshir (since 1989)
*Head of government:* Omar Hassan Ahmed el Beshir (since 1989)
*GNP per capita:* $330 (1987)
*Currency:* Sudanese pound (£1 = 7.13)

Premier Sadiq al-Mahdi was overthrown and imprisoned in a late June military coup. He and several other former Sudanese leaders were freed in November by the new military junta, which remained faced with a desperate economic situation and renewed fighting in the south, where rebels led by Colonel John Garang seized several strategic cities.

# Suriname

South America
63,250 sq. mi
Pop: 415,000
UN, OAS

*Capital:* Paramaribo (Pop: 67,905)
*Official languages:* Dutch, English
*Religions:* Moslem, Hindu, Christian
*Political status:* Republic
*Head of state:* Ramsewak Shankar (since 1988)
*GNP per capita:* $2,510 (1986)
*Currency:* Suriname guilders (£1 = 2.83)

In August, a Canadian pilot was seized by Amerindian rebels who control most of the west of the country. He was freed in early October. In November, the government called for peace talks with the rebels.

# Swaziland

Southern Africa
6,705 sq. mi
Pop: 676,049
UN, OAU, CW

*Capital:* Mbabane (Pop: 23,290)
*Official languages:* Swazi, English
*Religions:* Christian 77%, traditional 23%
*Political status:* Monarchy
*Head of state:* King Mswati III
*Head of government:* Sotja E. Dlamini (since 1986)
*GNP per capita:* $730 (1984)
*Currency:* emalangeni (£1 = 4.20)

Swaziland, a kingdom whose economy relies almost exclusively on trade with neighbouring South Africa, continued during 1989 to expel to South Africa members of the anti-apartheid African National Congress.

# Sweden

Northern Europe
173,731 sq. mi
Pop: 8.4m.
UN, EFTA, OECD

*Capital:* Stockholm (Pop: 663,217)
*Official language:* Swedish
*Religion:* Lutheran 95%
*Political status:* Constitutional monarchy
*Head of state:* King Carl XVI Gustaf
*Head of government:* Ingvar Carlsson (since 1986)
*GNP per capita:* $18,607 (1987)
*Currency:* Swedish krona (£1 = 10.17)

In July, Christer Pettersson, a 42-year-old drifter and drug addict, was found guilty of the February 1986 murder of Prime Minister Olof Palme. However, he was released from jail in mid-October after his conviction was overturned.

# Switzerland

Western Europe
15,943 sq. mi
Pop: 6.6m.
EFTA, OECD

*Capital:* Bern (Pop: 300,316)
*Official languages:* German, French, Italian, Romansch
*Religions:* Roman Catholic 47.6%, Protestant 44.3%
*Political status:* Federal state
*Head of state:* Jean-Pascal Delamuraz (since 1989)
*GNP per capita:* $17,840 (1986)
*Currency:* franc (£1 = 2.58)

A scandal over charges that her husband was involved in the laundering of drug money, which led to the late 1988 resignation of Justice Minister Elisabeth Kopp, continued to rock the country. Mrs Kopp's parliamentary immunity was lifted in February. In October, the extreme-right Vigilance party lost Geneva elections.

# Syria

Middle East
71,498 sq. mi
Pop: 11.4m.
UN, AL

*Capital:* Damascus (Pop: 1,251,028)
*Official language:* Arabic
*Religion:* Sunni Moslem 90%
*Political status:* Republic
*Head of state:* Hafez al-Assad (since 1971)
*Head of government:* Mahmoud Zubi (1987)
*GNP per capita:* $2,000 (1984)
*Currency:* Syrian pound (£1 = 33.29)

The presence of thousands of Syrian troops in Lebanon caused serious tensions with the US, which blamed Damascus for much of the bloodshed in that war-torn country. In November, the Soviet Union, for years Syria's main arms supplier, urged President Assad to abandon his quest for military parity with Israel and put more emphasis on defence. Syria has an estimated 15-billion-dollar military debt to Moscow.

# Taiwan

East Asia
13,969 sq. mi
Pop: 19.7m.

*Capital:* Taipei (Pop: 2.64m.)
*Official language:* Chinese
*Religions:* Buddhist, Taoist, Christian
*Political status:* Republic
*Head of state:* Lee Teng-hui (since 1988)
*Head of government:* Lee Huan (since 1989)
*GNP per capita:* $5,075 (1987)
*Currency:* new Taiwan dollar (£1 = 40.70)

Relations with China warmed slightly in 1989. In May, Finance Minister Shirley Kuo was able to attend a meeting of the Asian Development Bank in Beijing. In October, all 54 people aboard a China Airlines Boeing 737 were killed when the aircraft hit a mountain and caught fire in the east of the country. At year's end, Taiwan was set for parliamentary elections.

# Tanzania

Eastern Africa
364,886 sq. mi
Pop: 23.2m.
UN, CW, OAU

*Capital:* Dodoma (Pop: 45,703)
*Official languages:* Kiswahili, English
*Religions:* Christian 40%, Moslem 33%
*Political status:* Republic
*Head of state:* Ndugu Ali Hassan Mwinyi (since 1985)
*Head of government:* Joseph S. Warioba (since 1985)
*GNP per capita:* $240 (1986)
*Currency:* Tanzanian shilling (£1 = 228.00)

The government in September said it was launching an all-out war against rampant corruption caused by the drop in government employees' income. Citizens were asked to help stamp out bureaucratic graft.

# Thailand

Southeast Asia
198,456 sq. mi
Pop: 53.9m.
UN, ASEAN

*Capital:* Bangkok (Pop: 5,609,352)
*Official language:* Thai
*Religions:* Buddhist 95%, Moslem 4%
*Political status:* Constitutional monarchy
*Head of state:* King Bhumibol Adulyadej (since 1946)
*Head of government:* Chatichai Choonhavan (since 1988)
*GNP per capita:* $810 (1986)
*Currency:* baht (£1 = 40.50)

Following a 42.9 per cent cut in US military aid, Thailand in 1989 turned to China for some of its military needs. The country played a major role in regional peace efforts undertaken by the Association of South East Asian Nations. In November, Thailand was hit by a typhoon that left more than 300 dead.

# Togo

West Africa
21,925 sq. mi
Pop: 3.25m.
UN, ECOWAS, OAU

*Capital:* Lome (Pop: 366,476)
*Official language:* French
*Religions:* Animist 46%, Christian 37%, Moslem 17%
*Political status:* Republic
*Head of state:* Gnassingbe Eyadema (since 1967)
*GNP per capita:* $250 (1986)
*Currency:* franc CFA (£1 = 499.13)

The country's former interior minister, who enjoyed strong popular support, was dismissed for alleged misappropriation of government funds and mismanagement. The economy was boosted by good crops and increased production of phosphate.

# Tonga

South Pacific
289 sq. mi
Pop: 95,200
CW

*Capital:* Nuku'alofa (Pop: 28,899)
*Official languages:* Tongan, English
*Religion:* Christian 90%
*Political status:* Constitutional monarchy
*Head of state:* King Taufa'ahau Tupou IV (since 1965)
*Head of government:* Prince Fatafehi Tu'pelehake (since 1965)
*GNP per capita:* $580 (1986)
*Currency:* pa'anga (£1 = 2.09)

International relief aid began arriving in mid-January to help finance reconstruction of vital fishing facilities that were destroyed in December 1988 when Cyclone Gina battered the South Pacific island.

# Trinidad and Tobago

Caribbean
1,978 sq. mi
Pop: 1.24m.
UN, Caricom, CW, OAS

*Capital:* Port-of-Spain (Pop: 58,400)
*Official language:* English
*Religions:* Christian 48.6%, Hindu 25%, Moslem 5.9%
*Political status:* Republic
*Head of state:* Noor Hassanali (since 1986)
*Head of government:* Arthur Robinson (since 1986)
*GNP per capita:* $5,120 (1986)
*Currency:* Trinidad and Tobago dollar (£1 = 6.74)

Unknown assailants in September tried to assassinate President Hassanali's wife in what the government later said was an attempt to destabilize the regime.

# Tunisia

North Africa
59,664 sq. mi
Pop: 7.32m.
UN, AL, OAU

*Capital:* Tunis (Pop: 596,654)
*Official language:* Arabic
*Religion:* Mainly Moslem
*Political status:* Republic
*Head of state:* Zine el Abidine Ben Ali (since 1987)
*Head of government:* Hamed Karawi (since 1989)
*GNP per capita:* 1,300 (1986)
*Currency:* dinar (£1 = 1.51)

April elections brought added legitimacy to President Ben Ali's government, which seized power in November 1987. In a September reshuffle, Justice Minister Hamed Karawi was appointed premier. Mr Ben Ali in 1989 sought to balance greater democracy with a perceived threat from Moslem fundamentalist groups.

# Turkey

Southeastern Europe
300,947 sq. mi
Pop: 50.67m.
UN, NATO, OECD

*Capital:* Ankara (Pop: 2,251,533)
*Official language:* Turkish
*Religion:* Moslem 98.2%
*Political status:* Republic
*Head of state:* Turgut Ozal (since 1989)
*Head of government:* Yildirim Akbulut (since 1989)
*GNP per capita:* $1,020 (1986)
*Currency:* Turkish lira (£1 = 3,545)

Turkish Prime Minister Turgut Ozal was elected president for a seven-year term after a late October ballot that was largely boycotted by the left-wing opposition parties. He promised to press ahead with badly needed economic reforms and to work for his country's early membership of the EC. However, French President Francois Mitterrand indicated in November, while he held the EC's rotating presidency, that the Turkish government's request to join the 12-nation European Community should be postponed until at least 1993.

# Tuvalu

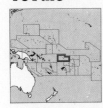

South Pacific
9.5 sq. mi
Pop: 8,229
CW

*Capital:* Funafuti (Pop: 2,620)
*Official languages:* Tuvaluan, English
*Religion:* Protestant
*Political status:* Constitutional monarchy
*Head of state:* Queen Elizabeth II
*Head of government:* Tomasi Puapua (since 1981)
*GNP per capita:* $500 (1984)
*Currency:* Australian dollar

As part of a multi-million dollar, three-year development aid project, Japan in early February handed over six brand new vessels to help train Tuvalu's fishermen in the use of modern fishing technology.

# Uganda

Eastern Africa
91,343 sq. mi
Pop: 15.5m.
UN, CW, OAU

*Capital:* Kampala (Pop: 458,423)
*Official languages:* English, Kiswahili
*Religions:* Christian 62%, Moslem 6%
*Political status:* Republic
*Head of state:* Yoweri Museveni (s. 1986)
*Head of government:* Samson Kisekka (since 1986)
*GNP per capita:* $230 (1984)
*Currency:* Uganda shilling (£1 = 315.96)

Local elections held in February, the first fraud-free ballot since 1962, further widened the powers of the ruling National Resistance Council. The following month, tension broke out with neighbouring Kenya, which accused Ugandan forces of launching cross-border attacks.

# Union of Soviet Socialist Republics

Eurasia
8,649,496 sq. mi
Pop: 284.5m.
UN, CMEA,
Warsaw Pact

*Capital:* Moscow (Pop: 8,815,000)
*Official language:* Russian
*Religions:* Christian, Moslem, Jewish, Buddhist
*Political status:* Federal union
*Head of state:* Mikhail Gorbachev (since 1988)
*Head of government:* Nikolai Ryzhkov (since 1985)
*Head of Communist Party:* Mikhail Gorbachev (since 1985)
*GNP per capita:* $6,000 (1985)
*Currency:* ruble (£1 = 1.01)

It was a paradoxical year for Mikhail Gorbachev. His popularity in the West soared to new heights while at home he was faced with massive strikes, a catastrophic economic situation, rising crime statistics, bloody ethnic clashes, growing conservative opposition to his reform drive and spreading nationalism. As the Soviet leader travelled to Rome in late November for a historic meeting with Pope John Paul II, and from there to Malta for his first summit conference with President Bush in December, he left behind a nation in unprecedented turmoil. In the Baltic states, under Soviet control since 1940, millions of Latvians, Lithuanians and Estonians were calling for total political and economic independence from Moscow. In Moldavia, a former province of Romania, there were growing demands for autonomy. Meanwhile, ethnic strife, which left scores of people dead, spread through Uzbekistan, Georgia, Azerbaijan and Kazakhstan. The economic situation worsened dramatically. For the first time since the post-war era, sugar was rationed on a nationwide basis, in addition to butter, meat and other staples. In July, Mr Gorbachev said over £10 billion would urgently be spent abroad to buy essential foodstuffs and consumer goods. A mid-year strike by thousands of coal miners, notably in Siberia, further threatened the ailing economy. By October, more than six million people had no steady employment. The country officially numbered nearly 20 million alcoholics and 40 million people were classed as heavy drinkers. Overall crime statistics shot up by more than 30 per cent nationwide.

# United Arab Emirates

Middle East
32,300 sq. mi
Pop: 1.77m.
UN, AL, GCC, OPEC

*Capital:* Abu Dhabi (Pop: 670,125)
*Official language:* Arabic
*Religion:* Moslem 90%
*Political status:* Federation of emirates
*Head of state:* Sheikh Zayed bin Sultan Al Nahyan (since 1971)
*Head of government:* Sheikh Rashid bin Said al-Maktoum (since 1979)
*GNP per capita:* $14,410 (1986)
*Currency:* dirham (£1 = 5.79)

In August, Sheikh Zayed criticized the West for not doing more to end the war in Lebanon. In June, the government freed two Irishmen who had been arrested for the attempted kidnap of an Arab-Irish girl.

# United Kingdom

Northwestern Europe
94,226 sq. mi
Pop: 55.78m.
UN, CW, EEC, NATO, OECD

*Capital:* London (Pop: 6,770,400)
*Official language:* English
*Religions:* Church of England, Roman Catholic
*Political status:* Constitutional monarchy
*Head of state:* Queen Elizabeth II
*Head of government:* Margaret Thatcher (since 1979)
*GNP per capita:* $8,920 (1986)
*Currency:* pound sterling

The personality and policies of Margaret Thatcher dominated the year, as they have the decade. Yet her critics believe that the Iron Lady, who in May celebrated ten years in Downing Street, is betraying signs of metal fatigue. She even faced her first challenge for the Conservative Party leadership.

During the year she lost a foreign secretary (when she reshuffled Sir Geoffrey Howe) and a chancellor of the exchequer (when Nigel Lawson resigned). Differences over Europe were factors in both changes and Mrs Thatcher found herself in a minority within the EC and the Commonwealth. Relations with Mikhail Gorbachev remained warm, but the post-Reagan "special relationship" with the US cooled somewhat with disagreements over the "boat people".

Europe was also the focus of the Tories' first national defeat in ten years when a resurgent Labour won the elections for European MPs. These elections also brought bad news for the former Alliance parties, both of which were beaten into third place by the Green Party.

Environmental issues played an increasingly important role in politics, but concern over the economy remained paramount. High interest rates, which reached 15 per cent in October, failed either to quell fears about the trade deficit or to curb inflation. Privatization, health service reforms, the poll tax and food safety also caused problems for the government, as did action by railwaymen, dockers and ambulance crews, amongst others. For most people, though, the summer was memorable for its record hours of sunshine rather than its strikes.

Britain was also afflicted by yet more disasters: an air crash on the M1 following that at Lockerbie, two more train crashes, Hillsborough and the sinking of the *Marchioness*. And the IRA campaign of terror brought bloodshed to West Germany, Deal and Northern Ireland itself.

# United States

North America
3,539,289 sq. mi
Pop: 238.7m.
UN, NATO, OAS, OECD

*Capital:* Washington DC (Pop: 638,333)
*Official language:* English
*Religions:* Protestant 56%, Catholic 36.7%, Jewish
*Political status:* Federal republic
*Head of state:* George Bush (since 1989)
*GNP per capita:* $16,710 (1986)
*Currency:* dollar (£1 = 1.58)

As Mr Bush in November marked the first anniversary of his election to the White House, he could look back on a year marked by improved East-West relations, the fall of the Berlin Wall, rising anti-communist sentiment in East Bloc nations, decreased but still-present trade tensions with Europe and Japan and a well-established peace process in Southern Africa. On the home front, Mr Bush was faced with a devastating drug problem, a growing violent crime wave, the spread of Aids and often-acrimonious national debates over abortion and the flag-burning issue. The economic situation remained reasonably stable, despite an October Wall Street panic and a small but worrisome rise in inflation. On the foreign affairs front, the year saw a crisis in US-China relations after Washington responded to Beijing's anti-democracy crackdown in June by imposing sanctions. Relations with Britain remained fairly good and in November Mrs Thatcher discussed events in Eastern Europe with Mr Bush. In December, Mr Bush held his first summit meeting with Soviet leader Mikhail Gorbachev. This focused on the historic changes sweeping through Eastern Europe's communist states which called into question the post-war partition of Europe. In the Middle East, pro-Iranian terrorists executed a US hostage in July.

Washington suffered two important foreign policy setbacks: in Nicaragua, where it practically abandoned all hopes of seeing the US-backed Contra rebels prevail, and in Panama, where General Noriega continued openly to defy Washington. At home, victory seemed far from assured in the war against drugs, despite a massive, 20-ton September cocaine seizure in Los Angeles. The nation's capital was rocked by an unprecedented crime wave, much of it drug-related. The country was in 1989 hit by two major natural calamities: the rampage of Hurricane Hugo through South Carolina in September and the October San Francisco earthquake.

# Uruguay

South America
72,172 sq. mi
Pop: 3.08m.
UN, LAIA, OAS

*Capital:* Montevideo (Pop: 1,246,500)
*Official language:* Spanish
*Religion:* Roman Catholic 66%
*Political status:* Republic
*Head of state:* Julio Maria Sanguinetti (since 1985)
*GNP per capita:* $1,860 (1986)
*Currency:* Nuevo Peso (£1 = 1,089)

Uruguay's first fully democratic elections in 18 years were won in late November by Luis Alberto Lacalle of the opposition National Party. Outgoing President Julio Sanguinetti is to step down in March 1990.

# Vanuatu

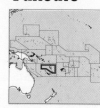

South Pacific
5,700 sq. mi
Pop: 149,400
UN, CW

*Capital:* Vila (Pop: 15,000)
*Official languages:* Bislama, English, French
*Religion:* Christian 80%
*Political status:* Republic
*Head of state:* Fred Timakata (since 1989)
*Head of government:* Walter Lini (since 1980)
*GNP per capita:* $350 (1981)
*Currency:* Vatu (£1 = 189)

The country's former president Ati Sokomanu was found not guilty in April of having attempted in early 1989 to overthrow the government of premier Walter Lini.

# Vatican City

Southern Europe
108.7 acres
Pop: 1,000

*Capital:* Vatican City
*Official languages:* Italian, Latin
*Religion:* Roman Catholic
*Head of Roman Catholic Church:* Pope John Paul II (since 1978)
*Secretary of State:* Cardinal Agostino Casaroli (since 1979)
*Currency:* lira (£1 = 2,162)

The Vatican's finances took a turn for the better in 1989, with a budget deficit of £27.9 million. This was approximately £10.9 million less than had been expected.

# Venezuela

South America
352,143 sq. mi
Pop: 18.77m.
UN, LAIA,
OAS, OPEC

*Capital:* Caracas (Pop: 1,044,851)
*Official language:* Spanish
*Religion:* Roman Catholic
*Political status:* Republic
*Head of state:* Carlos Andres Perez (since 1989)
*GNP per capita:* $2,930 (1986)
*Currency:* bolivar (£1 = 59.01)

The drug problem worsened considerably for Venezuela in 1989 despite government attempts to fight trafficking. In November, security forces seized more than 4,500 pounds of extremely high grade cocaine.

# Vietnam

Southeast Asia
127,245 sq. mi
Pop: 61.4m.
UN, CMEA

*Capital:* Hanoi (Pop: 2m.)
*Official language:* Vietnamese
*Religions:* Buddhist, Taoist
*Political status:* Socialist republic
*Head of state:* Vo Chi Cong (since 1987)
*Head of government:* Du Muoi (since 1988)
*GNP per capita:* $200 (1989)
*Currency:* dong (£1 = 7,132)

For Vietnam, the year brought new hopes that the country, which has been at war for nearly half a century, would at last know a period of peace. In September, the last Vietnamese troops sent into Cambodia in 1979 to support the Phnom Penh regime against anti-communist, China-backed guerrillas, left that war-ravaged country. An estimated 60,000 Vietnamese soldiers were killed and many more wounded in Cambodia.

# Western Samoa

South Pacific
1,093 sq. mi
Pop: 163,000
UN, CW

*Capital:* Apia (Pop: 33,170)
*Official languages:* Samoan, English
*Religions:* Congregationalist 47%, Roman Catholic 22%, Methodist 16%
*Political status:* Constitutional monarchy
*Head of state:* King Malietoa Tanumafili II
*Head of government:* Tofilau eti Alesana (since 1988)
*GNP per capita:* $770 (1985)
*Currency:* tala (£1 = 3.61)

The small island nation, faced with continued economic woes, in 1989 invested heavily in tourist facilities, hoping to attract visitors from Australia and the US.

# Yemen (North)

Middle East
73,300 sq. mi
Pop: 8.6m.
UN, AL

*Capital:* San'a (Pop: 427,151)
*Official language:* Arabic
*Religion:* Moslem (Sunni 39%, Shi'a 59%)
*Political status:* Republic
*Head of state:* Ali Abdallah Saleh (since 1978)
*Head of government:* Abdel Aziz Abdel Ghani (since 1983)
*GNP per capita:* $550 (1986)
*Currency:* riyal (£1 = 15.45)

North Yemen in 1989 worked for closer ties with Marxist South Yemen. By year's end, the two neighbouring states were on the verge of creating a single confederated state.

# Yemen (South)

Middle East
130,065 sq. mi
Pop: 2.3m.
UN, AL

*Capital:* Aden (Pop: 318,000)
*Official language:* Arabic
*Religions:* mostly Moslem, Christian, Hindu
*Political status:* People's democratic republic
*Head of state:* Haidar al-Attas (since 1986)
*Head of government:* Yasin Sa'id Nu'man (since 1986)
*GNP per capita:* $270 (1987)
*Currency:* dinar (£1 = 0.54)

Disastrous April flooding in central regions caused damage estimated at £48 million, killing thousands of head of cattle and destroying dozens of schools and hospitals.

# Yugoslavia

Southern Europe
96,835 sq. mi
Pop: 23.41m.
UN

*Capital:* Belgrade (Pop: 1,470,073)
*Official languages:* Serbo-Croat, Macedonian, Slovene
*Religions:* Orthodox 41%, Roman Catholic 32%, Moslem 12%
*Political status:* Federal socialist republic
*Head of state:* Janez Drnovsek (since 1989)
*Head of government:* Ante Markovic (since 1989)
*GNP per capita:* $2,300 (1986)
*Currency:* dinar (£1 = 64,380)

In May, a 38-year-old economist from Slovenia was appointed president, thus becoming Europe's youngest head of state. Throughout 1989, he battled against the country's worst-ever economic crisis, with inflation nearing 1,000 per cent, high unemployment and a spiralling foreign debt. The year was also marked by continued and violent ethnic clashes in the southern Kosovo province. In November, 92 coal miners died in the country's worst-ever mine disaster.

# Zaire

Central Africa
905,365 sq. mi
Pop: 32.56m.
UN, OAU

*Capital:* Kinshasa (Pop: 2,653,558)
*Official language:* French
*Religions:* Mostly Roman Catholic, Protestant, Moslem
*Political status:* Presidential republic
*Head of state:* Marshal Mobutu Sésé Séko (since 1965)
*Head of government:* Pida N'bagui Sambwa (since 1989)
*GNP per capita:* $160 (1983)
*Currency:* zaïre (£1 = 652.68)

During a June visit to Washington, President Mobutu rejected charges of human rights violations, saying Zairians supported him 100 per cent.

# Zambia

Southern Africa
290,586 sq. mi
Pop: 7.12m.
UN, CW, OAU

*Capital :* Lusaka (Pop: 818,994)
*Official language:* English
*Religions:* Christian 66%, Moslem
*Political status:* Republic
*Head of state:* Kenneth David Kaunda (since 1964)
*Head of government:* Malimba Masheka (since 1989)
*GNP per capita:* $300 (1987)
*Currency:* Kwacha (£1 = 27.5)

Former Interior Minister General Malimba Masheka was appointed premier in March and said he was committed to sweeping economic reforms.

# Zimbabwe

Southern Africa
150,699 sq. mi
Pop: 8.87m.
UN, CW, OAU

*Capital:* Harare (Pop: 656,100)
*Official language:* English
*Religions:* mostly Anglican and Roman Catholic
*Political status:* Republic
*Head of state:* Robert G. Mugabe (since 1987)
*GNP per capita:* $780 (1984)
*Currency:* Zimbabwe dollar (£1 = 3.55)

Despite improved performance by the crucial mining sector, the country remained faced with high unemployment and a heavy debt burden.

| Abbreviations | | | | | |
|---|---|---|---|---|---|
| | AL | Arab League | | LAES | Latin American Economic System |
| | ANZUS | Australia, New-Zealand, U.S. | | LAIA | Latin American Integration Association |
| | ASEAN | Association of South East Asian Nations | | NATO | North Atlantic Treaty Organization |
| | Caricom | Caribbean Community and Common Market | | NC | Nordic Council |
| | CFA | African Financial Community currency | | OAS | Organization of American States |
| | CMEA | (or Comecon) Council for Mutual Economic Assistance | | OAU | Organization of African Unity |
| | CW | The Commonwealth | | OECD | Organization for Economic Cooperation and Development |
| | ECOWAS | Economic Community of West African States | | OPEC | Organization of Petroleum Exporting Countries |
| | EEC | European Economic Community | | UN | United Nations |
| | EFTA | European Free Trade Association | | WP | Warsaw Pact |
| | GCC | Gulf Cooperation Council | | | |

124

125

## Photo Credit

The position of the pictures are indicated by two letters: fp = full page b = bottom, t = top, l = left, r = right, m = middle, x = middle left, y = middle right

**Cover**
- Allsport bl
- Topham/Associated Press tl, tx, ml
- Rex Features ty, tr, mm, mr, bx, bm, by, br
Allsport 13 bl, 18 bm, 18 bx, 20 br, 24 tr, 30 bm, 39 mr,

39 bl, 42 bm, 45 bl, 48 br, 51 bl, 52 br, 55 bl, 57 br, 61 mr, 61 bl, 63 bl, 65 br, 72 mr, 78 mr, 83 mr, 93 ml, 95 bl
Andy Warhol Estate 74 br
BBC Enterprises/Julian Charrington 105 bm
Beken of Cowes 65 ml
Chronicle UK New 4 mr, 18 br, 23 br, 33 bl, 80 ty, 90 br
Clive Barda 34 by
Empics Nottingham 7 tl, 71 ml
Foote, Cone and Belding 41 bl
Impact 88 tr
Independent TV News 21 mr
Kobal Collection 35 bx, 73 bl, 85 br

Network Photographers 70 bx
Popperfoto 11 br, 15 tm, 16 by, 22 tx, 30 mr, 37 bx, 40 mm, 55 tx, 55 mr, 56 tm, 56 by, 57 tl, 59 tl, 60 mx, 63 tl, 64 by, 66 br, 67 tl, 68 br, 69 tr, 71 tl, 71 bx, 75 tr, 79 br, 79 bl, 84 my, 85 tr, 89 tm, 93 tm, 94 mr, 96 br, 97 tx, 99 my, 102 tm, 102 bx, 103 mr, 103 br, 104 tr, 104 mr, 105 ml
Leslie E. Spatt 105 tm
Rex Features 4 tr, 5 tl, 6 bx, 6 br, 8 br, 9 tm, 10 mr, 11 tl, 11 mx, 12 mr, 12 by, 13 tm, 13 br, 14 ty, 14 mr, 15 bm, 17 tr, 17 bl, 19 tl, 19 mr, 19 bl, 20 tm, 21 tm, 21 bl,

22 tr, 22 bm, 24 bx, 24 by, 25 bx, 26 mm, 27 tr, 27 bl, 27 br, 28 by, 29 bl, 31 tr, 31 br, 32 tm, 34 tm, 35 tx, 36 ty, 36 mr, 37 tl, 37 tr, 37 br, 38 ty, 39 tr, 40 mr, 41 tm, 41 mr, 42 tr, 43 tl, 43 ml, 43 my, 43 mr, 43 br, 44 tr, 44 mm, 45 by, 46 tr, 46 mr, 47 tm, 49 tm, 49 br, 50 bm, 51 br, 53 mr, 53 bl, 54 tx, 54 ty, 54 by, 56 mr, 57 tr, 58 ty, 59 bl, 60 mr, 61 my, 62 mr, 63 ml, 64 mx, 64 mr, 65 tm, 66 tx, 66 tr, 67 mr, 68 bx, 69 ml, 70 ty, 70 tr, 72 tm, 72 by, 73 tr, 74 tm, 75 ml, 75 br, 76 br, 76 mr, 77 tm, 77 mm, 77 br,

80 mr, 81 br, 83 mr, 84 tm, 84 tr, 86 mr, 87 bl, 87 ty, 87 my, 88 mr, 89 br, 90 tr, 91 fp, 92 br, 93 tr, 93 ml, 94 ty, 94 bm, 95 tm, 95 mm, 97 br, 98 ml, 98 bm, 99 tr, 99 my, 100 tm, 100 tr, 101 tm, 101 br, 101 bl, 103 tr
Science Photo Lib/NASA 68 tr, 68 mr
Select 82 br
Sipa Press 5 bl, 6 tm, 15 mr, 25 tr, 29 tm, 35 mr, 36 br, 45 tl, 46 bx, 60 tm
Solo 83 tr
Topham/Associated Press 5 tr, 8 tm, 9 tm, 10 tr, 12 ty, 16 tm,

17 tl, 23 tr, 23 ml, 27 tm, 28 tr, 30 ty, 31 tl, 32 ty, 48 tl, 50 mr, 52 tm, 53 tm, 53 br, 59 tl, 61 ml, 73 tm, 78 ty, 78 br, 79 tm, 81 tr, 81 mr, 82 tm, 85 tl, 85 bl, 90 bl, 92 tm, 96 tm, 97 tr, 102 tr
Topham Picture Library 9 bl, 11 tr, 14 bm, 17 br, 25 mm, 26 mx, 26 tr, 29 br, 33 tr, 33 br, 34 mr, 38 mr, 45 mr, 50 tm, 51 tr, 57 bl, 58 br, 62 bm, 63 mr, 67 ml, 76 tm, 80 br, 81 bx, 86 ty, 87 tr, 87 mr, 87 my, 95 br, 104 br
Viz 97 bx